SUFI
Therapy of the Heart
A TRANSCENDENT EXPERIENCE

DAVID HEINEMANN

A Sterling Paperback

STERLING PAPERBACKS
An imprint of
Sterling Publishers (P) Ltd.
A-59 Okhla Industrial Area, Phase-II,
New Delhi-110020.
Tel: 26387070, 26386209
Fax: 91-11-26383788 E-mail: ghai@nde.vsnl.net.in
www.sterlingpublishers.com

Sufi Therapy of the Heart: A Transcendent Experience
© 2003, David Heinemann
ISBN 81 207 2468 2

Published by Sterling Publishers Pvt. Ltd., New Delhi-110020.
Printed at Prolific Incorporated, New Delhi-110020.

CONTENTS

iii

iv

COLOUR PHOTOGRAPHS

1. *'It all began in Malaysia'*
2. An Islamic cleric (*Mulla*) rebukes a Dervish
3. The Egyptian gods Osiris and Thoth
4. Sufi craftsmen leave cryptic messages in their designs
5. Sufi craftsman's Guilds are of ancient origin
6. Transcending all divisions, including Life and Death
7. The temple of Abraham
8. A Perfect Master radiates the Divine Light
9. Prophet Muhammad's Night Journey
10. The Sphinx of Giza, Egypt
11. *'Love is the Wine'*
12. Inside a Sufi Centre
13. God as the Beloved as a Universal symbol
14. Wool(*sūf*) symbolising the mystics (*sūfī*) self sacrifice
15. The Brethren of Purity (*Ikhwān as–Safā'*)
16. Though the rose dies its perfume remains

LINE DRAWINGS

ACKNOWLEDGMENTS

The author gratefully acknowledges the following authors and their publishers, for permission to quote from their works:

Laleh Bakhtiar, *Sufi: Expressions of the Mystic Quest.* Thames & Hudson, London, 1976.

C.M.Bowra, *Heroic Poetry.* Macmillan, London, 1952.

Titus Burckhardt, *An Introduction to Sufism: The Mystical Dimension of Islam.* Crucible, Wellingborough, 1990.

------------------ *Letters of a Sufi Master* (translation). Perennial Books, Middlesex, 1969.

Anthony Clare, *Psychiatry in Dissent.* Tavistock Publications, London, 1976.

Afkham Darbandi & Dick Davis (translators), *The Conference of the Birds.* Penguin, London, 1984.

C.Glassé, *The Concise Encyclopaedia of Islam.* Stacey International, London, 1989.

Paul Jackson (translator), *Sharafuddin Maneri: the Hundred Letters.* SPCK, London, 1980.

Martin Lings, *A Sufi Saint of the Twentieth Century: Shaikh Ahmad al-Alawî, his spiritual heritage and legacy.* George Allen & Unwin, London, 1971.

SOURCES OF COLOUR PHOTOGRAPHS

2: Bodleian Library, Oxford; Elliot, 254 folio 9r. **4,5,11,14,16**: Turkish Ministry of Tourism **9**: Museum of Islamic Art, Istanbul; MS no 1941 **12**: Topkapi Library, Istanbul MS no H 1365 **15**: Suleymaniye Library, Istanbul; Esad Effendi MS no 3638. The remaining illustrations are the authors.

For Bob, Balrama, Alister, Arjay, Arun, Danni, Fida, John, Jelal, Lalagee, Mark, Markus, Ruth, Sigrid, Suha *and others like them.....*

....in memory of my Grandmother *and* Uncle, *whose grave sites were never found; my* elder sister, *incinerated at 18 months; my physically and mentally scarred* parents *- and the millions of others like them - who bear witness to the results of prejudice, bigotry, religious hatred, racism, nationalism and the injustices of war....*

....to all these is this book dedicated, with the hope that their sufferings were not in vain - and that the world may learn to TRANSCEND *such limitations....*

INTRODUCTORY PREFACE

As long ago as 1923, the Orientalist Nicholson, acknowledged in his *The Idea of Personality in Sufism*, the difference between the Oriental concept of personality and our own. He observed that the Western Christian idea of personality is based upon the values derived from the notion of Jesus and his relationship to God.[1] Yet despite this, he went on to examine Sufism in these terms, turning Muhammad into a poor substitute for Jesus. For this and other reasons, investigators since his time, have seen Sufism as being a derivative of Islam,[2] or in some cases as a synthesis between Islam and some other religion.[3] However, as the spiritual Master *Bābā* Dovid Yūsuf pointed out in a discourse, one of his predecessors whose teachings he carried on,[4] never met Muhammad, yet taught the same doctrine independent of him. In other words, the mystic experience that is responsible for the esoteric tradition is something independent of any religion, its establishment as such, or even its founder.

The essential difference between Western (Christian or secular) concepts of personality and those of Sufism lie in the nature of how these concepts are obtained. The pioneering psychologist of religion, William James (1902), whilst showing the importance of the mystical experience for the origin and existence of established religion, also made a distinction between mystical experience and mysticism in general, paying special attention to the Sūfī experience.[5] It is the nature of this experience which was – and still is – of primary concern to me as a psychologist and practising psychotherapist, whose own life experiences – including research in other cultures – has demonstrated the inadequacy of the Western psychological model. Although I sought for many years to explain in psychosociobiological terms, the bizarre phenomena I encountered, I was finally forced back into looking for an alternative framework, or paradigm, to do so. For this reason, much of what follows might seem to be an apology, or justification for a particular religious perspective, but to view it in this way is a mistake. It is rather, that explaining in rational terms, what is for the most part non-rational (sometimes, even irrational), requires a semantic framework adequately developed to do so. Sufism – as part of the ongoing Universal Esoteric Tradition – benefits from having developed an explanatory framework at a crucial time in history, when Islamic, Jewish and Christian societies, were forced to interact with one another – that is just prior to the Renaissance. In fact, it was because of this interaction that the Renaissance took place. Since that time, the Christian Church has succeeded – for the most part – in efficiently eliminating Christian esotericism,[6] either by murder, persecution, or persuasion: including creation of the erroneous belief that science has *explained away* the spiritual, while Judaism, which has faced such opposition for centuries, even prior to the creation of Christianity, has been unable because of this, to develop an adequate explanatory framework that can be understod by non-Jews. Only since the emergence of the Chasidim in the last three centuries,[7] has such a system now begun to develop. But even here, the influence of Islamic mysticism upon this system is apparent, for it is dependent upon the earlier creation of the Kabbalah, which itself arose in Islamic Spain.[8]

For all these reasons, only in the Islamic world did the esoteric tradition develop to such an extent that a philosophical framework emerged capable of conveying in semantic terms, what is essentially an undefinable experience. It is the transcendent nature of this experience which is of central concern in this book, and not Sufism as such. However, the reader will have to bear with me as I fully develop the semantic and philosophical framework (which is essentially Sufism), in order to make such experience translatable; but it should not be assumed from this, that this is in itself a sufficient means of comprehension. It is here that the Sufi Teacher assumes a central role, for such a teacher will adapt time-honoured techniques to individual differences; allowing for the fact that it is only the transcendent experience itself that makes such comprehension truly possible.

Much of the above can be illustrated in the example of the enigmatic spiritual Master, *Bābā* Dovid Yūsuf. He is affiliated to over forty Sufi Orders, and also claims spiritual authorisation from all the World Religions, including recognition by tribal teachers. Unlike the leaders of some pseudo-Sufi groups (Islamic cults) he makes nothing of this pedigree and gives no weight to an *Isnād*, or document claiming transmission of authority;[9] for it would fill a whole volume, containing not only the names of Islamic teachers, but of those from all of the world's religious traditions, including the tribal. *Bābā,* claims that his teaching is a culmination of the Sufi tradition, which having served as the major (not the only) transmitter of the inner doctrine since the time of Prophet Muhammad, will now be conveyed by a new world religion, just as the Sufis themselves carried on an esoteric tradition existing prior to Muhammad, that was conveyed by the Christians, and before them the Jews and the Zoroastrians.

This claim is likely to be true, for in his study over thirty years ago of Sufism, Spencer Trimingham noted that it was in rapid decline.[10] The Sufis have given birth to external religions apart from Islam. The Hindu Sufi saint Kabīr gave rise to the Sant tradition of India; the Sufi *Bābā* Nanak, to the Sikhs in the Punjab; and many of the followers of Sayyīd 'Alī Muhammad the *Bāb,* of Iran (from the Sufi city of Shiraz) were dervishes, one of whom created the Bahā'i religion. Jewish Sufis have also helped sustain Judaism by their considerable influence on it, which has continued in Turkey until the present time.

That there is a need to transcend the nationalism and religious strife with which our world is plagued at the present time is clearly evident. Increasingly, intermarriage and the breaking-down of ethnic groups and community bonds, necessitates that there be a value-system that can transcend these difficulties. Not to mention the environmental and ecological problems that require an international coordinated effort to resolve. *Bābā* Dovid Yūsuf respects and acknowledges the differences present within the existing World Religions, providing an umbrella under which they could be resolved, rather than ignored, or eliminated. In this sense he claims to bring no new religion, but recognises that there is a common basis to them all.[11]

This need for a new value-system in the social sphere is paralleled by the need for a new paradigm in psychology and medicine – especially psychiatry. Failure to create such a framework has led to a return to Behaviourism, which has long ago been shown to be inadequate. Just as in the political sphere, rather than creating a new socio-economic framework after the rejection of Socialism, there has been a return – a regression we might say – to the outdated, and outworn shibboleths of Capitalism. The consequences of this are that our whole fragile ecosystem is under threat, just as our society is being rent apart by increasing violence and moral decay. This book is an attempt to show that there is another way of looking at the world. A way which overcomes these problems, and that has within it the groundwork for a new paradigm.

In writing this book, I have tried to write it in such a way, that in addition to it being a source book for academics, or students who might like to use it as a basis for their own investigations, that it is understandable by the public at large. This means, that whilst I have omitted unnecessary abbreviations and technical terms, I have also provided a full source of references, including those in the original languages. I have also given – where possible – an alternative source in English, and when rendering the original text into English, I have used words which bring out the sense of the original in a clear and understandable form, rather than being a pedantically accurate, or stylised translation. Quite often translators of the past have used Old English (as in the *King James version of the Bible*), which while conveying a sense of the sacred, has also obscured the meaning of the text. However, in an attempt to capture the shades of meaning of the Arabic, or Persian texts, I have used the original terms in brackets beside their translation, which academic researchers should find useful. This has illustrated their holistic meaning which makes such translations so difficult.

It is likely, that scholars who confine themselves to their own narrow field, will be irritated at finding references drawn from a variety of disciplines – though I have limited this much more than was the case with my own investigations.

In addition, I have sometimes used conjunctive terms such as his/her; s/he; or wo/man, in order to overcome the problem of male dominated terms, which as explained in the text, are not representative of Sufism. Notes and references are extensive, so that those who are unfamiliar with the academic background can follow the text; as well as fuller information for subsequent researchers being provided. Whatever the case, they should be read in conjunction with the text, for many of the concepts utilised will be unfamiliar to Western readers, and in other cases are likely to be confused with traditional interpretations, which are often quite different than those employed by the esoteric practitioner. These differences can be seen in the **Glossary**, where Arabic, Persian, or Turkish words can have an entirely different meaning than that usually employed (compare, e.g., *Hajj, Ka'aba, Hulūl*, with dictionary definitions).

Much of what is presented is likely to be challenging to orthodox Muslims (or those pseudo-Sufi groups which are really nothing other than Muslims in disguise). For this reason, the original Arabic has been used alongside its translation, for crucial *Qur'ānic* passages. Space has prevented this for other languages. Where I have used transliteration, it is based on the Classical system, with the following modifications. As differences in pronunciation are dependent on context, dialect and interpretation short vowels have not always been distinguished from one another, whilst occasionally letters have been added to assist in pronunciation, such as in, e.g., *Ka'aba*. The *hamza* has been represented by a pause ' since a glottal-stop is not a part of common English; though I have occasionally used an h, where meaning or convention dictated it. Similarly, since the *'ayn* is unique to Arabic and has no European equivalent, it has been represented as '. I have also neglected to use diacritical marks (i.e., dots under letters distinguishing long and short sounds) because of reproduction difficulties. However, they have been included in the **Glossary**, and the **Index of Persons**, for those who wish to discover the precise pronunciation of the word, or name in question. As italics have been used for Arabic transliteration, quotations, and occasionly emphasis, foreign words and those having a meaning other than the usual, have been emboldened in their first instance – the meaning of which can be found in the **Glossary**. Names and titles are sometimes also distinguished by emboldening. The numbering of **Qur'ānic** passages is that generally used and not as in Arberry's system. Conversely, I have used Arabic, rather than Latin numerals for references, except where they are used in the original. Bibliography dates are as in the publication quoted, which sometimes means that the C.E. (Common or Christian Era) date is not given. In the use of sayings of Prophet Muhammad *(Ahadīth)* I have only used *Tawatur* *hadīth* (that conveyed by Sufis), as *Sunnī* and *Shī'ah* compilations differ. For the same reason, I have not provided a chain of transmission for such sayings, though their source is generally quoted. The numerous references to the **Mathnawī** are to Rūmī's, unless stated otherwise.

Much of the source material for this book is oral, and has been gained through an intimate association with Sufi *Shaykhs,* or their disciples, and others involved in the esoteric tradition. To this material has been added an acquaintance with Classical texts, ancient sources and contemporary works. But it is participation in and membership of, esoteric groups and Sufi Orders, which has provided the most valuable information. Most misunderstanding of the esoteric tradition has arisen because those academics who have investigated it, have not themselves been initiates; or in the rare cases that they have been, have had a limited experience of one group only. This is especially the case with Sufism, for nearly everything that has been written about it in recent years, has been by someone who has become acquainted with either a Muslim sect, or syncretist cult, masquerading under the label of Sufism. In fact, this writer would argue that to understand Sufism as part of the ongoing esoteric tradition, it is necessary to both examine it from various perspectives, as well as have acquaintance with other expressions of that tradition. Only by so doing, will wrong conclusions be avoided, or what is obscure become clear.

xvi

For example, whilst academics (and even Muslims to some extent) glibly quote about the supposed influence of Christianity upon Muhammad, they remain totally unaware of Jewish sources which are much more significant and cannot be realised without knowledge of that tradition, while both groups - including Jews - are generally unaware of how all three traditions draw upon Egyptian and Persian sources.

Although one may not necessarily accept all the conclusions and beliefs of Sufism as presented in this book, in my own case, it would not have been possible without my full participation - so to speak. If the text is understood, it will be seen that it is not the external beliefs of Sufism as such, that characterise it, but its attitude to life - and this I fully endorse. I submit it with the hope that it can contribute to a greater understanding between Jews and Muslims; just as there is also a necessity for both Christians and Jews, to acknowledge their common basis.

Only by participation in a complete sense in Sufism, is it possible to understand the similarities with, as well as the differences from, Islam. For the genuine Sufi group will be secretive, for its adherents have been persecuted and often brutally murdered in the past, and are still vehemently opposed throughout most of the Islamic world. Contributing to the demise and distortion of Sufism, has been the rise of Islamic fundamentalists - *Wahhābī* and

Shī'ah – including the control by such jurists, of Islamic, Arabic and Persian, studies departments. Opposed to Sufism, since it challenges the basis of their authority and status, they have made large financial endowments to Western universities labouring from a shortage of funds. Anyone who has a contrary point of view and submits research, or applies for a position in such universities will soon find either rejected.

The concepts employed in this book are by their transcendent nature holistic. In order to make them accessible to reductionist language and concepts, I have presented them from a variety of angles, so that there is some repetition. This should be borne in mind when coming across unfamiliar terms or concepts, for what may at first be obscure will with perseverance become clear. I have also provided an exhaustive **General Index**, which can be consulted to facilitate understanding.

Last, but by no means least, apart from the publishers whose sources I acknowledge, I would like to thank all those persons who over the years have assisted me in my endeavours in a variety of ways, but most especially my wife, who has laboured for many years as my unpaid typist, counsellor and confidant and without whom this book would never have come into being.

Notes and References

1) R.A.Nicholson, *The Idea of Personality in Sufism*, Mehtab Publishers, Lahore, 1987, p, 59.

2) See the following books (full details in the **Bibliography**) Shah 1964, & 1968, Rushbrook Williams 1973, Ansari 1986.

3) See the compilation of various views in Archer 1980.

4) *Shaykh* Uways al-Qarānī, from Yemen (died c 634).

5) William James (1902), *The Varieties of Religious Experience*,, Fontana, London, 1960, pp,66-91;412-413;387-391;405,467.

6) The esoteric groups that exist within the Christian world, cannot show any continuity with those that existed during the Middle Ages. The exception to this is Freemasonry, which whilst it can show some continuity, has significantly changed from the *Illuminati* and other groups which brought it into existence. In any case, it cannot really be said to be Christian, since like Islam, it recognises a common basis to the world's religions, which is one of the reasons why it has been opposed by the Roman Catholic Church.

7) Although the *Hasīdīm* (pious ones) existed prior to the movement founded by Israel Baal-Shem Tov, in the eighteenth century (see **Appendix 4**) their effect on the world at large (including Judaism) was minimal. One exception to this was Baruch Spinoza (1632-1677), whose beliefs were very similar to Sufism, but not being understood, led to him being excommunicated from Judaism and ostracised by Christians.

8) For further details on the links between Sufism and Chasidism, see Louis-Jacobs, *The Jewish Religion: A Companion*, Oxford University Press, 1995, pp, 500-501 & 44-45.

9) A supposed chain of transmission of authority traced from Prophet Muhammad, through a line of authorised *Shaykhs*. In actual fact, a thorough examination of such *isnāds* will show gaps, or contradictions, for some of the individuals could never have met, or must have lived very long periods of time (e.g. ,250 years).

10) *The Sufi Orders in Islam*, Clarendon Press, Oxford, 1971, pp, 246-259.

11) Adherence to the teachings of *Bābā* Dovid Yūsuf, does not impede the practise of any religion, e.g., becoming influenced by him, many have become practising, rather than token Jews, Muslims, Hindus or members of other faiths, discovering that there is a common source to them all, that transcends external dogmas. This subject is explored in later chapters.

Rabbi Hayim ben Moshe Becerano Efendi (1846–1931), last Chief Rabbi of the Ottoman Empire and first of the Turkish Republic. Fluent in 16 languages, he knew the *Tanakh* (Jewish Bible), . Christian **New Testament** and the *Qur'ān* by heart. A key figure in the preservation of sacred music – Jews having lived in Turkey for over 2,300 years – he is associated with a Sufi (Rūmī's followers) Jewish tradition of music*(Maftirim)* – that continues in the synagogues of Istanbul until the present day.

THE TRANSCENDENT EXPERIENCE

"Die before you are dead"

Muhammad the prophet

An Incident in Sarawak

Although I cannot recall the exact year, I remember the place, Sarawak, in South East Asia, which was once known as Borneo. Although a part of Malaysia, which is a highly developed and thriving modern society based upon the Western economic model, there still remains much of the original indigenous culture - a blend of tribal spirit worship, Hinduism, and the later acquired Islam.

Travelling through this jungle territory, as one with a background in social anthropology, as well as being a practising psychologist, I had made acquaintance with its people, who had rewarded me with a hospitality, generosity and genuine warmth, that was in sharp contrast to my own Western culture with its individualistic orientation. Having been befriended by a local family, I was about to experience, what to these native people was not unusual, but to my Western eyes, beyond usual experience.

Arising one morning from my hammock, I was greeted with a hive of activity on the part of my host family. The old man, or Grandfather, they said, was preparing to die that day! Surprised, I asked, had he suddenly become sick?

1

"No" - they informed me, he was his usual sprightly self - *"But this was a good day to die,"* he had said. Anyway they said, *"What was so unusual about dying?"*

As the old man was of sound mind and they as respectful and typical Orientals were obedient to parents wishes, they began to make preparations for the funeral. There was much to do: family from other villages had to be called; a large celebratory meal to which everyone in the village was to be invited had to be prepared; as well as all the usual paraphernalia that went along with such an occasion.

Intrigued, I watched as later that day the old man in apparently good health, washed, said his prayers and lay down on his bed. Calling his extended family to his bedside, he bade them farewell, subsequently dying with a smile on his face. [1]

Though there was the usual mourning, nobody was quite as upset as I was. The old man had looked as if he might have gone on living for at least another ten years. He had not succumbed to an illness - there was not even a fever - and as a strictly religious Muslim, self-inflicted poison was out of the question: yet he had died! What is more, he had done so without pain or fear, and at a time of his choosing! Such an incident was more than puzzling, it was highly disturbing, for it did not fit into my usual Western experience of death. In some way or another, he had overcome Death's power to terrify and control. He

2

had *transcended* the Western experience of death!

The Martyrdom of Hallāj

The old man had practised a form of esotericism known as *'Sufism'*. Whilst persons from many cultures, creeds and all levels of society have been its practitioners,[2] my researches showed that Sufism had generated a number of unusual and mysterious figures. It is from this tradition that we get the English word *faker*, a word derived from the Arabic term *faqīr* meaning 'poor one'. A word coined by the English colonisers of India, who unable to comprehend such feats as sticking knives in flesh without drawing blood; sleeping on beds of nails; handling hot coals and other incredible phenomena; put it down to conjuring-tricks. Today, we are much more knowledgeable and numerous psychological studies have shown that such feats can be genuine and not necessarily fake.[3] Although I had researched such phenomena, including Healing, over a number of years, I had not come across this approach to death. I became interested to learn more about who the Sufis were.

Writing at the beginning of the last century, Frenchman Louis Massignon pointed out,[4] that unlike the mysterious aspects of the life of Jesus the Nazarene (which are contestable as they were recorded solely by his followers), the Sufi martyr, Husayn ibn Mansūr al-Hallāj's (died 922 C.E) life was very well documented by his

3

enemies, as well as his followers. A life which strangely paralleled that of Jesus the Nazarene, in many respects.

Born in Persia in 858 C.E in the village of Tur near Bayda, Hallāj travelled extensively throughout Persia, Iraq, Central Asia and India, visiting many holy men and spiritual masters of the time. Later he began to preach, attracting large audiences and performing many miracles. As a result of his popularity and unorthodox beliefs, he found himself in conflict with the Islamic clergy, who, afraid of losing their power and position of privilege, branded him a heretic. Just as Jesus had aroused the wrath of the compromising clergy of his day – who together with the political power Rome, had him put to death [5] – so did Hallāj create opposition. Thrown into prison twice, he was finally condemned to death after a controversial trial of seven months.

When the sentence was carried out, like Jesus, he was whipped, spat upon and ridiculed, before finally being crucified. The religious and political authorities – intent on making him an example to others who might wish to challenge the system – had his body dismembered and burnt, scattering the ashes in the river Tigris. A number of legends grew up around this event, including the story that the ashes, when sprinkled upon the water, formed one of the words for God in Arabic, *Al-Haqq* – the Real or True. Significantly, it was his use of this term to describe himself, that allowed the religious authorities to condemn

4

him on the charge of *shirk* (i.e., making himself equal to God), a charge also levelled at Jesus.[6] Some days later, he was seen walking around, in much the same way that Jesus was claimed to have done after his resurrection.

Whatever we might think of these mysterious appearances, one thing is certain - for it was remarked upon by several witnesses, including his espoused enemies - that is, that he died forgiving his executors. whom he believed (like Jesus) did not really understand the full import of what they were doing. According to Hallāj, the truths he spoke were not his own, but those of God - the Universal or Transcendent Self within:

> May God forgive those who crucify me... .I am completely annihilated in God....*only His words* remain as they proceed from me.[7]

It is this linking of himself with God, that makes so many of his comments parallel those of Jesus. Also, like Jesus he accepted his fate with resignation and as enevitable. Speaking to the onlookers who were amazed at his tranquil state as he was led to the point of execution, he said:

> It is the right time to be happy, for now I am going back home.[8]

All the accounts tell us that he died with a smile on his face.

Who was this man, and how was he able to die such a painful and ignominious death without remorse, regret or fear? Since he grew up in an Islamic culture and would have known little about Jesus[9] probably never even having

5

read the Bible, which in his time – as is still the case in some Islamic countries – would have been unobtainable – why does his life and death parallel so closely that of Jesus? Was there something in common between them; something which also allowed the ordinary old man from the distant steaming jungles of Malaysia, to transcend the normal Western experience and fear of death? To answer these questions, let us turn to another example.

Al-Hamadhānī and the Sufi Experience

'Ayn al-Qudāt al-Hamadhānī (died 1131), lived some two hundred years after Hallāj. Also imprisoned for heresy, he was executed by being skinned alive and hung upon a gibbet, at the entrance of the college at which he had previously taught Islamic Jurisprudence, by order of the vizier of Iraq. He was only 33 when he died, which was also Jesus's supposed age at death.

What is significant about the Judge of Hamadhān's martyrdom, is not that he had predicted it, just as Jesus and Hallāj had predicted their own deaths. Nor that he endured it willingly and without fear, but that he was able to do so because *he had already experienced and survived death.*

Sometime before his martyrdom, Al-Hamadhānī's disciples, for a period of about one month, considered that he had died already. In a state in which he seemed to be

6

suspended in Time, and during which all visible signs of life had ceased, just like Jesus, he came back from the dead! This was a physically observable experience, which but for the failure of decay to set in, would have resulted in his disciples burying him. [10]

Explaining this experience to his disciples, as well as later would-be followers, he described it as a mystic state during which the self with its usual limited experience, is transcended:

Here (in this state) the ease of dying is shown to the disciple's (**Transcendent Self**). As he is subjected to this experience - which is beyond his control - he gives up, cutting all connections with that which is created (within Time) ... You must realise that there is another kind of life beyond the physical and the body's frame ... in this above and beyond world, *everything is perceived as life within Life,* whereas, to those who can only see this (limited) world, everything is as death within Death. Until you transcend death, you will never really have life ... *when you realise this (state) within yourself, then you will realise how death occurs (what it really is).* [11]

It was his realisation of a greater **Transcendent Self** in which the limited self of everyday experience is contained, that enabled Al-Hamadhānī to experience martyrdom without fear. It was for him a proof that bodily death can be transcended, a fate which he himself predicted, in his desire to follow in the footsteps of Hallāj.[12] His previous experience of a death-like state was that of transcending Time and the limited self. But is such an experience really possible? Is it not simply a case of a different culture with

7

different expectations? Or has anyone in the West, in contemporary times, experienced it?)

A Western Example of the Experience of Transcending Time

It was questions such as these, that led to my own experience of transcending Time and the limited self as a result of discovering Master *Bābā* Dovid Yūsuf, (a *maggid)* Sufi *Grandshaykh* and 'Teacher of the Age'.[13] Although I had investigated Healing and allied phenomena for over 20 years, here was someone who defied all the usual explanations. Unlike other healers whom I had met, this man avoided the limelight and for the most part worked anonymously. In many cases, he even practised healing without the recipient being aware of his existence. There was the case of the lady in hospital, dying of cancer, whose daughter had approached him without the mother being aware of it. To the amazement of the medics, she made a sudden recovery after having seen the *Shaykh* standing at her bedside (interpreted by the hospital staff as an hallucination). She was able to describe him graphically, even before she had any knowledge of his existence, let alone his appearance. Only later, when in conversation with her daughter, was the mysterious bedside figure identified.

There were many similar incidents like these, yet in every case, the *Shaykh* assured me that he could not heal

8

anyone. *"I have nothing whatsoever to do with it,"* was how he usually responded to questions about his healing powers. [14]

It was not until much later that I realised what he actually meant. According to the *Shaykh*, real healing - as opposed to self-induced states of wish fulfilment (what we might call faith-healing) - did not depend upon him (his limited self) at all. It was the **Greater Transcendent Self** (what in colloquial terms we refer to as God) that he held was responsible. Although this **Transcendent Self** did operate through and by him, it did so ONLY WHEN he ceased to be his limited self. To put it in the words of Al-Hamadhānī, it was when he ceased to be a *you* that he truly became *His Self:*

> *Do you understand what I say?* I say that as long as you are *'you'* and attached to your (limited) self, you do not really exist! When you cease to be *'you'* then you (truly) become yourself.[15]

Slowly, it dawned upon me, that it was this loss of individual limited consciousness, together with acquisition of a larger shared consciousness - the **Transcendent Self** - that the so-called 'mystic experience' was about, an experience not confined to any culture, time-period, or religion, but which is difficult to come by in our materialistic society, where everything is reduced to its lowest components. A society which sees symptoms of an illness as the illness; rather than as a result arising from the person as a whole being sick. In a society in which we

9

are controlled by, treated by and seen as machines, the holistic (whole) view of the mystic has no place.

I began to realise, that it was this view of the self that accounted for such cryptic phrases as Jesus's *"I and my Father are One"* – or, *"He who has seen me has seen the Father"*.[16] It was for similar reasons that Hallāj was branded as a heretic, for he had claimed that he was the *Truth, the Real(Haqq)* – a word that Jesus had also applied as an epithet to himself [17] – and an expression for God in Islamic culture. Much later, I was to understand how such a perception could occur, with my own experience of the **Transcendent Self**.

It was November 1984. I had led a Peace Walk from London to the tomb of the Patron saint of Ecology, St.Francis, in Assisi, Italy. It was part of a plea to world leaders to halt the arms race and to spend money on helping the poor in Ethiopia – a country that was having, what up until that time, was the worst famine the world had seen. Travelling back from Assisi, on a train through Switzerland to Germany, I was engrossed in meditative thought, when suddenly I found myself transported through Time. I saw *and experienced* myself speaking another language, in another place and another time.

To explain in words exactly what happened on this occasion is not really possible, despite the insistence of my publisher. Part of the Dictionary definition of the word TRANSCENDENCE is *to excel, or to surpass description, reason, belief, or usual range of human experience.* Yet, this does not mean that such a state does not exist. The fact that we have a word for it indicates that we are talking about something. Philosophers such as Kant, Schelling, and the American poet–philosopher Emerson, have all in their own way, established it as a part of human experience. What concerns us here, is not whether philosophy can establish the existence of such a state, but rather, what it means in terms of human experience and existence.

What can I say that would convey the overwhelming sense of such an experience? All I can say is that I became aware that what we normally experience as Time & Space – our physical and material reality – is in fact a partial, incomplete, and distorted view. There was a realisation, that all selves – including my own – were/are a part of/subject to, a **Greater** underlying and **All-Encompassing Self**. This **Greater Self**, was/is inseparable from cognition. I seemed to stand outside of my limited self, moving backwards and forwards in Time, as I viewed/participated in a series of lifetimes, experiencing them in their entirety, including death – each as real, in every sense of the word, as the present one, which from time to time, I came back to. I was living for hundreds of years, yet on coming back to present reality, I was aware that only minutes had passed in this time-space. It was this aspect which made the whole episode so disturbing.

Moving in and out of Time, I became aware that rationality, as it is generally understood, is no more than an economy of thought. (A total/holistic/All-encompassing view, cannot be explained, conceptualised, or grasped, within the limitations of reductionist thought.) Furthermore whilst absorbed in the state of TRANSCENDENCE, emotions as they are generally defined, ceased to have any meaning. Returning to everyday existence, meant experiencing a profound sense of loss. Of moving from a multidimensional REALITY, to a partial, limited and distorted one. Much later I was to learn - as we shall discuss in a later chapter - that Prophet Muhammad also experienced this sense of loss after his 'Night-time Visionary Journey'.

Now, such an incident could be explained as an hallucination, imagination, etc - but for one thing - the other people travelling with me in the railway carriage saw that something was affecting me physically, as well as mentally. I seemed to move from life to death - from one time-space to another - and then back again. It was my inability to convey to others what I was experiencing; together with my physically and mentally exhausted state, that caused those who accompanied me on the train, to insist that it be stopped. And that I be taken to hospital for an examination. When the train halted, an ambulance was sent for and I was hastened into the emergency department of the local hospital. A number of tests were taken, all of which showed that I had suffered a severe trauma – yet there was no apparent physical cause – and all psychological tests showed me to be of sound mind.

"We were convinced from your appearance, that you were on drugs and had had an overdose," said the consultant, "but your blood is entirely clear. I'm afraid I have no explanation whatsoever," he said. "If you had been an hysteric, then perhaps we could put it down to an hysterical seizure – but the problem is you aren't. Anyway, there are no signs of cardiac arrest, neurological disturbance, or anything that would explain it – You are the psychologist, you explain it!" he said, walking away puzzled.

Later that day, I was told I could leave. The mystery – at least for the Western medical system – remained. But for me, it was not a problem – but a solution! I had experienced a **Greater Self** – a self that was not confined to a limited time space – but a **Transcendent Self**, that operated in and through my own limited and bodily self. It was an experience that changed my life – an experience I shall never forget!

Quite clearly, my own Western model of psychology and therapy was lacking, since it could not account for, nor explain, such an experience. Could it be that somewhere, Western medical science, with all its technological wonders, had gone wrong? Was there, perhaps, an explanation that could account for both the

13

religious experience, the mystic's vision, paranormal phenomena and other seemingly bizarre incidents that seem to defy our view of the world as containing discreet entities, or limited selves?)

If Healing – in the fullest sense of the term – is in actuality, a concern with the whole person, then perhaps the clue to understanding such phenomena lies in understanding that the present general lack of trust in the orthodox Western medical model – the turning to alternative approaches to medicine and the mushrooming of new and/or different therapies – results from a failure to understand what it is that people are seeking. Whilst interest and involvement in religion is declining in the West, interest and participation in alternative therapies is increasing – Is there a correlation? Are Religion, Psychology and Medicine interdependent and related concerns? What is it that those who utilise alternative therapies are really seeking?

Plato (427–347 B.C.E.), disciple and biographer of the esoteric Master **Socrates**, who conveyed that Ancient Wisdom which ultimately became identified with Sufism. He travelled to Egypt, where according to Jewish tradition he became acquainted with Prophet Jeremiah's teachings.

Notes and References

1) I was later to learn, that Fātimah az-Zahrā', Muhammad's daughter had died similarly without sickness at age 29.

2) As we shall see, Sufism is a practice, or a spiritual discipline, and not a religion as such. Its adherents have been members of all faiths - and some of none. So that Sufism counts amongst its Masters; Socrates, 'Obadiyāh Maimonides - grandson of the famous Rabbi - St.Francis of Assisi, Kabīr the Indian saint, the original Sai Baba (not the present day one) a Hindu saint, Erich Fromm the Jewish American analyst, Goethe, Francis Bacon (the real Shakespeare) and many others.

3) For some examples, see *Arthur Clarke's World of Strange Powers*, John Fairley & Simon Welfare, Guild Publishing, London, 1984.

4) *Al-Hallaj Martyr Mystique de L'Islam*, Librarie Orientaliste, Paul Geuthner, Paris, 1921.

5) It should be noted, that it was not the Jewish people, as a whole, who were responsible for his death, a distortion that can be attributed to the later Christian Church, who wished to sever all links with the Jewish Faith that Jesus and his followers had practised.

6) John 5:18.

7) *La Passion d'Al-Hallaj*, Louis Massignon, first edition, Paris, 1922, pp, 759-761 & *Akbar 'Al-Hallaj* (Arabic text edited by Louis Massignon, Paris 1957). Compare these words with those of Jesus in Luke 23:34 & John 8:19,27-32,42-43 & 10:31-39.

8) Massignon, as above, compare with John 14:2; & 17:1-4,11 & Luke 23:43.

9) Although the Islamic Holy Book, the Qur'ān, does mention Jesus as a prophet and martyr, it gives few details.

10)'Ayn al-Qudāt al-Hamadhānī, *Zubdat al-Haqā'iq; Tamhīdāt; Shakwā 'l-Gharib*, edited by Afif Usayran, Tehran, 1962, pp, 231-232.

11) See the above, pp, 52,319,419 (emphases mine).

12) *Tamhīdat*, as above, pp, 232 & 235-236.

13) The Sufi say, that every hundred years, or so, a 'Teacher of the Age' appears who has the sole authority to speak for God, as did the prophets Moses and Muhammad, events being affected by his/her presence in the world. Although it is the duty of all Sufis to look for that Teacher, who takes precedence over all others, his existence often goes unrecognised but for a few disciples. About such Teachers, Prophet Muhammad is reputed to have said:*"God has hidden the men of greatest knowledge."*

14) Compare these words with those of the Biblical hero Joseph, in Genesis 41:16.

15) *Tamhīdāt*, as above, p,287.

16) John 10:30 & 14:9-10.

17) John 14:6.

16

SEEKING THE TRANSCENDENT

"Every Quack's hand makes you ill; come to me that I may treat you. "

Mevlana, Jalāl ad-Dīn ar-Rūmī

What are those who Utilise Alternative Therapies, Really Seeking?

There has been a gradual realisation that religious experience and psychology are not separate fields. Various books have flooded the market endeavouring to transcend the traditional distinction between psychology as an objective and materialistic science, and the highly personal and intersubjective world of religious experience. In addition, a number of more serious academic studies of non-Western forms of psychiatry have been undertaken over the last thirty-five years. Shafii, an American child psychiatrist, showed that non-Western forms of psychotherapy, including meditation techniques, whilst dealing with the range of human development as covered in Western psychiatry (though using different terms), also went far beyond aspects of the human psyche as covered in Western psychological theory.[1] This was also the conclusion of the eminent psychiatrist Deikman, who, after studying all non-Western psychotherapeutic methods over many years, concluded that Sufism was pre-eminent, going far beyond Western methods and theories.[2]

17

The study of religion, from a psychological point of view, goes back as far as 1902, with a classic work by William James,[3] that showed that religion and psychology are not in reality separate fields, but joint endeavours looked at from different perspectives. This is illustrated by the religious experience - the subject matter of James's book - that can only be understood by examining both fields. Whilst the book was in effect little more than a literary survey, containing no empirical studies, the late Sir Alister Hardy and his successors continued this enquiry, collecting thousands of examples of persons who had a religious, or mystical experience, most of which resulted in promoting their general well-being, if not actually profoundly changing their lives.[4] It was Sir Alister Hardy, an eminent Biologist and world-respected scientist, who in discussing with me at Merton College, Oxford, a paper that I had written as a young man, pointed out that my inclination towards always looking for the materialistic explanation was foolish, and not really objective as science is supposed to be. This encouragement and advice has, over the years, continued to be reinforced by my own findings.

Philosophers, going back to Ancient Greece, have always understood - as expounded by the injunction found over the temple at Delphi - that to *Know yourself is to know the Universe*. Over a thousand years later, Prophet Muhammad was reported to have said, *"Those who know*

18

themselves know God. "[5] In other words, the search for self-knowledge is the search for *Transcendence* : being an acknowledgement that it is the desire to understand those aspects within us that link us to the **Infinite** – however it may, or may not be defined. The experience of physical illness, or emotional trauma, causes us to consider our mortality, our vulnerability, and to seek to understand the meaning of our illness, as an experience in an ongoing experiential field called 'Life'. From the temple physicians of ancient Egypt, through the philosophers of ancient Greece, down to more recent figures such as the physicians Paracelsus and Nostradamus – and in our time to Lawrence LeShan and Linus Pauling – an understanding of life as a whole (religion and its philosophies), has never really been separated from an understanding of the individual's experience in the world (psychology and its allied sciences).

With the development of the Industrial Revolution and a science based upon looking at human beings as machines, medicine was reduced to a practice without meaning. Technological excellence replaced human understanding and feeling. Now in our time, it is the rejection of this attempt to make everyone into a lifeless, souless lump of matter – motivated solely by economic concerns – that has created the desire for something more, something else, translated in practice, into an interest in alternative-medicine, New Age groups, and other forms of consciousness expansion.

19

In other cases - especially the young - where such natural needs have not been obliterated, eliminated, pacified, or institutionalised, there has been a turning to drugs, Or a belief in extra-terrestials, poltergeist, or other forms of transcendent experience, in an attempt to retrieve this loss.

I would suggest that what is being sought is meaning in life; a relationship with the Universe; a fuller experience of the self; something beyond the limited everyday confinements of the material world. In short, *it is Transcendence that is being sought.* It is this experience of that which lies beyond the self that has formed the basis for the value-systems upon which cultures and civilisations have been erected for most of human history.

The failure to realise that Transcendence is something basic and necessary for human fulfilment,[6] has led to a crisis in Western psychiatry and medicine. Whilst we may see the closing down of mental hospitals and the so-called open door approach of psychiatry, as evidence of a fresh wind of change, it hides the bitter truth. Such an approach is motivated by a desire to reduce costs. It has little to do with concern for the patients, who having been institutionalised and unable to cope with our increasingly competitive lifestyle, now commit suicide in large numbers and even in some cases, murder.[7]

The reality is that drug therapy has become more sophisticated and acts so as to restrain people without the

20

need to lock them up, shock them, or surgically destroy their brain, though should drugging not be sufficient, these methods can be, and still are, sometimes used.

Religion and Psychiatry

An examination of medical history and anthropological texts will show the relevance of the spiritual - the transcendent factor - to human well-being. Whilst we generally term such concerns as religious, the word 'religion' is not sufficient to cover what is meant by spirituality. In other societies, it has a holistic or complete meaning; applying to concerns that go beyond the immediate, and which subsume within them, the social, individual and physical. The separation of the spiritual from everyday life, from political and scientific concerns (and even increasingly from moral and social ones) in our society, has led to the erroneous belief that this is necessary and beneficial. The truth is that in other societies - and in earlier times in our own - such a separation did not exist and this was not *in itself* harmful. The opinion that this is to society's benefit is based upon the dissemination of materialistic propaganda and is untrue, often involving a complete falsification of history. The ecological destruction, genocide, terrorism, violence, crime, marital disharmony and other associated phenomena that is characteristic of our society, show that this is not the case.

21

The endeavour to separate such concerns is in fact artificial: for it is the effects of death; anxiety over life in terms of its meaning; sexuality; family violence, and other associated matters, that are of primary concern to the psychologically disturbed. Such matters have always been in the past (and still are in many societies) a spiritual concern.

Social anthropologists like Lewis,[8] have explored the world of the Tribal Healer, and compared such examples with those in Classical times, discovering that spirituality is of fundamental importance to such societies and irretrievably linked with the medical belief-system. We assume, to our cost, that our medical system - including psychology and psychiatry - is objectively free of spiritual values, but is this really the case?

Social systems and their cultures depend upon values which underpin the structure of the society in question, and which by their expression, continuously reinforce it. The culture reminds; recollects; and perpetuates these values; together with the institutions which arise from them, and which in turn validate them. When the materialist argues that we are motivated by greed, self-concern, or power, he or she is basing such a viewpoint upon beliefs - a set of values - which enable that person to both conceptualise and express such views. Further-more, when the materialist does so, he or she utilises terms and ideas, which, originally and traditionally, were

22

the province of the spiritual teacher. Though we may change the terms - the words employed - in the end they do not alter the situation. For any system necessarily depends for its existence upon shared values; values that originate within the mind.

The underlying problems of all societies are to do with states of mind. Unless we begin to look at how such states arise; can be understood, explored and utilised (not ignored, controlled, abused or invalidated) can problems be dealt with. It is the mind - *the self* - what it may, or may not be, and how it operates, that traditionally was the concern of both the medical specialist, as well as the spiritual teacher. In the past - which is still the case in some societies - doctor and priest were the same person.

We may define such persons as 'Healers'. Their continuation and proliferation in our own society [9] is an indication of their importance to human well-being. My own experience in alternative-medicine, over the past 30 years, has shown that when persons seek out an alternative, or complementary practitioner - regardless of what therapy is involved - what they are seeking is healing - in the fullest sense of the term. (There is a need to talk about and share; personal concerns, incidents and events, of which the presenting problem - the physical malady - is just a symptom, or aspect of, the whole pattern and process involved.)

A concern with the whole person by such practitioners,

is a continuation of the ongoing healing tradition of ancient times, even though it might not be recognised as such. It is an expression of frustration at a mechanistic and meaningless existence, and a desire to discover something more.

That something more, something outside ourself – yet which continually interacts with it – does exist! The claim it does, is the *oldest and most emphatic claim* of persons from every type of culture and civilisation, dating back to the dawn of history. The fact this claim has been universally made, still persists; and has been responsible for some of the greatest acts of humanity and greatness; that people have given their lives – and still do – for it, argues for its existence. Furthermore, persons who lay claim to having accessed it, have been involved in healing – miraculous cures – and other strange (phenomena, that defy our limited and reductionist perception of the self and its world.)

Could it be that the understanding of such experience is to be found in a different conception of the world, that also allows us to be different; to transcend the everyday world of existence?

To answer these questions, we need to discover the roots of the ongoing and underlying esoteric tradition, which Gurdjieff and others have connected with Sufism,[10] a basis upon which the world religions were later built.

The Continuity of Esoteric Egyptian Teaching

While it is not our purpose to fully examine the history of ancient Egypt and its relationship to earlier – and influence upon – later, civilisations – a subject that has been adequately dealt with elsewhere [11] – a few facts are needed to establish our theoretical base, before expounding the teachings and methods employed in Sufism.

According to the esoteric Master – the Sufi *Shaykh* and statesman, Abū Hafs 'Umar Suhrawadī (died 1234), there has been a transmission of the Ancient Wisdom, by a succession of teachers, going back to *Hermes of Egypt.* Disciples have gathered together to study and learn from what remains of this transcendent knowledge, using time-honoured methods. These teachings are emulated and expounded by the Master of the Age – *Al-Insān-al-Kāmīl;* the Perfected, Complete, or Universal Teacher – who always appears at the necessary time.[12] This Teacher is a reappearance of Divine Wisdom personified, as epitomised in *Khidr* (the legendary teacher of Moses),[13] *Idrīs* – the Biblical Enoch – and also, Melchizedek and Elijah.[14]

The name *al-Khidr* literally means 'the green one'; referring to the continual growth and freshness of Divine Knowledge; always transcending the limited knowledge and ossified religions, of the time at which it appears. The link with ancient Egypt is clearly apparent here, for the god Osiris was painted green (the colour of Islam) to represent the annual rebirth, or flooding, of the river Nile.

25

That Suhrawardī should claim that Sufism's source is *Hermes of Egypt*, is of great interest, for as any student of the esoteric (regardless of what external tradition is followed) knows, *Hermes* reputation as a Healer, and author of esoteric texts, is legendary. Generally referred to in the Greek texts as *Hermes Tristmegistos*, meaning 'thrice born', the Church Fathers were unable to decide on whether or not he preceded Moses. This problem is resolved by realising that there is an ongoing substratum of esoteric knowledge, independent of the external religions.

Hermes was the Greek name for the Egyptian *Thoth/Osiris* who became deified as a god.[15] *Thoth* was called *Theuth* by Plato,[16] who stated that he was a man of great wisdom who lived in Egypt. Cicero tells us he was from Thebes and was a 'Lawgiver'. Reputed to have lived in the town of Khumunu (modern al-Ashmūnayn) in Upper Egypt, he can be identified with the spiritual Master *Djhowtey*, the original source of the esoteric tradition that later came to be identified with Sufism. [17]

Viewed from this perspective, Sufism can be identified with mainstream esotericism, passing through *Hermetic*, *Pythagorean* and *Platonic* traditions.[18] Thus, *Hermes* is born *thrice;* first in Egypt, then as Moses the Hebrew, before finally being reborn in ancient Greece. It is therefore equivalent to the Greek *Hagia Sophia* (**Divine Wisdom**),[19] differences being accounted for on the basis of

26

different social contexts, circumstances and needs of the time.[20]

As we shall see, there are many parallels between the ideas of Socrates and the teachings of the Sufi, who have claimed him as one of their own.[21] In more recent times, the analytical psychologist Jung, utilised the concept of archetypes, which is similar to that of Socrates, Ideal Forms, having derived the notion from the esoteric tradition of Sufism via his study of alchemy.[22] Philosopher and psycholinguist Chomsky, has arrived at similar conclusions from his study of language.[23]

In Plato, stories (the myth) focus the mind on what cannot be proved by logical argument.[24] These are to Socrates *beautiful discourses* through which the mind is *charmed* and the fear of death overcome.[25] This *telling of tales* parallels Sufi stories, which cannot be understood in a purely logical way, for they are designed to work at a different level. Similarly, Sufis have intimated that Shakespeare's tragedies were based on Sufi stories,[26] for, like the Greek tragedy, they act so as to affect one on a deep level, by showing the comic-tragic nature of life.

Sufism and the Continuity of the Therapy of the Ancients
Seeing Sufism as a continuation of mainstream esotericism, whose repository and source was Egypt, does not mean we need to see Egypt as its exclusive source, but rather as the civilisation that secretly preserved, through its esoteric

masters, the Ancient Wisdom of earlier ages, that subsequently became the basis of later civilisations. The story of Moses in the Bible, as also of Joseph's and Abraham's sojourns in Egypt, are *mythologised* (history plus legend) accounts of this. [27]

The remnants of these earlier ages are to be found in Persia, India and Central Asia, as well as in the practices of the Shaman healers of traditional societies. Though these practices have become obscured and distorted over time, there is still preserved within them the elements of an authentic, original and primal tradition that show a common psychological origin.

A characteristic of such healers is their use of inspired poetry; sometimes sung or chanted. This has an ancient lineage and the religious books of the world are simply the development (and often distorted) remnants of this tradition. [28] Still a practice of genuine Sufi Masters, [29] it shows the same pattern as the Greek *demioergoi* and *Homerids* and the Hebrew *moshelim* who preceded them. [30] In addition, like the early Freemasons – for whom Shah claimed a connection [31] – Sufis are often artists and specialist craftsmen, as well as being poets and/or musicians, as was the case with the Greek bards, a fact which is reflected by the names of some of the Orders. [32]

The fact that the *Bard* has existed in a variety of traditions – geographically, as well as historically – is indication of a common origin. Its psychological basis is an acknowledgement of the creativity of the ecstatic utterance, that depends for its existence upon a universal underlying experience - the transcending of individual consciousness. Note what a nineteenth century, Kara Kirghiz Bard, from north of the Hindu Kush, had to say regarding this experience: [33]

> I can sing every song; for God has planted the gift of song in my heart. He gives me the word on my tongue without my having to seek it. *I have not learned any of my songs; everything springs up from my inner being, from my Self.*

The Christian might point to the ecstatic experience of speaking in tongues, and we are also reminded of the Biblical accounts of Deborah's song, of the song of Moses, and of the book of Psalms.[34]

To understand the universal psychophysiological basis of this phenomenon, we need to witness the Sufi's use of the breath, which reflects both Yogic practices as well as the recitation of Japanese love chants, where a charmed expression is recited three times on the one breath.[35]

نفس *nafs*, the Arabic and Sufi word for self, is akin to *nafas* (breath), being derived from the same root. The latter word also means; "freedom" and "liberty", so that in every case, there is a recognition, a realisation, that life - the expression of a limited individual self - is but a manifestation of a Greater underlying Unity - a **Transcendent Self** . To control the breath is to become aware of the essential nature of **Reality**, just as in all cases,

29

chanting involves a spontaneous natural rhythm that parallels baby rocking, sexual intercourse (where breathing rates also change) and tidal movements.

Sufism could be described as inducing birth *(nifās)* – meaning a *realisation* of the **Transcendent Self** –by creating a recognition of the inevitable death of the limited individual self, a fact which is usually ignored, or pushed away from consciousness. It does this by giving up, or controlling – breath*(nafas)*, freedom*(nafas)*, liberty*(nafas)*, of the limited self, just as the Cuna Shaman of South America, uses a rhythmic chant to induce childbirth.[36]

The echoes of other forms of spiritual experience, such as Buddhism and Christianity, are examples of the common origin of these later traditions, who have developed the One Transcendent Truth – expressions of a **Transcendent Self** – in their own culturally specific way. So that, the Sufi martyr, 'Ayn al-Qudāt al-Hamadhānī, referred to in **chapter one**, uses a saying of Jesus on being *born again*, when discussing the Sufi experience. Such parallels are for the Sufi deliberate. Seen as expressions of a Transcendent Truth, they do not require that there be actual knowledge – in a scholarly sense – of alternative traditions.[37]

We have seen in **chapter one**, how, not only Sufi martyrs, but also ordinary Sufi individuals have been able to face death without fear. Here we have linked this overcoming of the fear of death with experience of a **Greater Transcendent Self**. We shall expand on this in due

30

course, but let us note for the moment that Sufism is an expression - a continuity - of a primordial and essentially therapeutic process. By confronting the death of the individual limited self - dealing with its capacity to create an underlying anxiety and power to destabilise the personality - anxiety is decreased, and awareness created of a **Transcendent Self** that permeates all Existence. The Sufi would say that it is not sex (as in Freud) that is repressed, but the fear of death. This is akin to the Shaman, or tribal healer's technique of initiation, in which death is participated in by the overcoming of a traumatic, or life-threatening experience.[38] Sufi practices - as in the temple rites of ancient Egypt, and preparations for death in Tibetan Buddhism[39] - can be seen as a means of rehearsing death.

This confrontation with the death of the limited self is vividly illustrated by the story of the famous Sufi Master, Farīd ad-Dīn 'Attār (died 1229), told here by *Bābā* Dovid Yūsuf:[40]

> Before he became the famous Suf Master, poet and author, Farīduddīn was a Medical Herbalist. He also produced perfumes - notably from roses - which gave him his name '*Attar*. It was whilst working in his shop, that something happened that was to dramatically change his life.
>
> A bedraggled Dervish came into the shop, intent on the collecting of alms. Farīduddīn was busy attending his customers, oblivious to the poor man desperate for some small change with which he could buy something to eat.

"Can you not serve me?" said the Dervish.

"Wait, for I am busy at the moment!" said Farīduddīn.

"How will you have time to die?" said the Dervish,

"When my time comes I shall die just like you", said Farīduddīn.

"Do you mean what you say; if I die will you die also?" said the Dervish.

"What foolishness is this?" said Farīduddīn irritatedly, *"Of course I shall die, just like you!"*

At this point, the Dervish ignoring customers in the shop, put down his begging-bowl, bottom side up. Resting his head on it, he lay down on the floor, and saying *"There is no god, but THAT which is!"* [41] he expired.

Farīduddīn was so taken aback that he dropped everything, closed up his shop, gave all that he had to the poor and dressing himself in a sack from his shop, took up the life of a Dervish.

When later he gathered a group of disciples around him, he would explain to those who came to listen, that it was because he had died on that day with the Dervish, that he had been resurrected, to a new life, a new beginning.

Notes and References

1) M.Shafii, *Freedom from the Self: Sufism, Meditation and Psychotherapy*, Human Sciences Press, New York, 1985.

2) A.Deikman,"Deautomatization and the Mystic Experience", *Psychiatry* 1966 (29),pp,324-338 & "Sufism and Psychiatry"*Journal of Nervous and Mental Diseases* 1977 (165), pp,318-329.

3) William James, *The Varieties of Religious Experience*, Fontana, London, 1960.

4) Sir Alister Hardy, *The Spiritual Nature of Man*, Clarendon Press, Oxford, 1979 and *The Divine Flame: An Essay Towards a Natural History of Religion*, William Collins, London, 1966.

5) According to the Sufi Master, Abū Bakr Muhammad Muhyī-d-Dīn ibn 'Arabī (died 1240), in his *Treatise on Being*. Also in Rūmī's *Mathnawī* 5:2114.

6) One exception to this was R.D.Laing (see his *The Divided Self* & *Transcendental Experience in Relation to Religion and Psychosis* in **Bibliography**) whose psychosis and premature death from alcoholism, is sometimes used as an example, to justify seeing and treating psychological disturbance as simply a case of biochemical abnormalities within the brain.

7) **MIND** (the society for the psychologically disabled), annual reports for 1993 forward. Available from **MIND**, Granta House, 15-19 Broadway, Stratford, London E15 4BQ.

8) I.M.Lewis, *Ecstatic Religion: An Anthropological Study of Spirit Possession and Shamanism*, Penguin, Harmondsworth, 1971.

9) When I began to investigate healing, over 30 years ago, it was a rare phenomenon and interest in religion was still strong. Today at the time of writing, only 4 per cent of the population of the UK regularly attend any form of Church, whilst there are over 10,000 registered 'spiritual' healers and an equal number of 'secular' healers, i.e., alternative therapists.

10) See Rafael Lefort, *The Teachers of Gurdjieff*, Gollanz, London, 1969 & Idries Shah, *The Sufis*, Octagon Press, London, 1964.

11) David Rohl, *Legend: The Genesis of Civilisation*, Arrow Books, London, 1999.

12) *'Awārif al-Ma'ārif* (**Bounties of Divine Knowledge**) 'Alāmiyya Press, Cairo, 1358/1939. Also to be found in Al-Ghazālī's *Ihyā'*, etc.,(see **Bibliography**) 1334 A.H. edition. Perfected does not mean perfect.

13) The account is to be found in the *Qur'ān* 18:65-82.

14) *Qur'ān* 21:85, **Genesis** 5:21-24; 14:18, **2 Kings** 2:1-18, **Hebrews** 11:5, **Jude** 14-15. There is also a *Book of Enoch* amongst the Dead Sea Scrolls (see **Appendix 4**).

15) Bernal 1991 (see **Bibliography**), Vol. 1, pp, 144-145.

16) *Phaedrus*, in Plato (I) (see **Bibliography**), pp, 561-563.

17) See above, also Bernals 1991, p, 139.

18) According to the Platonic view, the things and people we love on

earth are reminders to us of the Paradise from which we come and to which we will return. Unlike the Peripatetics, Stoics, Epicureans and other schools of Greek philosophy, the Platonists (Plotinus, Neopythagoreans, Gnostics) believed in revealed doctrines, revered their teachers as masters of higher learning, and believed that this knowledge was inaccessible to the logical mind. All these beliefs - as we shall see - are characteristic of Sufi teaching.

19) This term should not be confused with the *Sophists* of ancient Greece, despite some similarities (see note below). It should be realised that in the interaction between Socrates and the Sophists (many of whom turned to Socrates) the influence of the former upon the latter, was likely to have been considerable. This parallels the situation between Sufism and pseudo-Sufis, many of whom derive their influence and/or origins and teachings from genuine masters.

20) Gorgias the Sophist (brother of the physician Herodicus of Leontini c 500 B.C.E.) taught that the rhetorician had to speak according to the *eidê* (species, type) and the *kairos* (occasion) of the minds of the hearer, a concept which is basic to Sufism and has been repeated by Masters, such as Ibn 'Arabī, Jalāl ad-Dīn ar-Rūmī, Idries Shah & *Bābā* Dovid Yūsuf (see *Eulogy of Helen* 10-14).

21) F.Sezgin, **Geschichte des Arabischen Schrifttums**, Brill, Leiden, 1971, pp, 58,77,96-110.

22) Titus Burckhardt, **Alchemy**, Element, Shaftesbury, 1986, pp, 8-9, 18-19 & R.Landau,**The Philosophy of Ibn 'Arabi**, New York, 1959, p, 4 ff; C.G.Jung, **Modern man in Search of a Soul**, Routledge & Kegan Paul, London, 1961, pp, 5 & 15 and R.J.Evans, **Jung on Elementary Psychology**, Routledge & Kegan Paul, London 1979, pp, 68-70. However, unlike the Sufi, Jung did not acknowledge that the **Divine (Transcendent)** is *a priori* but considered symbols as part of our *psychic heritage* (see Evans 1979, pp, 65-74).

23) A.N.Chomsky, **Syntactic Structures**, Mouton, Hague, 1957.

24) **Phaedo** 77e, 78a, 144d.

25) **Charmides** 157a-157c.

26) Martin Lings, **The Secret of Shakespeare**, Aquarian Press, Wellingborough, 1984, pp, 134-140.

27) See **Genesis** 11:1-9 & **Qur'ān** 2:213. Persia and later Egypt, were repositories of this knowledge transmitted in abbreviated form, i.e., code (mythology, oral tradition, ritual systems) the decipherment of which has to a large extent been lost. See Bernal 1991, Vol. 1,pp, 24-26 & note (11).

28) For the history of such see: Parry 1970, Lord 1960, Bowra 1952, Chadwick 1942 (full details in the **Bibliography**).

29) This is one of the hallmarks of the genuine Sufi Master. The fact that with few exceptions, original poetry that is chanted, or sung in an extemporaneous way, can rarely be witnessed (*Bābā* Dovid Yūsuf is an exception), is an example of the demise of genuine Sufism at the present time.

30) *Demioergoi* - literally 'workers for the people'; travelling craftsmen

and poet-musicians (*Odyssey* 17:382-385). The *Homerids* were the preservers of their Master Homer's text (Plato's *Phaedrus* 252b) and the two groups were essentially the same; see M.I.Finley, *The World of Odysseus*, Chato & Windus, London, second edition 1977, pp,36-40,55-56. For the *moshelim*, see **Numbers** 21:27-31.

31) Idries Shah, *The Sufis*, Octagon Press, London, 1964, pp,172-191; 225-227;399.

32) The *Naqshbandiyya*, who in a variety of ways are linked to all the Orders - i.e., they alone have the authority to initiate into other Orders - are named after Muhammad Bahā' ad-Dīn Naqshband of Bukhara (died 1389), whose name means Designer. Its members originally formed a craft guild *(asnāf)* that specialised in mosque building. For a fuller examination of the connection between Sufism, artisans and musicians, see Spencer Trimingham, *The Sufi Orders in Islam*, Clarendon Press, Oxford, 1971, pp, 234-235,238.

33) C.N.Bowra, *Heroic Poetry*, Macmillan, London, 1952, p, 41.

34) **Judges** 5 & **Exodus** 15.

35) For the *Yogi*, life is determined by the number of breaths taken; for the Japanese *Shamon,* all breaths are linked in the One Breath

36) Claude Lévi-Strauss,*Structural Anthropology*, Basic Books, New York, 1963, pp, 186-205.

37) Compare **John** 3:3 & 'Ayn al-Qudat al-Hamadhānī's words in his *Tamhīdāt* (see **Bibliography** re-details), 1962, p, 319.

38) Parallels between the experiences of the realised Sufi and those of the Shaman are striking; see Iona Lewis, "What is a Shaman?" in *Folk* Vol. 23, 1981, pp, 30-33 & his *Ecstatic Religion*, Penguin, Harmondsworth, 1971, pp, 188-192 & 198-199.

39) W.Y. Evans-Wentz (Editor), *The Tibetan Book of the Dead*, Oxford University Press, Galaxy edition, New York, 1960 (originally published 1927) & Rohl (as above) 1998, pp, 387-395.

40) Alhough this account may be allegorical rather than historical - a factor which is common for many of the stories of the masters, including the links in the chain of transmission of teachings *(isnād)* - it is actual in that it teaches an essential truth as realised by 'Attar. His famous *Conference of the Birds* is referred to in our last chapter.

41) This is the actual -as near as possible in terms of meaning- translation of the first part of the *Shahādah* or Islamic creed.

3

THE SUFI EXPERIENCE

"The people are asleep - when they die they wake-up!"

Muhammad the prophet

Muhammad and the Sufi

The Sufi recognises that there are different levels of consciousness, and all Sufi practices are designed to produce an awareness of this fact. This is done by allowing the centre of consciousness - the innermost being, or Spirit - to transcend the limitations of the earthly and conditioned self. This means rising above the ordinary self, so as to experience the **Transcendent Self** that permeates all Existence.

To achieve a state of perpetual awareness of the **Transcendent Self** - and consequently of the Unity of Existence (*Tawhīd*)- the Sufi practises withdrawal *(khalwah)* : solitude and fasting - including abstinence from sexual relations. During such periods of isolation, there will be a constant reflection on the Unity of Existence, by a repetitive chanting of invocatory phrases (Names of God),[1] that induce a recognition, remembrance, recollection, of the **Transcendent Self**. The Arabic word for this practice, *Dhikr*, literally means 'to cause to remember'; also 'to mention, or state'. In Persian it is *Zikr*, and in Hebrew *Zeker*.

Very often this takes place as a series of night vigils *(Tahajjud)*, and it is likely that the Holy Book of Islam *(Qur'ān* – literally 'Recitation', i.e., a revelation chanted in poetic form) began as a response to such invocations.[2] For it was whilst living in a cave known as *Hirā'*, when taking part in the traditional yearly retreat of *Takhannus* (involving a withdrawal for a month, by men, from social responsibilities, including fasting, isolation and sexual abstinence, so as to meditate on problems of living) that the merchant Muhammad was overwhelmed by a realisation of his **Transcendent Self**, that ultimately led to him becoming the Prophet of Islam. Whilst Muslims will interpret this as a description of the angel Gabriel, a close examination of the text will reveal that this is not the case. Gabriel is not mentioned anywhere in these verses.[3]

In the mythology of ancient Greece, as in the Bible, there is a reference to Hagar,[4] the *Egyptian* second wife of Abraham and mother of his first son Ishmael. There was thus a realisation of the Egyptian origin of the esoteric tradition in ancient Greece – so that Muhammad as an initiate of this tradition, looked to the same cultural origin for his beliefs as Socrates. Muhammad belonged to the *Hunafā'*, who in contrast to the polytheistic idol worshippers of his time, were monotheists, that practised a form of mysticism that they claimed went back to Ishmael, the half–Egyptian ancestor of Muhammad's clan.

Bābā Dovid Yūsuf pointed out that the story of Hagar

37

being turned out into the desert to wander, by Abraham's jealous first wife Sarah,[5] is an esoteric description of how the original pure teaching (Ishmael was the first son) originating in Egypt (Hagar), though rejected by the *externalists* (i.e., Sarah, symbolic of the dogmatic power-seeking clerics - *of all religions* - in contrast to the self-sacrificing teachers of underlying spiritual truths) survived, despite its wandering (from one cultural expression to the next) to ultimately flourish by Divine protection (God made a spring well-up to preserve Hagar and her son Ishmael) in the desert (Muhammad in Arabia). It is from this source - the esoteric tradition transmitted by (though distinct from) Islam -that Sufism comes. The common origin of both Judaism and Islam is symbolised by the figure of Abraham. Significantly, Muhammad's family had connections with Yemen, an ancient trading people, that - like Abraham - travelled throughout the Middle East, including Israel, and contained a large and influential Jewish community. It was probably these links that enabled Muhammad to settle in the predominantiy Jewish town of Medina - and also to settle the disputes between them and the Arabs - when he took refuge there, after fleeing for his life from Mecca. The *Qur'ān* (16:103) also tells us that Muhammad had a Teacher of *foreign tongue* who spoke Arabic with an accent, which together with the fact that Muhammad, to begin with, followed Jewish practices, such as praying three times a day in the

38

direction of Jerusalem - and especially the way in which these prayers are chanted - makes it probable that this Teacher was a Jew. [6]

By the time of Muhammad(570-632), *Takhannus* had degenerated into self-indulgent speculations over problems thought to be set up by the rival gods of the *Ka'aba*, the temple of Mecca. As ancestral idols (anthropologists would say totems) they reflected Arabia's warring factions fighting for dominance and control. Muhammad's 'Revelation' was that these differences could be transcended by uniting clans in the worship of One God.

Thus the *Hunafā'* were Sufi forebearers, and in this sense Muhammad was a Sufi before he was a prophet, and a Muslim in the way we now understand this word. [7] Moreover, his ecstatic utterances, melodically chanted - which form the basis of the Islamic Holy Book *(Qur'ān)*, were expressions of his **Transcendent Self**, and parallel those of the bards of all traditions that existed before him, a fact testified to in that Revelation itself (*Qur'ān* 41:43).

Muhammad taught that the *Ka'aba* had been erected on the site of what had originally been a temple to the One God, built by his forefather Abraham and son Ishmael. [8] Like the masters before him, Muhammad expounded his teachings by stories that dramatised the point he wished to make, reciting in poetry, rather than prose, so transcending rational thought processes, a pattern that has subsequently been followed by all genuine Sufi Masters.

39

Later, after a lifetime of struggle, during which he had to flee for his life, he triumphantly returned to his city, together with an enormous following, so causing Mecca to capitulate without war. It was then that he gave orders for the *Ka'aba* to be cleansed of its 360 ancestral idols, uniting the warring clans in the belief in One God, so overcoming their bloody feuds by the *Way of Transcendence*.

This masterful stroke of genius was a visible sign of a realisation within himself! For the Sufi, the idols, which Muhammad cast out of the *Ka'aba*, were the tangible manifestations of the attachments, desires, fears and expectations, by which they were enslaved. Sufism is a cleansing of the heart, or *Ka'aba*, which in Western psychological jargon would be defined as deconditioning. We should notice that in order to obtain unity amongst the warring tribes, it was necessary that there be a Unity of Spirit. Establishing it depended upon overcoming not only petty tribal squabbles, but also internal psychological divisions. A unified *psyche* was the route by which internal national divisions were transcended; for polytheism is a reflection of an internal psychological dualism, as much as it is of a social one.

For the above reasons, it can be seen that Muhammad is central to the continuity of the esoteric tradition. Not only does he provide an outstanding example of a 'Teacher of the Age' (as Moses, Jesus, etc., were of theirs) – *Al-Insān al-Kāmīl* ; the Perfected, Complete, Universal, or

Transcendent Teacher - but he also became the continuator of the esoteric tradition, for which Egypt had become the repository. (Whilst the esoteric traditions of Judaism and Christianity - whose links with Egypt cannot be doubted [9] - had by this time, for the most part, died out, Islam, through Muhammad, retained and restored them.

The importance of Sufism to this revival cannot be over estimated.) For example, in the case of Judaism, the great Rabbi Maimonides(1135-1204), had a grandson, 'Obadiyāh, who wrote a treatise on Sufism (see **Bibliography**), and an Order can be traced to him. The concept of the 'Hidden Teacher' that began with a saying of Muhammad, was passed on, through both *Shī'ah* Islam, and the Jewish mystic book, the *Zohar*, compiled in Islamic Spain.[10] The common source to both traditions has been acknowledged by informed Kabbalists,[11] whose use of the term *En Soph* אין סוף for the Infinite - a word that is unsemitic in its construction - shows a link to Greek thought (*Hagiah Sophia* Divine Wisdom) as well as to Sufism. The **Book Jetzira**, which the Kabbalists claim as their oldest document (prior to the **Zohar**) was shown as long ago as 1832, to belong to the *Geonim* period, i.e., about the ninth century C.E.[12] - and nothing since this time has been found to invalidate this claim. Much later, this same Jewish mystical tradition, with its Islamic roots, was to influence Sigmund Freud (though he distorted it), by his creation of Psychoanalysis. [13]

41

In Christianity's case, it was primarily because of persecution, and the adoption of Pauline Christianity, by Emperor Constantine, that this link was lost. However, since discovery of the *Gnostic Gospels* and the *Dead Sea scrolls*, it has become apparent that original Christianity was a form of Judaism very similar to early Islam. The *Theraputae of Egypt* and the *Essenes of Qumran*, like the Sufi, wore wool as a symbol of sacrifice (the Passover lamb) also conducting sacred dance.[14] That there is a likely link between the *Essenes* and John the Baptist in the desert has often been pointed out.

This does not mean that Islam represents Muhammad's teachings - quite the contrary - like the other religions, Islam is a distorted and debased expression of what in origin is One pure primal Truth. For this reason, Sufis who have professed an outward allegiance to Islam (some have not) have often been brutally persecuted, murdered, or suppressed.

An example of the difference between Sufism and Islam can be seen in the life of the eminent Islamic jurist and theologian, Abū Hāmid Muhammad al-Ghazālī (died 1111). Whilst his contribution to the continuity of Islam is widely acknowledged - and his books often quoted by orthodox Muslims - his 40 volume monumental work *Ihyā 'Ulūm ad-Dīn* (The Revival of the Religious Sciences), was burnt in Cordova, during the reign of the Islamic ruler 'Alī ibn Yūsuf Tashfīn (died 1143). Yet, he had spent most of his life reconciling Sufi beliefs with Islamic theology.[15] The continual harassment, ostracism and ridicule, that the Sufi experiences, occasioned the exoterically and orthodox grounded Sufi, Abū'l-Qāsim ibn Muhammad al-Junayd (died 910), to state that *"None reaches the rank of Truth until a thousand honest people testify that he is a heretic,"* this being a veiled reference to the later Sufi martyr Al-Hallāj (see **chapter one**), whom he openly excluded from his circle for reasons of safety.[16]

Discovering the Transcendent Self

What distinguishes Sufism from all external religious sytems is its ability to transcend the definition of *finite* self and *Infinite* Self. It is this capacity, that despite its primary use of the Islamic format as a vehicle for its teachings (sometimes it has used other religions) is what marks it out as something different from Islam.

This ability of Sufism to transcend limitations can be discovered by examining one of the symbols employed in Sufism - the double-headed axe *(tabar)*. Its meaning - like the symbols of Freemasonry - is of many levels and interpreted according to the degree of progress of the initiate. This symbol, which occurs in connection with many Sufi Orders, but most significantly in the *Khalwatī* and *Ni'matullāhī*, in essence, refers to the active capacity of the realised human being, to act as an agent of Divine knowledge. In other words, the ability to discriminate, or

43

what we would define as consciousness, brings with it the knowledge of, and capacity for, *both* good and evil (as in the story of the Garden of Eden). Understanding this symbol by Sufi decipherment shows how Sufism – though it has used Islam for its transmission – precedes and is independent of, any of the existing religions. To discover the crucial meaning, we need to remember that the Sufi Master, Suhrawardī, traced Sufism back to ancient Egypt, which has many connections with both the external aspects of Islam, as well as the esoteric tradition. Apart from Muhammad – whom we have seen was a continuator of the esoteric Egyptian teachings, and whose ancestress was the Egyptian Hagar (in the mystic tradition she is seen as an Egyptian princess, a fact acknowledged by the Jewish Rabbis) and the obvious geographical, historical and other ethnic links – there are also many parallels between the external religions of both Islam and Egypt, as well as with Sufism. This should not surprise us, in view of what we have already discovered.

Râ, the original primary God, associated with the sun (see *Qur'ān* 24:35-36), is spoken of in the *Egyptian Book of the Dead* (17:1-4) as *One* and also as a *composite of Names* – all characteristics of the Islamic *Allāh*. Thoth, the founder of the Egyptian religion, is personified as the moon (a symbol of Islam) and acts as a spokesman for *Râ*. Thoth, is also credited with being the inventor of writing, founder of the social order, scribe, interpreter, and *Râ's* representative on earth. When he speaks for *Râ*, he speaks with *Words* (or Names) *of Power* (E.B.D. = *Egyptian Book of the Dead* 23:30), the invoking, or use of such Words (Names of God), being the means of *Râ* being known/revealed/remembered(E.B.D.110), concepts that are paralleled by the notion of God's messenger – prophet (Muhammad) and the sacredness of the *Qur'ān*.

(Both have the concept of a bodily resurrection after death)(E.B.D. 1:1; Pyramid text: *Teta* 1:248,270; *Papyrus of Nebseni* 177-178). Each depicts judgment after death as the weighing of deeds on a scale (*Qur'ān* 21:47;23:102-103), with the reward of an *earthly* Paradise, that is well-watered (*Qur'ān* 3:15,198; 4:57; 5:122; 15:45; 18:31; 22:23; 43:70-73). In the vicinity of *Râ* (under his many Names) is a sacred tree -- a Tamarisk or *Unbu* –(E.B.D. ·42; & 28:2; Pyramid texts: *Unas* 107, *Teta* 66; & 39). According to a saying of Muhammad, the *Tuba* is a tree planted by *Allāh* in Paradise, into which He breathed His spirit, whilst the sacred *Lote Tree* (Tamarisk?) is planted at the *farthest reaches of Paradise* and is *enshrouded in mystery* –*Qur'ān* 53:14-16.

In the *Qur'ān* (20:70-73; 26:46-52) Moses converts the magician priests of Egypt, who shaved their heads and wore a white unseamed garment over one shoulder (Maspero 1904-1906, Vol.9, p, 357), just as the Muslim does when going on pilgrimage to Mecca. Also, the ancient Egyptians greeted one another in the street by making a ritual bow, sinking the hands to the knees, in the same way as Muslims do during communal prayer (*Herodotus Book 2*), etc.

In ancient Egyptian heiroglyphics, *Osiris/Thoth*, the deification of the spiritual Master *Djhowtey*, is represented as a ram = *ba* and/or Ibis (heron-like bird) = *ba*. The word for soul or inner essence is also *ba*. *Ba* is represented in hieroglyphics as a heron, because a heron *cleaves* the water with its bill when spearing a fish, just as the ram, also *ba*, digs with its head. In every case, the meaning is: piercing; splitting; or cleaving power, and from this is derived the symbol of the axe. The soul – or *ba*, according to this concept – penetrates; pierces; divides = **The Intellect** *('Aql)* according to Sufism; where it equates with the Divine faculty of *Knowing*, having reference to the power of discrimination, implying separation through the consciousness of both Good and Evil.[17] We should also note, that this *knowledge of good and evil* – as in the Garden of Eden – has sexual connotations, for in Arabic, the word *ba* is used as a 'Word of power' to explain the conception of Jesus.[18] In the Bible to *know a woman* meant to have sexual relations with her.[19] The Latin for axe is *securis*, from *seco* meaning to cut, and is etymologically akin to *scio* (I know). The Greek κειω, κεαω (split, cleave) is similar in meaning. (In medieval magic the axe is replaced by the sword, as in *Tarot* cards and Chinese symbolism, all having connections to Sufism.)

46

For Sufism is essentially a system for cutting through apparent meanings into the underlying Reality/Unity (*Tawhīd*). The symbol illustrates, that while elements of Sufism can be found in a variety of systems, since the basis of all experience is One; Truth can only be known as an inner (piercing/splitting/cleaving/powerful) experience.[20] Some developmental systems have got stuck in symbols as a reality (religion), others have separated symbols and meanings from reality (science). Sufis seek the **Underlying Reality** beyond all forms, including Life and Death.

Illustration of the *rose that gives honey to the bees* (the conveyors of essential truths) as a symbol of the esoteric tradition, in the book **Summum Bonum**, published 1692, by the Rosicrucian exponent Dr. Robert Fludd (see *Qur'ān* 16:68-69).

47

Notes and References

1) See **Appendix 1**, for Names of God in Arabic.

2) This is indirectly implied in the *Qur'ān* 73:4-6; 74:1.

3) *Qur'ān* 53:4-7;81:19-23. Where Gabriel is mentioned in the *Qur'ān*, it is in connection with inspiration (2:97) and can be seen as a metaphor for such. See also *Qur'ān* 26:192-195, where a title used for Muhammad is there used to describe the *embodiment* of that inspiration: i.e., **Transcendent Self**.

4) M.C.Astour, *Hellenosemitica: An Ethnic and Cultural Study in West Semitic Impact on Mycenaen Greece*, Brill, Leiden, 1967, pp, 86-87,388.

5) **Genesis** 21:9-21.

6) Despite the separation of many Jewish communities from each other for 2,000 years, the way in which their sacred texts are chanted shows very little variation, demonstrating a continuity going back to temple times 3,000 years ago. The similarity to Islamic chanting of the *Qur'ān* is striking. Incredible similarities between temple songs and Gregorian tunes have also been found.

7) Martin Lings, *A Sufi Saint of the Twentieth Century: Shaikh Ahmad al-Alawī, his spiritual heritage and legacy*, George Allen & Unwin, London, 1971, p, 34 ff.

8) *Qur'ān* 2:124-129.

9) See Bernal, 1991, Vol 1, pp, 23-27, 124-130, 145-151.

10) Regarding the Hidden Teacher, see note 13 in **chapter one**. For the development of the idea of the hidden sage from Sufi and *Shī'ah* sources into Jewish mysticism, see Mach 1957 pp, 134-146 & Wineman, 1998, pp, 95-97.

11) The connection between esoteric Judaism and Sufism has been acknowledged by such authoritative sources as the *Encyclopaedia Judaica*, & Gersham Scholem, *The Messianic Idea in Judaism and other essays on Jewish spirituality*, Schocken Books, New York, 1978, pp, 251-253.

12) S.Zunz, *Die gottes-dienstlichen Vorträge der Juden*, Berlin, pp,165ff.

13) D.Bakan, *Sigmund Freud and the Jewish Mystical Tradition*, Schocken Books, New York, 1958.

14) Philo, *Contemplative Life* 38, 85-87 & **Appendix 4**.

15) Many Sufis have attempted to reconcile Sufism with Islam. However, despite the efforts of the Sufi 'Abd al-Wahhāb ash-Sha'rānī (died 1565) to subsume the Sufi within the Islamic orthodox framework, by making the sanctity of the Sufi saint dependent on observance of the *Sharī'ah* (Islamic Law), this like the efforts of others in this regard (see, *Sufism and Shari'ah: A Study of Shaykh Ahmad Sirhindi's Effort to Reform Sufism*, by Muhammad Abdul Haq Ansari, Islamic Foundation, Leicester, 1986) failed, because the sanctity of the Sufi is not dependent on any mediation whatsoever, but is independently obtained.

16) In C.Glassé, *The Concise Encyclopaedia of Islam*, Stacey International, London, 1989, p, 212.

48

17) *Mathnawī*   1:123.

18) *Qur'ān*   3:47, which as in the Egyptian case, as we shall see in later chapters, has an esoteric meaning for the Sufi.

19) **Genesis**   4:1 in the *Tanakh*   (Jewish Bible).

20) *Mathnawī*   1:2447.

4

TRANSCENDING THE LIMITED SELF

"He who denies God, denies himself. Who affirms God, affirms himself."

Taittriya Upanishad 2:6

Sufism as a Means of Establishing a Transcendence of Identity

It can be seen from what has already been discovered in our quest for the therapy of the Ancients, that Sufism, as an expression of the ongoing esoteric tradition, has an entirely different set of values and presuppositions than those which exist in most modern-day societies. This point cannot be over-stressed, because the judgements and assumptions often made by so-called neutral investigators – especially psychologists, sociologists, and medical research scientists – are actually Western (secular or Christian) ones. The notion of objectivity – as used in the Western sense of the word – is rejected by Sufism.

The reason for this is that such judgements are based upon a limited view of the world – a view which accords with the ego*(anā')*, or sense of pride arising from the limited self. According to Sufism, the intellect*('aql)* is not confined to those aspects of thought which are logical, as is the case in contemporary Western psychology. Its function – which can be defined in a loose sense as *Knowing* – includes aspects of thought not even considered

50

in Western psychology.) The faculty of choice *(nafs-i-natiqah)* - what is operating when Western researchers talk about being 'objective' - has the capacity, according to Sufism, of exerting an influence upon the individual, that can either arouse animal passions and emotions (hunger, thirst, lust, envy, anger), or alternatively, it can transcend the animal nature *(nafs al-haywāniyah)*. As we shall discover, from a Sufi point of view, perception is not simply a case of recording sense impressions.

It is in the notion of identity that Sufism shows its differences and superiority to Western psychology. (That Western psychological concepts of identity are inadequate is demonstrated by the identity confusion and subsequent social fragmentation that afflicts modern society.) The emphasis on nationalism, religious differences, and/or *ethnic cleansing,* and other sick euphemisms, betray an obsession over self, indicating this confusion.

In contrast to this, consider the example of the Sufi Master Jalāl ad-Dīn ar-Rūmī (died 1273), who counted amongst his followers, many who were not nominal Muslims. When at his death, multitudes of Christians, as well as Jews and Zoroastrians, followed his funeral procession, someone asked, *"Why should they weep for a Muslim?"* The reply given was: *"He is the Moses, the David, the Jesus of this Age, and we are his followers, his disciples. That is why we weep!"* [1]

Sufism has avoided religious intolerance, racism and the

51

excesses of nationalism, because it has the means for establishing a transcendence of identity. In fact, according to one investigative scholar: *"Sufism is the transcending of ordinary limitations."* [2] Sufi practice transcends the usual two modes of communication and activity – that is the intellectual and emotional – enabling a transcendent view of the world to take place. The Sufi neither discounts intellectual (in the narrow Western sense) nor emotional aspects of being/existence – *wujūd* [3] – and may use either; but the Sufi aims to transcend the limitations of both approaches, and Sufi practices are methods for doing this.

For this reason, Sufi writings (often described by ego-based academics as 'obscure') like Sufi stories, often have a meaning quite other than the obvious, (for their contradictory statements are designed to break through conditioned patterns of thinking) Their purpose is not to encourage arid intellectualism, but rather to promote healthy criticism (even of themselves) in order to avoid the fossilisation and idolatry, that arises from dogmatism.[4] Those who are unaware fail to realise this and often settle for an obvious, but limited meaning.

Unlike Western psychological and sociological concepts of self, as in the psychotherapeutic method of Kelly, known as 'Personal Construct Theory',[5] Sufism does not reduce the self to a socially created object, or something ephemeral (like the soul/spirit of Christian theology),[6] but

52

rather, considers it of central importance as an uncreated aspect of Infinite – **Divine Creativity** – or what is generally referred to as God. In other words, the **Transcendent Self** is asserted. Viewed from this perspective, creation and evolution become the same thing – what Master *Bābā* Dovid Yusuf, defines as *unfolding* – during which the necessary and inevitable, are continually emerging according to the needs, demands and contingencies of the time.[7]

The Sufi word for self *(nafs)* – which as we have seen is derived from the word for breath *(nafas)* – can also be translated as *soul* or *psyche*. Speech, carried by the breath, makes explicit what is implicit in consciousness, a fact which is recognised (directly or indirectly) in all the different vehicles for the esoteric tradition. The magic word **ABRACADABRA** (which is derived from a Sumerian term, via Hebrew) actually means, *as I speak so I create!* Tribal healing and magic depend upon invocations, or magic words, just as in the Indian tradition *mantras* (in the Persian *manthras*) are used in meditation and rituals. In Christianity, it is THE WORD which brings creation into being, an idea which is also found in the *Qur'ān*.[8]

In Sufism, the command *(Amr)* is contrasted to its creation *(khlaq)* – as is also the case in the *Qur'ān*.[9] They correspond to two distinct worlds: *Hāhūt* (Absolute) and *Lāhūt* (Manifest).[10] For this reason, we can acknowledge – or be aware of – the created world, for our essential

53

nature;[11] our Self, lies beyond, or outside of the created world. It is the Self that perceives, endowing objects with configuration, through experience of itself. There is no passive recording of sense-data: for perception must accept; encounter; participate in; penetrate; see through; evaluate - before it can subjectively discard; limit; delineate; or be affected by such data. Whatever it chooses to discard is not lost, but brought forward in a new light or perspective.

This ability is the result of the directive function of **The Intellect** – '*Aql*. The Persian Master, Sadr ad-Din al-Qunawi (died 1329), using the allegory of Adam and Eve, identified this '*Aql* with the original undivided self *(nafs al-wāhida)* [12] in its primal unity, its companion being Eve; meaning the **Soul/Self** from which all individual selves are brought into existence. (The meaning here is that the individual self contains within it, the means for being at unity *(wahdat)* with everything in existence.) This Transcendent potential can be realised by the self recognising its own inherent unity. **Thus at one and the same time, the self is individual as well as corporate.**[13] It is this potential that gives it the capacity for perception, recollection and discrimination.

In this conception, the self is an integral and integrated aspect of being, that is stable when true to its essential unified nature; yet which in its unfolding is transient. It is only by accepting its harmonious basis - the Unity of

54

Consciousness, or its Transcendent potential – that it can be free (in the true sense), from both inner and outer oppression. The power to act is not the result of a suppression of blind instincts, as in Freud's psychology, but rather a given natural capacity, to move forever forwards, upwards and outwards. By such action, the self as an act of **Infinite Creativity**, defines itself.[7] It is a self-directed movement, based on responsibility and initiative. Such action is purposeful; creating from within (the immanent), by reference to that which is without (the transcendent). Thought is not a corollary of the ego, as in Western psychology, but a necessary and contingent aspect of being. All that is necessary is that thinking be purified, in order for the limited self to be perfected and the **Transcendent Self** realised. It is this to which Sufi disciplines are directed.

The Concept of Personality in Sufism

The notion of psychotherapy, however it is employed, arises from a belief that there is some kind of disturbance within the *psyche*, giving rise to abnormalities of behaviour, cognition, or feeling – or a combination of these aspects. How such abnormalities are defined, will differ according to the school of thought being followed,[14] generally because there is an avoidance of any kind of metaphysical frame of reference – including as the Sufi saint and French philosopher, René Guénon, put it that:

"In all true metaphysical conceptions it is necessary to take into account the inexpressible." [15]

Sufism does not avoid the obvious, including realising that it is the *psyche* itself, which must necessarily be of primary concern in any consideration of perception, behaviour, feeling, or cognition. Sufism acknowledges in its concept of personality, an inexpressible, veiled, or hidden element within the *psyche*/soul/ self/*nafs*, [16] as well as not ignoring the importance of experience in the visible worlds, of which according to Sufism there are many. [17]

The self having its source in the Archetypal world (*A'yān ath-thābitah* [18] as the immutable essence, as well as having a potential, or possibility of being, could be said to be both created and eternal, in that both aspects are contained within it. In referring to the transcendent nature of the self, a saying of Muhammad (in which he speaks in place of God) and which is referred to by the Sufi, says:

"*I am* a hidden treasure and *I seek* to become known." [19]

The *I* referred to here, is that present within the **Absolute**. It refers to the Self beyond differentiation, the Real Self, in which and from which all personality and individual selves arise. For the **Transcendent Self** is outside of Time, and in the Sufi conception, existence is continually being created and re-absorbed. [20] Consequently, the self is potentially in a state of unison *(ittihad)*, undifferentiated from the **Divine Creativity**, while at the same time, the emergence into the world of differentiation/

form *(Nāsūt)* brings with it the tension of differentiation. This state of tension has been described as a battleground.[21] The Spirit – meaning the *Knowing* Principle (**Intellect** in a Sufi sense) which transcends the individual nature – fights with the self-centred limited self and its compulsive tendencies, that are responsible for its diffuse and changeable nature. It is a fight for possession of the heart. The heart – *qalb* in Arabic, *dil* in Persian – is the inner capacity for perceiving the true nature of things (supra-rational intuition) as centred within the individual, coming from the same root as *qābil*, meaning passive receptacle. It can be likened to the organ of orientation, in the literary sense of saying: " *I have set my heart upon something.*" The heart is at the point at which these two forces intersect, or cross. This for the Sufi, is the true meaning of the Christian symbol of the cross, whose origins go back to ancient Egypt (see plate 3).

If the individual heeds Transcendent beckonings immanent within the self, its passive habits and ambitions can be overcome. The mundane passions and desires that hide the true nature of the self – what Sufism calls, "veiling *(Hijāb)* [22] the heart" – can be recognised for what they are (illusory limitations of perspective) and the principle of **Reality** – the Spirit – will separate itself from appearance. Realisation of a **Transcendent Self** transmutes and suffuses the orientation, so that intuition becomes recognition: (Knower, knowledge and known are as One.[23]

57

From the Sufi perspective, self-knowledge and the spiritual quest (or what is mis-defined as religion) are inseparable. This, because it is love, which according to Rūmī, is "*the physician for all our ills*"; [24] love for all things in existence, both the beautiful*(jamāl)* aspects of Nature, as well as the vigorous*(jālāl)*, awesome and fearful.[25] Perceiving the Unity of Existence externally, the Sufi comes to know*(ma'rifa)* **Reality**, at the same time as knowing the inner self. This is the meaning of a saying of Muhammad:

"He who knows himself, knows (God) his Lord." [26]

Consequently, we find that the great Egyptian Sufi, Dhū'n-Nūn Misrī (died 859), informs us that *ma'rifa* (knowledge of **Reality**) must be distinguished from intellectual knowledge*('ilm)*, [27] for the former is only possible through the love*(mahabba)* of God/**Reality**. By learning not to rely on ourselves (as is the case in Western ego-enforcing psychology),

> but trusting in God *(tawakkul* [28]*)* a man knows God. It is a secret*(sirr)* Divine mystery *(sirr)* that must not be spoken of to the profane... True knowledge of God is not the knowledge that God is One, which is possessed by all believers; (exoteric Islam) nor the knowledge of Him derived from proof and demonstration, which belongs to philosophers, rhetoricians and theologians, but it *is the knowledge of the attributes of Divine Unity,* which belongs to the Saints of God (the Sufi), those who *behold God with their hearts* in such a wise that He reveals unto them what He revealeth not unto any one else in the world ...... Real knowledge is God's

illumination of the heart with the radiance of knowledge....They that know God are not themselves and subsist not through themselves (they have passed away to all but God – *fanā'*) but insofar as they are themselves, they subsist through God *(baqā').* [29]

From a Sufi perspective, confused individuals, having a dualistic orientation (in Western parlance the mentally disturbed), [30] are afflicted not so much by a lack of love, as by the fact that they do not love. The solution is a change in orientation; an appreciation of a relationship which transcends all others, i.e., that with the **Ultimate Self** (God). Such an appreciation cannot be apprehended by – to put it in Western psychological terms – rationality (is not achieved by the reinforcement of a limited ego), but is a mysterious and overwhelming experience (spiritual experience). To achieve unity of self, one must become a *muwahhid* – one who is unified with **Reality**/God. In order to know and love God, the Sufi must lose self (limited self) in the love and the knowledge of God. Such love and knowledge cannot be separated. The realisation of God's Oneness – which is also a realisation (in the fullest sense of the word) of one's own essential unity – cannot come about except by losing the self in the Oneness of God.

Ibn al-Fārid (died 1235) writing of his love for God,[31] in his *Tā'iyyutu'l Kubrā* , distinguished three forms of consciousness experienced on the Sufi Path. First, the shifting multiple consciousness of *ordinary perception* that, when engaged in on the Sufi Path, leads to *ecstatic consciousness,* so losing the former state. This in turn leads to a higher mystical *unified consciousness,* arising only (but not necessarily) when the former state is persisted in, on return to everyday consciousness. This can be summated by saying, that in the first stage there is an awareness of being an individual distinct from **Reality**/God. In the second stage all such distinction has vanished, while in the third stage, there is an awareness of being one with the **Creative Intelligence**, yet as a creation distinct. In the *ecstatic consciousness* stage all attributes of self are negated; but in the final stage they are restored, *transmuted and spiritualised*.

FORMS OF CONSCIOUSNESS	DEGREES OF SELF-AWARENESS	STAGES ON THE SŪFĪ PATH
UNIFIED CONSCIOUSNESS	**Transformed Self**	Beyond love
At one with Reality yet distinct from it	Unified state*(ittihād)*	Saint*(muwahhid)*
	Sobriety of union (sahwn'i-jam)	Realised Sufi*('Arīf)* baqā'
ECSTATIC CONSCIOUSNESS	**Self Negated**	Sufi*(fanā' fī-Llāh)*
Feeling of being merged with God	Intoxication *(sukr)*	fanā' al-fanā
	In love with God	fanā'
ORDINARY PERCEPTION	**Self in Duality**	Seeker*(sālik)*
Individual feels separated from God/Reality	Sobriety *(sahw)*	Believer in Externalist Religion
	In love with self	Unbeliever

It becomes clear from this explication, that Sufi self-knowledge is essentially different from Western concepts of personality formation. It does not proceed from below, so to speak, that is from our base animal nature*(nafs al-haywāniyah)* - with which according to Western concepts, we must seek to be integrated with in some way or another [32] - but from a higher level. It is this higher level - the **Transcendent** within us - that makes us human. Only by striving forever upwards, in this sense - rather than distorting this natural capacity into a striving to gratify base desires (competition, status) - is it possible for the self*(nafs)* to be at peace with its Self*(Huwa)*. Consequently, the Sufi says: *"lā anā wa lā anta: Huwa"* (not I and not you: *THAT!*).[33]

Bābā Dovid Yūsuf explained that *Huwa* is a term frequently used by the Sufi, because in its esoteric understanding, it means *Hū* - the sacred breath - as expressed - *aaah!* In other words, only by negating, expressing, giving up, sacrificing the limited self, or sense of I*(anā')*, can the **Ultimate Self** be manifest*(Hū-wā')*.

Self-knowledge, is from this perspective, nothing other than the knowledge of a **Greater Self** - a knowledge of **Reality**/God*(ma'rifa)*, which in turn is inseparable from the love of God/**Reality***(mahabba)*, so that Sufism, according to one definition, is *"a Way to God through love."* [34] The word Sufism now becomes explicable, for using the science of the relationship between the numerical values of letters

61

and their meaning, known as *Abjad* (**Appendix 2**), the Arabic word pertaining to mysticism *(tasawwuf)*, from which the word *Sūfī* is derived, can be seen to correspond to the value of the words *al-hikmah al-ilāhiyya* (Divine or **Transcendent** Wisdom). That is to say, it is the result of, is concerned with that knowledge which God - in His Love - dispenses to His lovers, a term, which reflects by its very nature(esoteric), that the outer is contained within the inner, just as the kernel is contained within the nut *(haqīqah* - inner, essential, intrinsic truth). It is a concept of personality that elevates, rather than lowers the fulfilment of potential, a concept which encourages responsibility, morality, accountability, and enrichment of personal relationships; rather than debasing them to the level of personal self-seeking. [35]

The Sufi Approach to Personal Difficulties and Illness

According to Sufism, human beings are the way they are because there is an **Infinite**, or **Transcendent** element, within their finite, limited and mortal form. As the **Infinite** is - by definition - *Absolute* perfection, limitlessness, that capacity is also present within the human being. However, whatever capacity is reached within this realm of existence, will be Destiny *(Kalimat)*, in that it is both a matter of effort and experience, as well as of individual potentiality. Having traversed a multitude of realms, ultimately, that **Infinite** Life Spirit will return to its **Source**. Ascending as it does so, through all the stages of existence,[36] it is an evolution taught long before Darwin, which is impelled not by base drives (Freud's *trieb*), but by inherent potential, unfolding itself in the manifestation of Existence, so that for the Sufi, the past is not the determiner of action. Rather it is the future, inherent in the present, that determines by means of orientation (*al-qalb*).

Once this is comprehended, it also becomes clear that existence in this realm - including its pain and discomfort - is not a suffering that can be avoided. Body and spirit are both essential, and pain has a purpose. Rūmī explains to his disciples:[24]

> If a seed does not have a kernel it fails; so too will it fail if it does not have a skin. If you plant a seed in the earth without its husk it will not germinate. Whereas, if you put it in the earth together with its husk, it will germinate, so becoming a great tree. Seen from this point of view, the body is a necessity, for without it what is great - the necessary principle within it - will fail, and its purpose will not be attained.

As to what that purpose may be, is made more explicit by Rūmī, when later in the same discourse, he quotes the account of Mary giving birth to Jesus under the shade of a palm tree, as mentioned in the *Qur'ān* (19:23) - explaining its esoteric meaning:

> It is pain that guides us in every enterprise. Until there is an ache - a passion and a yearning - for something within us, we do not strive to achieve it. Without the pangs of desire (pain), whatever we wish for remains unprocurable: whether it be

success in this world, or salvation in the next; whether we wish to be a merchant, king, scientist, or an astronomer. It was not until childbirth pains arose in her that Mary made for the tree – *"And the birthpangs drove her to the trunk of a palm tree"*. Those pangs brought her to the tree, and the tree which was withered became fruitful.

This body is like Mary. Everyone has a Jesus within him, but *unless we feel* these pangs, that Jesus is not manifest, returning to the mysterious source from which he came, leaving us at a loss and without fulfilment.

Life on earth is the means by which the human can become aware of the **Source**; the **Origin**; the **Divine** and **Infinite Creativity** within us. Rūmī explains this process of growth in awareness as a form of evolution. The human, although always potentially human, has proceeded in a process of development and *unfoldment*.

> In the beginning we were without existence, then we were brought into existence, written with the pen of existence upon the inanimate world; then from this pen into the vegetable; then from the vegetable to the animal; then from the animal to the human; and then from the human to the angel; and so on, ad infinitum.... *You shall with certainty ascend from stage to stage. What is the matter with them* (the unbelievers) *that they cannot believe?"* (*Qur'ān* 84:19-20). This present world has been shown to you, that you may see and acknowledge the other stages which lie ahead. It was not shown to you that you might disbelieve and say, *"This is all there is!"*

Similarly, in another discourse, Rūmī explains:

> As long as you recognise this pain and emptiness within yourself, this is proof for you that there is an Almighty that loves you and cares about you.

As to why there is pain and suffering? Rūmī answers:

> From the viewpoint of God (**The Supreme Good**), all things are good and perfect, it is only from our viewpoint that this is not so.....Things are made clear by their opposites; it is impossible to make anything known without its opposite...... *In times of difficulty everyone calls upon God..... when there is fear, anxiety and insecurity.* In secret everyone (even the unbelievers) call upon Him, trusting He will hear them and grant their request...but when He has restored them to health and peace of mind, *that faith departs and their illusions creating anxiety return.* [24]

In this radically different approach - what would be seen as negative experience, in Western and other forms of psychology [38] - there is an acceptance of the limitations of the material world, which limitations - together with the associated experience - are seen as positive when viewed from a transcendent perspective (Sufism). Everyone has a different capacity or potential, but, to quote another Sufi Master:

> If capacity had consisted in the possession of healthy limbs, every person so endowed would be of equal attainment: but experience shows that a man may possess healthy limbs, but his actions may not be similarly sound. It follows, then, that capacity does not derive from faculty and express itself in healthy limbs: faculty is a thing which varies in degree at various times, as any man may observe with regard to himself..and this being so, the inevitable conclusion is that the faculty of each single action is different from the faculty of any other action. Had the case been otherwise, men would have had no need or necessity of recourse to God at the time of their actions, and (the)

words, *"And to Thee we pray for help"*
(*Qur'ān* 1:4) would be meaningless.[39]

In these passages, from the earliest extant treatise on
Sufism, Abū Bakr al-Kalābādhī (died 995) argues that
neither capacity in the terms of genetic endowment, nor
experience(the chain of single actions) are what determines
outcomes. We cannot lay the claim for (or be grateful for)
causes as the basis of how we are - of events - for it is
the **Ultimate Reality** beyond causation who determines the
outcome:[40]

> (Sufis) are agreed that God does not do things for
> any cause: for if they had a cause, then that cause
> would have a cause, and so *ad infinitum;* and that
> is false..(Consequently) what restores thee to God
> from things[41] is fair (though it may seem
> otherwise), and what restores thee to things and
> not to him is foul.[42]

For the above reasons, in Sufism cognition takes on a
different meaning than in Western psychology, in the
sense that it is inseparable from attitudes.[43] *"The world is
a mirror,"* it is said, meaning that it reflects back to you
what is in yourself.[44]

This becomes explicable by examining Rūmī's discussion
of health and sickness. Rūmī, in a discourse, shows how
nebulous is the concept of health. How the essence of what
we mean by health - of pain, sickness, joy and suffering
- cannot be understood without recourse to the *Ideal
world* - in other words, the **Plane of Infinity**. It is only
the *essence* of things that is real and makes communication

and joint experience possible, he argues. The material realm is a manifestation, a consequence and not a cause. Rūmī illustrates this by a story designed to show that without considering the *World of Infinity* – the spiritual – we could make no real sense of things:[45]

Once there was a philosopher who denied **Reality**. One day he became ill and incapacitated. This illness went on for a very long time. Now a certain Islamic cleric went to visit him.
"What is it that you are seeking?" he asked the philosopher.
"Health," the sceptic replied.
"Tell me what shape is this health, describe it to me so that I may purchase it for you," said the clergyman.
"It has no shape, it cannot be described," said the philosopher irritatedly.
"If it's not possible to describe it, then why are you seeking it?" the cleric said emphatically, *"tell me what is this health?"*
"All I know," said the philosopher wearily *"is that when I am in health, I have strength, I have weight and colour, my cheeks are red and blooming."*
"That's not what I am asking, I am asking you about the spirit of health. What is the essence of health?" said the cleric.
"I don't know!" said the philosopher angrily.
"If you become a Muslim and change your views, then I will treat you and will make you well, bringing you back to health," said the cleric.

As is the case with most Sufi tales, there is a twist in this story, for the real meaning is not the obvious one. The essence of the Sufi experience is its multifacetednesss. The apparent contradictions contained within the tale are designed to enable the seeker to break through the self-conditioned attitudes, or superficial appearance, to the real meaning underneath. (By contravening the confines of logic, it becomes possible to speak on several levels at once.) The surface explanation is as given above – i.e., it is the essence which is Real and not its limited manifestation. However, the perceptive amongst Rūmī's followers would have realised that Rūmī had little in common with the formalities and the external formalised thinking of the cleric, and much more in common with the attitude of the philosopher. The rigid Muslim would have seen in the story, the moral that Islam (in the sense of a limiting religion) is the only source of truth. But Rūmī – in common with the philosopher – was continually pointing out, that the essence of things IS indescribable; beyond form and logic. Thus the essence of things cannot be known without form. The manifest IS the means by which the underlying essence (unknowable as/in itself) makes itself known.

(Yet for all this, what might appear to be heretical to the Muslim (Rūmī has often been condemned by them) is a basic tenet of Islam.) Islam condemns the use of images of any kind in worship, because *Allāh* (the Arabic word for God) is beyond any form that we might conceive. *Allāh* is not dependent on anything, but we are utterly dependent on *Allāh*, which is why without Revelation, we cannot know **Truth/God** *(Haqq)*. Rūmī explains:

> When the Prophet (Muhammad) - may God bless him and grant him peace - was carried away out of himself so that he spoke; he always used to say; *"God says"* (this or that). From outward appearance it was his tongue that was speaking, but in reality he was not there (was not himself) for the speaker was God.[24]

If we apply this conception to health, it is clear that illness, suffering, pain of any kind, is as much as, joy, happiness, laughter, a way of knowing that God exists. It is a breaking through of the self-conditioned experience, to an awareness of the mutual experience, the underlying *Unity* of all things, which shows the **Source** as **One**, i.e., God/**Reality**. Illness especially, cause us in a very fundamental way, to acknowledge our dependence on that **Reality**, by actually showing us, how impermanent the material state is. We are forced back on ourself so to speak, by our seeing how, that, without that underlying essence, we could not exist. The closer that experience of illness brings us to death, the greater is our need for a belief in an essence, a spirit that survives death. So it is that the Sufi thanks God for calamities and illness, since they deepen dependence on God and make the Sufi more aware of the illusory, transient and impermanent state of the material realm.

Although in the Sufi concept of personality there is an emphasis on transcendent realities - of spirit rather than form, of motivations rather than actions, of attitudes and meanings rather than experience - this does not mean that

69

experience is totally disregarded. There is a recognition as in Jewish mysticism, that: *"The past is always present"*, but that past goes beyond this limited existence - even beyond Time itself. Although there is a recognition of the animal within us (though even during this stage we were always potentially human), we are required to use the rational*(nafs-i-nātiqah)* to exert a positive, rather than a negative influence, so as to transcend our animal nature *(nafs haywāniyah)* and utilise our spiritual capacity.[46] Whatever we experience in this realm, must be viewed as a secondary cause, the real essence*(ar-rūh)* underlies this, and its **Source***(Adh-Dhāt)* is essentially non-limiting; non-discriminatory; not Timebound.

It is precisely because of this internal factor, that the Sufi has no need of concepts like Super-ego, repression, and the like. To become oneself is to transcend the limiting animal nature*(nafs al-haywāniyah)*, as well as the ego's whims*(nafs al-ammārah)*, to be beyond the feeling of self-reproach*(nafs al-lawwāmah)* and to be at peace with one's Self*(nafs al-mutma'innah)*.

In a unique way, the Sufi goes beyond both the treatment of symptoms (modern allopathic medicine - including psychiatry) and secondary causes that contribute to these symptoms (homeopathy and other alternative systems), to the origin of these causes themselves, that is to say beliefs - metaphysical, supra-rational and intuitive factors(a truly holistic approach). In doing this there is no

70

flight into fancy, no discounting of the material realm, but a consideration of both inner and outer realities. While not becoming bogged down, or debased by the materialistic tendency of reducing everything to its lowest level, it also anchors itself in the real (total) experience of the person concerned. Form and spirit are not separated:

> When the physician comes to examine the sick person, he questions their inner physician. There is within you a physician – your natural temperament which accepts or rejects. So that the outer physician questions your inner one: *"Was there anything that you ate which upset you? How does this feel? How is your sleep?"* From what this inner physician tells him the outer physician makes a prescription.
>
> Hence the root of the matter is to be found in that inner physician – the patients temperament. Now when this inner physician is weak and the temperament has been corrupted, because of this weakness, everything is reversed and the indications given are twisted (and incorrect): *sugar is bitter, vinegar is sweet.* Then is the outer physican needed to bring back the natural harmony, restoring the temperament to what it was. *After this* we can show ourselves to our own Inner Physician and listen to what we are told from within....the Sufi are physicians who return health to its natural balance; until the spirit has been strengthened and the heart restored.[24]

Notes and References

1) The source of this account is oral, the most exhaustive bibliography on Rūmī is by Mehmet Onder in Turkish (Istanbul). Otherwise see the *Manāqib al-'Arifīn* by Mevlana Shams ad-Dīn al-Aflākī (2 vols), Ankara, 1959-1961.

2) P.E.Anderson, "Sufi Studies"; *Library Journal of American Institute for Continuous Education*, March,1974.

3) For Sufis, strictly speaking, this can only be said of God: i.e., only God (the **Transcendent Self**) exists.

4) Sufi Master *Bābā* Dovid Yusūf, often deliberately encourages hostile attitudes on the part of externalist Christians, Muslims and Jews, as well as would-be Sufis, in order to avoid genuine Sufism being identified with religious dogmatism. Yet, he is able to influence those who criticise him.

5) Sufism does not disregard social-psychological aspects of experience, but rather does not consider them primary. For Kelly G.A., see *A Theory of Personality: The Psychology of Personal Constructs*, Norton, New York, 1963.

6) Similarities are not coincidental; both are developments of Christian philosopher Descarte's dualism of Mind and Matter.

7) Sufism draws a midway path between the absurdities of a cynical materialism and the childish emotions of the religious dogmatist. Dissolving the barrier between an unthinking belief in an anthropomorphic Deity and the arrogant assertions of atheism. It – to use Sufi Master Ibn 'Arabī's words - defines God as: *"the Name which is given to the creative impulse that is found expressing itself everywhere and in all kinds of development."* The full implications of this perspective, which was also enumerated by Rūmī, have as yet to emerge in Western scientific theory, though their rudiments have already been grasped by the philosopher and psycholinguist, Naom Chomsky, although not himself a professed Sufi (see his 1957, work in **Bibliography**).

8) John 1:1 & *Qur'ān* 2:117.

9) *Qur'ān* 7:54; 14:32; 16:77; 17:85.

10) In his *Mirat 'l'Arifīn* (**Reflections of the Awakened**).

11) The essence, was referred to by 'Abd al-Qādir al Jīlānī(died 1166) as *al-'ama* (the dark mist), which Sir M. Iqbal (1873-1938) - who acknowledged his debt to the Sufis - writing in, *The Development of Metaphysics in Persia*, Luzac, London, 1908, p 48, equated with the concept of the Unconscious.

12) *Qur'ān* 4:1; 6:98; 7:189; 31:28; 39:6.

13) Abū Nasr Muhammad ibn Tarkhān al-Farābī (died 950), in his *Risālah fi-l-'Aql*, regarded the Intellect, as used in Sufi parlance, as being the **First Existent**; the **First One**; the **First Reality**. The similarity to these ideas and those of Plato, shows a link between them and an ongoing esoteric tradition.

14) Many of the problems confronting clinical psychologists as well as psychiatrists, arise from the fact that there is no general agreement

over what constitutes a symptom, or a syndrome; or even a cure. Words which may be variously and loosely used in different contexts, by different and even by the same individual on different occasions, because: "(mental) *diseases do not exist independently of the people who are sick*...the variety of ideological positions, within psychiatry, the biological, the dynamic, the social, the behavioural, represent different emphases."*Psychiatry in Dissent,* Anthony Clare, Tavistock Publications, London, 1976, p, 69 (italics mine).

15) From "Oriental Metaphysics" in, **The Sword of Gnosis**, edited by Joseph Needleman, Baltimore Press, 1982.

16) The Arabic *nafs* corresponds to the Greek *psyche,* or Latin *anima,* so that in translation, *self* and *soul* can be used interchangeably. However, as we shall see, according to Sufism, there are several selfs*(nafs):* i.e., the soul manifests or passes through several stages.

17) Sufism believes in many worlds of existence, visible and invisible, each having different laws, perceptions of reality and experiences of Time. All things being in a state of constant change and flux. Pervading all these worlds is the **Sustainer** and **Source** *(Rabb al-'Alamīn - Qur'ān* 1:2). Sufism, has divided these worlds into three primary divisions: *Nāsūt* ; the human, physical and mortal worlds, accessible to the senses, *Malakūt* ; the subtle, animic and mental worlds, of angelic and other associated beings - usually invisible, but which interact with, surround and permeate the sensory worlds and *Lāhūt* ; the **Divine World of Reality** in which all worlds are contained. Sometimes, these three divisions are made into five (*al-hadārāt al-ilāhiyyah al-khams* - the five divine presences) by adding *Hāhūt* ; the **Essence** or **Absolute** beyond Being *(adh-Dhāt).* Plus subdividing *Malakūt* into *Jabarūt* - the world of angels - from *Malakūt,* the subtle world. The complete explication of the 80,000 worlds of existence, is beyond the scope of this book. Sufism aims to experience them, rather than learn about them intellectually.

18) From *'ayn* - literally a *spring,* or *eye,* referring to something which exists potentially, but whose existence can only be known when that potentiality has been fulfilled.

19) Such sayings are not always found in traditional compilations but are considered to be of primary importance for they are vouched for by an unbroken line of Sufi oral transmission. Constantly repeated in writings of the Masters, they are known as *tawatur.* When sayings of Muhammad reproduce what God has said, they are known as *al-e-Qudsī.* This saying is both and referred to as *tawatur hadīth al-e-Qudsī,* is a key element in Sufi teaching.

20) Rūmī, **Mathnawī** 1:1142.

21) Ibn Arabī's, **Fusūs al-Hikam (Facets of Wisdom)**. Also see Titus Burckhardt's, **An Introduction to Sufism**, Crucible, Wellingborough, 1990, pp, 26-27.

22) From the Arabic term for the garment which totally covers women in Muslim countries.

23) In Sufi terminology, the heart becomes a receptacle or tabernacle *(mishkāt)* of the **Transcendent Mystery**(*sirr* - literally; *secret).* This latter word is a reference to the fact that there is a point of contact

between the individual and the **Creative Principle**. It was the revealing of this "secret" that the Sufis say, condemned Al-Hallāj; meaning that by openly proclaiming it, he undermined the power of the Islamic clergy who naturally executed him. Just as in the Christian world – even though the essential humanity of Jesus is admitted – no-one, not even the liberal Christians, would dare say that Jesus's realisation of the Divine within him, was no more than is possible for anyone (even if unlikely).

24) *Fīhi mā fīhī* (**In it what is in it**, see **Bibliography**). As we shall see, he illustrates this by the story of Mary giving birth to Jesus. Meaning that the realisation/birth of our **True Self**, is a giving up of the burdens of the limited self that we carry around with us.

25) *Jamāl* is the feminine: soul; form; the passive = **Eve**; *Jālāl* the masculine: spirit; vitality; the active = **Adam**.

26) *Mathnawī* 5:2114. Also Ibn 'Arabī, in his *Treatise on Being* (see the 1976 partial translation in **Bibliography**). This saying by Muhammad, is transmitted by Sufis *(tatwatur hadith)*.

27) Later Sufi, such as Ahmad ash-Sha'rānī(died 1565)see **Bibliography** Vol 1, pp. 52ff) - found it necessary to distinguish between *'ulūm al-kasbiyya* (the various forms of acquired knowledge); *'ilm al-wahab* (given knowledge, i.e., as the result of Sufi practise) and *'ilm al-laddunī* (knowledge received directly from the **Divine Reality**). The first is impersonal and various; the second individual and developmental, whilst the last is transpersonal. *Ma'rifa* is distinguishable from all these forms, in that it is experiential rather than sensory.

28) *Qur'ān* 65:3 & 14:13, showing that only God, can fulfil all trust placed in Him.

29) *The Tadhkiratu'l-Awliyā of Shaykh Faridu'din 'Attar*, translated by R.A. Nicholson (2 Vols. 1905-1907, London Vol. 1, 127:3-21 in brackets mine). This passage is not contained in Arberrry's later (1966), but partial translation.

30) The Sufi can agree with Freud, that all are neurotic (i.e., until arriving at the Unitary State).

31) The **Beloved**/God is here referred to as **'She'**(*Hiya*). Arberry (1956) has partially translated some of Ibn al-Fārid's poetry and Nicholson (1923, pp, 20-32) makes reference to some of the material outlined here, but the complete explication as used here, is Sufi Master, *Bābā* Dovid Yūsuf's.

32) Western psychology terms e.g.,sublimation; transposing; behaviour-modification; assertiveness; gratification; readjustment; or similar – depending on the school of thought followed - are based on satisfiying the animal nature.

33) The Arabic *Huwa* is usually translated as **He**, since it has no exact equivalent in English. It refers to the **Essence of Reality** *(Adh-Dhāt)* and the name of the **First presence** (*Hāhūt* - see note 17) is derived from it.

34) Javad Nurbakhsh,' *In the Tavern of Ruin': Seven Essays on Sufism*,

35) Duplicity of character is inevitable, when altruism is seen as non-existent as in Western psychological theory.

36) *Qur'ān* 2:156.

37) Sufis have often been accused of *shirk* (associating others with God, see *Qur'ān* 4:116) by Muslims. However, in reality it is the accusers themselves who have committed it by *(iblīs)* denying that humans can reach the position of worship. In so doing, they become Slanderers (*Iblīs*, see *Qur'ān* 2:34).

38) Even in Buddhism - with which Sufism has some similarities - suffering is to be regarded as not desirable, as *Dukkha* (unsatisfactoriness).

39) *The Doctrine of the Sufis*, translated by A.J.Arberrry, University Press, Cambridge, 1935, pp, 30-31.

40) This does not mean there is no free will, but rather that what free will there is, varies in each and every moment, and each and every existence, as part of that determination.

41) Worldly, or limited concerns, i.e., status, power, advantage, materialism, etc.

42) In Arberry, as above, pp, 35-36 (in brackets mine).

43) This may be one reason for the acceptance and use of hypnotism by Sufi physicians (taken over in Persia, from the Magians) long before its use in the West. For the use of hypnotism by the Sufis, see J.Hallaj, "Hynotherapeutic Techniques in a Central Asian Community", in *International Journal of Clinical and Experimental Hypnosis*, Vol. 10, No 4, Oct.1962, pp, 271-274.

44) *Mathnawī* 1:1306 & 4:2138.

45) For the full import of this story, it should be realised that the Great Sufi Masters of the past (to a limited extent this is still true today) were often holistic physicians, who treated both physical as well as mental conditions.

46) The two capacities we are born with, the "animal" and "spiritual", are referred to by Master *Bābā* Dovid Yūsuf, as *"the devil and the angel within"*.

5

THE WAY OF TRANSCENDENCE

"Jesus said: If anyone wishes to be a follower of mine, he must leave self behind... whoever cares for his own safety is lost, but if a man will let himself be lost for my sake, he will find his true self. What will a man gain by winning the whole world at the cost of his true self? Or what can he give that will buy that self back?"

Matthew 16:24-26 *(New English Bible).*

The Metaphysics of Sufi Psychology

As is well known, Sufi Masters have often been thought to have miraculous powers. Sometimes, these so-called miraculous powers arise from a knowledge of hypnotism, as well as the practise of telepathy, which, while not realised about by non-initiates of the past, and not even fully understood by such persons today - have been practised by Sufis and their predecessors, for thousands of years.[1] The Sufi philosopher - the world's first social anthropologist - 'Abd ar-Rahmān ibn Muhammad ibn Khaldūn (died 1406), refers in his **Kitāb al-'Ibar** (Book of Examples), to the psychological force which he believed emanated from those with miraculous powers. A force which he considered was neither good or evil, but which he thought was in some way related to the use of rituals that were designed to work up the emotions of participants into a hypnotic state.[2] Not only does this show that Sufis were concerned to comprehend - rather than just super-stitiously use, rituals - but it is also a scientific statement which has been partially verified,[3] and which points the way to something which Science does not yet fully understand,[4] this because - to use the Sufi expression - miracles are events which *'khāriq al-'ādah'* (break the habit) of the mind in its perception of reality. In contemporary Western psychological terms, we would say, "because of conditioning".

Sufi practices are designed to break through conditioned ways of thinking. These are the idols which trap the individual in dualism (as we have seen in **chapter three**) - so it is not surprising that Sufis should be ahead in understanding holistic conceptions, or be open to the utilisation of new knowledge. Many of what might be termed miracles *(karāmāt),* [5] are due to what is not sufficiently understood in Western Science, or which cannot be expressed in reductionist language.[6] This form of knowledge Sufism would define as that which is known through the senses, in contrast to that which is known only to the initiated, as the result of *receiving* [7] transcendent knowledge*(ma'rifa)* [8] and powers*(karāmah).* [9] The former*('ilm)* is natural; the latter supernatural, such being conceived as a gift, or endowment from God, as the result of God's friendship*(wilāyah)* [10] - hence *receiving.* The reason for such a difference in knowledge and powers, is found in motivation as well as dispensation. True/Real

77

Divine/Transcendent knowledge(ma'rifa) may begin with the intellectual pursuit, but only by purification of the self(mākhāfat-mahabbat) can such knowledge be obtained, for it is dependent on Divine Guidance. As the fourth Caliph and son-in-law of the Prophet, 'Alī ibn Abī Tālib (died 661) said: "I know God through God."

While the Sufi does not deny the usefulness of analytical knowledge, the Sufi knows that such knowledge is insufficient. The focus of concentration is not upon the acquisition of knowledge – which can be just another form of greed – no more than it is upon achieving a state(hāl), or a station(maqāmāt), but rather is upon God. The Sufi wishes to be as Muhammad was, a condition in which the whole concentration and focus is upon the **Divine Reality**, or **THAT WHICH IS !** as Bābā Dovid Yūsuf called it. A state in which as the **Qur'ān** (53:17) said of Muhammad:

His gaze swerved not,
nor did it go astray.   مَازَاغَ ٱلْبَصَرُ وَمَاطَغَىٰ

This form of concentration has as its aim, not intellectual superiority, self-glorification, but rather self-annihilation (fanā'). Reasoning and intellectualism can be a means of hiding(hijāb) Reality, by leading to the false belief that True knowledge(ma'rifa) can be gained by oneself. Since the **Infinite** cannot be compared to any idea, cannot be assimilated(tashbīh), nor nullified by intellectual argument (tahlīl), this cannot be the path to real, true, or complete

78

knowledge. Neither can such knowledge be attained by inspiration *(ilhām)*. If it could, then those who have claimed this as its origin, would have come to the same conclusions, and clearly they have not. Others have made intuition the source of knowledge, but if this is a faculty then we all must have it, and there would be no differences, or knowledge, to be obtained. How do we know that inspiration, or intuition, is not self-delusion?

This is illustrated in the **Qur'ān** (6:79), by the story of Abraham, who seeing that God could be known (manifest within Creation) through the majesty of the Heavens – the sun, the moon and the stars – came to see God in everything and did not therefore limit God to anything. The path of the Sufi, is to say as did Abraham:

My face is turned WHOLLY to THE Creator of heavens and earth. I will not make companions to God.

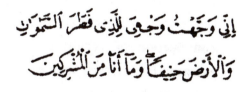

(The inability to comprehend Sufism – including its mysterious aspects – arises from a failure to realise that what may be termed real perception, is not. Conversely, what may be considered as abnormal, or unreal, may actually be more real than that which is perceived with limited sight *(hijāb).*) The Sufi points out that Muhammad called life in this world; *a dream* from which in the next life we will awake.[11] From this perspective, the perception of sleep may be imaginary, just as we can pinch ourself in a

79

dream to see if we are asleep. This may also arise because of a real event being perceived out of Time. Examples of this are visions of the prophets. Or the case of Abraham, who dreamt that he was sacrificing his son and the next day lived out what he had dreamt (*Qur'ān* 37:102-105). Such occurrences, like miracles, are linked not only to motivation - in that it is this (orientation, heart - *qalb*) which is the intermediary between the higher and the lower; the external and internal worlds - but can also be explained by the Sufi concept of Time.

While Western science, until relatively recently, had not realised the relativity of Time, for the Sufi, this has always been so. The Sufi believes all is dependent on and relative to God,as the only unchangeable and fixed point.[12] The Universe is therefore (to put it in Western terminology) a continuation of accidents [13] manifesting from a single essence; for at each and every moment, the Universe is born, annihilated and reborn.

Sufism aims to negate Time - and all that pertains to it, such as Death - by becoming aware, that while Creation is subject to time and space, and can therefore be said to be *then* and *there,* God is *Eternally Present,* being **Infinity** itself. All exercises in Sufism are designed to create direct perception of this **Reality/Truth***(al-Haqq).* A transcendent and holistic perspective, it WAS/IS summated by Muhyī'd -Dīn ibn 'Arabī (died 1240):[14]

> When the secret of an atom of the atoms is
> clear, the secret of all created things both external

80

and internal is clear, and thou dost not see in this world, or the next, aught beside God.

The Sufi Master of our Age, made a similar statement: [15]

The Source of all things is their end, for the end is as the beginning. Therefore did the Son of Man say, *"Before Abraham was I AM"*. This is the secret mystery of the Universe that holds the key to all science.

Bābā explained that since the **Source**/God/**Reality** is *The Source* of everything, then all is present potentially. The passing in and out of existence of neutrinos is like our perception of reality - UNREAL. (When the Sufi Master *Yesua* (Jesus) said as recorded in the Bible, *"Before Abraham was I AM,"* he was indicating that his essential nature lay beyond any limitations that those who are confined to a materialistic, or a dogmatic religious perspective, might put upon him.) Once science realises that everything is present potentially, it will no longer think in terms of *evolution* (acquisition of traits, another version of the politics of greed), but rather of an *unfolding* of inherent potential. Thus the basis for both religion and science, as well as self-knowledge, is One.

The Sufi goes beyond Time - endeavouring to experience something of the nature of immortality while still in this world - by passing away from self *(fanā')*, into the consciousness of survival in God *(baqā)* (see the table in chapter four). While the Sufi believes, in common with the foundation of all religious systems, that there will be a return to God in a future sense,[16] there is also a belief in a return to God in the NOW! Not just metaphorically speaking, but also in an external way. This return to God is outside of Time and goes beyond the religious perception of Heaven/ Paradise/*Nirvana*.[17] The Sufi Master Al-Ghazālī, writing in his **Mishkāt al-Anwār (Niche of the Lights)** explained it thus:[18]

> The Realised .... perceive directly face to face, that nothing exists but God and *"everything perishes except His Self "* [19] always and forever ... (but) the Realised do not need to wait for the Resurrection to hear the command of their Creator proclaiming:*"Whose will be the Dominion that Day? That of the One; God, the Irresistable!"* [20] (for this proclamation is forever in their ears.) Neither do they understand that the utterance *"God is the Greatest!"* means that He is greater than others - God forbid. As there is nothing other than Himself throughout existence, there can be no phrase to compare with His Greatness.

While empirical psychology focuses on external aspects of behaviour, looking for causes as a means of explanation, Sufism does not separate the self from the **Cosmic Order**. It does not seek to divide Truth from Beauty, or to give precedence to the functional over the aesthetic. For the Sufi "being practical" is to seek harmony. Paradoxically, this comes about by seeking an independence from the World - not in an ascetic sense of renouncing it - but by transcending its limiting orientations. It is in the concept of *Cause-Abandonment,* that this becomes clear.

Cause-Abandonment

Tark-i-sabab (Cause-Abandonment) is not a concept in the ordinary sense of the word, for it cannot be comprehended by discursive thought or logic. It is characterised by the ability of its practitioners to 'fly in the face of reason', to perform actions which seem to disregard common sense. In fact, this is only true when there is no belief in a Greater **Reality**. The Sufi by action, demonstrates that THERE IS such a **Reality***(Haqq)*, and that **Truth***(Haqq)* can only be known by experiencing that Greater **Reality**(*Haqq/* God). It is in placing trust in this **Reality**, that the Sufi is able to transcend – what appears to be – in the usual experience of life, the cause and effect relationship. It does not mean that the Sufi does not believe that cause and effect occurs, but rather that there is a belief in a **Greater Determiner** of all events to which the principle of causality is subject – the **Final Cause** (God).

According to the Sufi Master Ashraf 'Alī Thānvī (died 1943),[21] there are three kinds of causes. The first kind can be designated as the *absolute cause*, which is known by the fact that it is inseparable from its effect, e.g., the effect of drinking water, or eating food, is to appease the cause of one's hunger and thirst. While Sufi practices can be seen – in part – as ways of decreasing the effects of such causes on the personality, so as not to be controlled by them, these causes cannot be entirely ignored. Sufism does not encourage asceticism as an end in itself. To die, or become sick, - as has occurred with some so-called "holy wo/men" - is not considered admirable, but foolish. Such a practice being an indication of self-obsession, rather than the reverse. [22]

The second type of cause, is the *imaginary* one, derived from flights of fancy: e.g., If I do this, or believe this, about myself, then, I will get this. This illusory condition is typified by the numerous individuals who do the football pools, or take part in the National Lottery, firmly convinced that "one day" they will win. Such an attitude portrays a pre-occupation with the world, rather than with God,[23] and can be seen as a form of *self*-indulgence, or *self*-preoccupation, rather than the reverse.

The final type of cause is the *conjectural* one, and arises from the notion that a given chain of events, will necessarily cause the required effect: e.g., that our job "will" supply our requisites, that the crops "will" not fail; that the recession "will" end, etc. Quite often, the belief in such causes is tied-up with endeavouring to fulfil one's so-called "economic needs". This attitude is typified by the externalist Muslim, who trapped in a materialistic lifestyle, will glibly quote the saying of Muhammad, " *Trust in God, but tie your camel,* " totally unaware of its real meaning,[24] which is that God will provide our needs, providing that we put our trust in Him and not ourselves. To take precautions "just in case", is not a mark of faith *(īmān)*, but of disbelief *(kufr)*. The Sufi believes in subjecting the

84

will to God's direction*(istislām);* restraining the ego, or headstrong camel, accepting what God gives – good or bad – and the failure to do so as a mark of self–concern.

The Sufi, believing in a **Transcendent Reality**, neither flaunts the Divine decree as observed in Natural Laws, nor imagines that they conform to personal whim. Yet, at the same time, the Sufi does not limit the power of that **Reality**, believing smugly in the power of personal effort. 25 Similarly, there is no attempt to escape obligation by feigning an excuse based upon conjecture. The believer in God is not passive or timid in the face of difficulties, and does not invent a cause for failing to meet the obligation to grow and move towards God. This is the REAL obligation from which all else springs.

It is in this light that we can begin to understand *Cause- Abandonment,* which, rather than being an escape from the world and from obligation, is in fact a commitment to truth, plus, participating in action that demonstrates this. It means deciding in favour of a **Greater Reality**, and leaving consequences to it. By developing a trust*(tawakkul)* in that **Reality**, the Sufi is not determined by anxiety. Rather there is a contentment *(qinā'at)* that is not swayed by changes in circumstance, since it is rooted in the **Permanent** and the **Infinite**. Such an attitude enables the shackles of habit, conditioning and determinism to be broken.

There are numerous examples of Sufi, who in the face

of difficulties, have manifest equanimity: being indifferent to a lack of money; or showing great courage when confronted by insurmountable problems. In some cases, Sufis, have fought with and led armies against tyrants or colonisers. History is replete with examples of such individuals, who ignored the odds and practised *Cause-Abandonment*. The defeat of General Gordon in the Sudan; the Algerian revolution; the *Mujahideen* in Afghanistan; the Tunisian independence movement; the Libyan struggle against the Italian Fascists, are just a few examples of struggles in which Sufis were involved, or which were led by them,[26] just as there have also been Sufi martyrs who have refused to fight for corrupt governments and/or nationalist armies.

We have the example of the Berber, Tāriq ibn Ziyād, who under the command of the Arab General Mūsā ibn Nusayr, in defensive expansion of the Islamic world, invaded Spain in 711, just 92 years after the beginning of the Islamic era. On landing on its shores, he burnt all the boats, so making retreat impossible. His co-commanders questioned him, one of whom said:

How is Cause-Abandonment justified by religious law(Sharī'ah [27] *) ?* His reply was to laugh and say:
All land is mine because all land is owned by my God! [28]

This act was not an assertion of the right to invade, own, or conquer land - in fact the reverse.[29] Tariq, in defence of his faith, was demonstrating that ONLY God has rights of ownership; and that ALL things are held in trust for that rightful owner. Ibn Ziyād's apparently reckless action was rooted in a deep faith that God is the **Ultimate Controller** of affairs, who alone determines the outcome. It was not believing in those *false gods* of Nationalism, Patriotism, Arab expansionism, or Zionism; but an xpression of a trust in a **Transcendent Reality** that does not recognise humanly imposed and created national borders, a claim for the right of all persons, everywhere, to live freely under God.

So it is that the Sufi does not succumb to fears which would paralyse most, and is not trapped by circumstances, or some other supposedly causative factor. One Sufi, finding himself under attack, when supplying material needs to the starving of Bosnia, replied to his questioners as to why he should undertake such a dangerous mission, with the words which summate this belief in *Cause-Abandonment*:

> I shall not die unless God wills it ! And when He Wills it I cannot prevent it. What difference whether I die here, or in my homeland?

While Sufis acknowledge that not everyone has the same capacity, it is important to realise that from a Sufi perspective, these differences are not seen as causative factors. Eventually, *"all must return to God"* - which is not for them as for Muslims, simply a *Qur'ānic* expression pertaining only to death, but an irreversible Divine decree, referring to our given, innate and natural capacity, to be human and express transcendent values. Rūmī summates:

> It is *(the hū)* man's duty to radiate light and
> warmth, It is the base man's function to invent
> excuses and be shameless. [30]

The extent to which Sufism encourages and believes in this transcendent capability, can be observed in its word for saints(*awliyā'* plural, *Walī* singular), a term meaning friend, that can equally be applied as a title for a Sufi Master – living or dead – as to Sufis generally, who are referred to as the *friends of God* an expression found in the *Qur'ān* (10:62) as one of the oldest names for Sufis.

The Immanent Transcendent

It is this different metaphysical basis to Sufism that both explains as well as facilitates, the development of transcendent potentials within an individual undergoing transformation. In the Christian world, the Divine is separated from life in general, requiring God to "come down to earth", so to speak, a view of the world also propounded by the Greeks and Romans, on whose philosophies Western society, including its medicine, psychology, religion, science and politics, is built. This is contrary to Sufism, which achieved its peak in societies much older than the European. These societies – India, Persia, China – were in a highly advanced state, when Europeans were still living in the Stone Age. [31]

Sufism, like these Eastern societies, expresses a belief

88

in a **Transcendent Reality** that is **Immanent** within. The human being is not a base animal, subject to an external and higher Authority, who but for His condescension, we would have no dealings with, but rather, is him/herself, an expression of that transcendence.

Western philosophies like Materialism, Behaviourism, Empiricism, Rationalism and other similar notions, are simply variants on the theme of the powerlessness of the individual; we are controlled by something independent of ourselves, e.g., instinct, evolution, genetics, the State.

Developing the Shamanistic concept of the tree as symbolic of communicaton between the material and spiritual worlds – an idea which was in turn to be taken up by Kabbalistic Judaism, in its notion of, The Tree of Life – the Sufi sees the human being as the central expression of **Spirit** on earth. Like the trunk of a tree, that **Being** passes through the whole hierarchy of the world, with branches and leaves corresponding to the differentiation of that **Spirit** in its many states of existence. The process of unfoldment is the gradual perception and realisation of that **Reality**. Once realised, the disciple approaches each aspect of this unfoldment as an experience of the **Divine**. For this reason, symbolic life is not reduced to the thought impulses of a repressed mind, but is viewed as a means for mental/spiritual, health/growth, such symbols being considered with an attitude of sanctity.

For the Sufi, spiritual life is equivalent to symbolic life

that is regulated by the perception of different aspects of Spirit, with different forms expressing different facets of that Reality, each symbolic form, having the capacity to reveal something of that Reality, so that everyone IS a Name of God.[32] For this reason, symbolism was defined by Al-Ghazālī, in his *Mishkāt al-Anwār*, as, *the science of the relationship between the different levels of existence.* Following Socrates, the Master explained that behind each term, or manifestation in the material world, lay a reality in the Ideal or spiritual world:

> For everything that is in the *World of the Visible,* there is a corresponding likeness in the *World of the Supreme Nature.* For this reason, there is nothing in the world of sensations that is not a symbol of something in that beyond world. It can happen that one thing in this world may symbolise several things in the *World of the Supreme Nature;* and also that one thing in that world, may have several symbols in the *World of the Visible.* We call a thing symbolic, or typical, when it resembles, or corresponds in some way..[33]

The significance of this viewpoint lies in placing the emphasis, the responsibility, in a transcendent or elevated realm. The Sufi does not seek for total explanations in the visible realm, nor in some blind unconscious force such as the "I", "conditioned reflexes", or "instinctual behavioural patterns", because while Sufism acknowledges – we might even say, is primarily concerned with overcoming – conditioning, it does not lay the basis for such conditioning on blind instinctual impulses. Rather,

90

it sees the *habit of the mind* as the ploy of the ego, that is determined by a conscious desire for self-enhancement.

Thus symbols in dreams arise not as the result of distortion, but because:

> The effect of sleep, as is also the case in visions, is that the command of the senses over the inner self, the Divine Light within, is suppressed. For it is the tendency of the senses to preoccupy the inner self; to draw away its attention from the *Invisible World and the Realm above,* to the *Sensory World* ... but if it has attained complete perfection (as for prophets or saints) it is not limited to perceiving the visible form (symbol) alone, but passes directly to the inner idea.... [34]

For this reason, Al-Ghazālī in the **Mishkāt** and another of his works,[35] lists the faculties of perception as five, in the following ascending order: **sensory; imaginative; intelligential/cognitive, the rational/logical or propositional** and finally the **transcendent**.[36] Western psychologists will recognise these capacities, but it is noteworthy that in addition to the **transcendent** which is not at all recognised, a distinction is drawn between the cognitive and logical faculties, which, while implicitly recognised, has as yet no explicit semantic differentiation, or conceptual framework in Western psychology.

(It is the **transcendent** capacity that is primary to Sufis, and which in reality is the basis for all lower perceptions -- regardless of whom does the perceiving. Consequently, the Sufi Master in his/her capacity as the Complete or Universal Human (*Al-Insān al-Kāmīl*) , is recalling, or causing to remember *(dhikra)* the transcendent potential of the disciple, present WITHIN THEM BOTH. On this basis, symbols – visible, oral, or active – are *a bridge to the real* to use a Sufi expression.[37] Sufism thus becomes explicable by its methods – whether that be dream interpretation, recitation of Names of God, devotional exercises, or dance – as a means for returning the dualist back to the original primal state within *(fitrah)* : the **Immanent Transcendent**. A state of Unity *(Tawhīd)* existing ONLY within the **Source/ Creator/God**; a healing of the divided self.

Once the significance of the above has been realised, it will be seen why the Sufi claims God as the only **Reality** – the only **One** *(Wahad)* in **Existence** *(Wujūd)*. Similarly, it also explains the emphasis on self-annihilation *(fanā')* as a means for returning to the original state of Unity. Furthermore, it shows that difficulties in understanding, or interpreting Sufi doctrine, arise because of the different conceptual basis upon which Sufism is built. For the Sufi, dualism and its consequences – the divided self – results from the refusal to recognise that God is THE only **Source of Existence**. According to this conception, Humanism – in the truest sense of the word – is not an atheistic doctrine, just as the term Pantheism only has meaning IF one believes that something other than God exists. For the Sufi, God AND everything cannot exist; the existence of the other is illusory. Yet that IS NOT to say that God is everything. Once this has been grasped, the notion of the

92

Divine Man - of God on earth - whether that be in the Greek, Roman, Hindu, or Christian sense, is an inadequate - as much as an inaccurate - concept, just as the notion of therapy extracted from its metaphysical basis, is illusory from the Sufi point of view.[38]

Following Sufi Master, Shāh Walī Allāh (died 1762) - in his elucidation of this point,[39] in an explanation of dreams and symbols - Sufi Master, *Bābā* Dovid Yūsuf, explained to his disciples that the *Qur'ānic* (5:113) reference to Jesus as a *man strengthened by the Holy Spirit,* refers to that **Universal Power**, which manifests to the degree to which its recipients are able to reflect it, so that when the orientation is totally towards **Transcendent** concerns - when that individual's self-concerns have been negated - it then seems as if there is no difference between the individual limited self and the **Transcendent Immanent** within. In a case like this *it seems as if* we have seen God. He summated it cryptically by saying:

> the Perfect Master, being pure and selfless, is not visible to us except by the *Radiance of the Light Divine* which shines through that one.

Notes and References

1) See note 43 in chapter four.

2) Būlāq, Beirut, 7 vols, 1956-1959 (orig. published 1284/1868)

3) Claude Lévi-Strauss, "The Sorcerer and his Magic", in his *Structural Anthropology*, Basic Books, New York, 1963.

4) Western psychology has only just begun to realise that there are connections between the worlds of matter and mind; something that Sufi physicians realised and employed centuries ago. See Abū'l-Walīd Muhammad ibn Ahmad ibn Muhammad ibn Rushd's *Bidayah al-Mujtahid*, 2 Vols, National Publications, Cairo, 5th Edition 1981, (while Averroe's philosophy has influenced the West, his medicine remains to be discovered).

5) The display of these gifts has been associated with the word *fakir*, being a derivation of *faqīr* (one who aspires to spiritual poverty, i.e., free of religious conditioning), another term for Sufi. Showing them openly is a mark of degeneration and inauthenticity.

6) Because of attempting to limit the activities of the mind, or faculty of choice *(nafs-i-nātiqah)* to logical operations, and another example of the inadequacy of Western psychological concepts.

7) Understanding, conceptualising, or perceiving, are inadequate terms for this Sufi experience. Idries Shah called it *direct perception*, but I prefer the word 'receiving', in that it acknowledges that its **Infinite Source** is outside of, as well as within, the individual and cannot be attained by personal, or individual effort, alone.

8) See note 27 in chapter four.

9) The word *karāmah* also means grace. By extension it implies, that such powers as are displayed by the miracles *(karāmāt)* of the saint in question, are a gift (from God) and not something learned. Hence the word *karāmat* for charitable acts.

10) From this word is derived the name for a Sufi saint, or Master (*Walī*, i.e., friend of God).

11) *Mathnawī* 4:3628; 6:1450; 4:3637; 3:1268.

12) The esoteric/real meaning of circling around the *Ka'aba* for the Sufi (as the Muslim does when going on pilgrimage) is that God is the central fixed point (**The Unchangeable**) around which all is in flux.

13) There are no real accidents for God is the **Determiner**. However, since God is indeterminate, incomprehensible, immeasurable – not obliged to operate according to some fixed mechanistic principle – from the Western perspective, this is an "accident".

14) *"Kitāb al-Alīf* " translated by J.Weir, **Journal of the Royal Asiatic Society** 1901, p, 809. The significance of this profound passage lies in its ability to incorporate within one statement - infinity *in both directions* - at the same TIME as depicting something which has only recently been realised in Western Science; i.e., the fabric of the Universe is contained within sub-atomic particles - neutrinos - that both pass out of existence and then reappear again, in the same moment that they are perceived.

15) In *Leaves from the Tree of Life: Saying, Meditations & Prayers for*

a *New Age*,, spoken by *Bābā* Dovid Yusuf and Edited by David Heinemann, Rainbow Trust Publications, Northampton, 1995, 111:2.

16) *Qur'ān* 53:42; 96:8.

17) While the Muslim realises that there are many different levels in Paradise - based on *Qur'ānic* interpretation (56:7-38,88-91) - there is a failure to comprehend that this is because Paradise is a state, rather than a place (see *Qur'ān* 89:27-30).

18) Abū Hāmid Muhammad al-Ghazālī's *Mishkāt al-Anwār*, Cairo, 1322 A.H. p, 18.

19) *Qur'ān* 28:88.

20) *Qur'ān* 40:16.

21) *Al-Sihat-al-Wasāwis*, Mehtab Publishers, Deoband, 1965.

22) There have been numerous Sufis who have lived frugally, such as e.g., the renowned female saint, Rābi'ah al-'Adawiyya of Basra, Iraq (died 801) whose ascetic lifestyle is legendary. Muhammad, quite often went without food himself and is reputed to have eaten only every other day. However, in all these cases, such asceticism as was experienced, was not seen as an end in itself. Quite often, as in the case of the contemporary Master, *Bābā* Dovid Yūsuf, this occurs as a result of living as a Sufi without independent means, unsupported by any institution (many of his disciples are poor, some of whom he assists, in addition to his own family).

23) The Sufi ideal is expressed in the following saying, *"to be in the world but not of it"* - see, *Mathnawī* 1:388.

24) In Arabic, to restrain a camel by tying its foreleg, so as to hamstring it, is *'aqālā*, which has the same root as *'aql*, meaning that the **Divine Will** can only operate if the personal ego/will is constrained. The headstrong characteristics of the camel are proverbial, and the people of the time would have had no difficulty in understanding this colloquial saying. The *Qur'ān* (14:12; 65:3) clearly states that trust in God should be complete, with no reliance placed upon one's own efforts.

25) Rūmī, *Mathnawī* 5:1543 on this point.

26) Often these movements, while led and inspired by selfless individuals, were taken over at a later date by power-hungry materialists, who used the memory of these figures in order to enlist popular support, at the same time as compromising their principles. It is a common pattern throughout the Islamic world and helps to explain the rise to power of Colonel Mu'ammar al-Qaddāfī, and others like him. The same thing can be observed in the case of some Jewish and Christian militant organisations. This occurred after the death of Muhammad, giving rise to the *Sunnī* and *Shī'ah* factions of Islam, neither of which the Sufi believes represents Muhammad's teachings.

27) Islamic Law, which like the Jewish *Halakhah*, covers all facets of life; the political as well as the religious.

28) Muhammad Ajmal, **Muslim Contributions to Psychotherapy & Other Essays**, Psychology Research Monograph (5), National Institute Publications, Islamabad, 1986, p, 66 (italics mine).

29) To understand this event, it is necessary to realise that Spain's inhabitants at this time, were mainly non-Trinitarian, or Arian Christians, subject to absent Catholic landlords who ruled under the authority of the Pope. For this reason the Muslims were seen as liberators. For a list of references and a discussion of this point, see Ahmad Thomson, *Blood on the Cross*, Ta-Ha Publishers, London, 1989, pp, 144-147.

30) In Ajmal, as above, p,69 (in brackets mine). We should note the etymological derivation of the word *human*, as having reference to the *hū*, or breath of God, as manifest in the complete human being.

31) Many philosophical, ethical, political and even economic problems, now discussed in Western society, were long ago considered in the East. Technological developments such as printing, explosives, antibiotics in medicine, sewage systems, running water, hygiene, and astronomical charts based on knowledge that the world was round, preceded their use in the West. Colonisation by Western powers, together with the decay of these civilisations and the deliberate falsification of their history, has prevented a realisation of these facts (see e.g., Nasr 1976 in **Bibliography**).

32) This is why a Shaykh when conferring initiation gives the disciple a specific Name of God to be used in personal intonation *(Dhikr/ Zikr/Zeker)*. In some Orders, such as the *Khalwatiyya*, this will correspond to a stage in the initiation process, while in others like the *Nūrbakshiyya*, it will be specific to that individual. In the case of the *Bābā'iyya* (Fraternity of the Universal Way) both practices are utilised. It was this practice that was copied by the founders of the Hindu, **Transcendental Meditation movement**, just as Gurdjieff's methods, **Subud**, and Bhagwan's **Active Meditation**, were all derived from *Naqshbandī* practices (for everyone being a Name of God, see Rūmī's *Mathnawī* 1:1238).

33) Abū Hāmid Muhammad al-Ghazālī's, *Mishkāt al-Anwār*, Cairo, 1322 A.H. p, 30

34) *Mishkāt*, as above, Cairo edition, p, 38 (in brackets mine).

35) *Ihyā 'Ulūm al-Dīn* Cairo, 1347 A.H (2) **Marvels of the Mind**.

36) *Mishkāt*, as above, Cairo edition, pp, 43-46.

37) *Mathnawī* 5:3257,3277. Note the similarity to Jung's ideas.

38) From the Sufi perspective, difficulty in understanding this point, arises from a dualism within the mind, and only participation on the path of Oneness (Sufism) will clear confusion.

39) Translated by G.N.Jalbani, edited by D.B.Fry; Shah Waliullah *Sufism and the Islamic Tradition: the Lamahat and Sata'at of Shah Waliullah,* Octagon Press, London, 1980, pp, 68-70.

6

FOLLOWING THE PATH OF TRANSCENDENCE

*"The revelation of Self is the Revelation of the
Cosmos itself."*

Master *Bābā* Dovid Yūsuf

The Sufi Concept of Mental Health

Sufism is an expression of the *holistic vision,* a phrase I
use to describe that original, primal and integrative
experience, from which all creativity, and genuine
spirituality, springs. Sufis talk of **dhawq** (taste), referring
to a state of consciousness that transcends mental
knowledge: a state of direct perception. (It is for this
reason that the Sufi Teacher uses stories and poetry –
which being multifaceted and not understandable in a
concrete linear sense – encourages and is an expression of,
holistic perception.) Such holistic teaching methods are
designed to induce within the recipient, a realisation of the
Unitary Nature of Existence. This attempt to reduce
everything into separate elements, disregarding the process
as a whole (reductionism), is a sickness, even though it is
the common condition of most people in our society. It
results in tunnel vision; an inability to consider alternative
approaches to existence, and ultimately prejudice. It has
led to the spurious notion that knowledge consists of a set
of facts conveniently arranged into an hypothesis.
However, such knowledge depends for its existence upon

97

the means by which these facts can be so ordered. Knowledge consists of an identity between the knower and the object of knowledge. Put in another way, we can say that knowledge and being are one. Any attempt to separate them will lead to false conclusions and to that condition which Sufism sets out to cure, namely, dualism.

This sickness is a disease *(marad)* of the heart,[1] arising from a state of self-deception, in which there is an endeavour to hide inconvenient facts from self, as well as from others.[2] Resulting in being alienated from self, as well as (because of) being alienated from the Divine Unity, or in common language – God. It is a dualism expressing the distance between the human being and the object perceived; between the human being and others – and is equivalent to a belief in the separateness of the individual from Nature and God. (Mental health can therefore be measured in terms of an affinity with, or a psychological distance from, THAT WHICH IS)[3] (Reality/God), as holistically expressed in the *Qur'ān* (2:9–10):

They try to deceive God and those who believe, but only deceive themselves though not aware (of it)! (For) in their hearts is a disease that God has increased. Pain increasing is their punishment, for they are false.

يُخَادِعُوْنَ اللهَ وَالَّذِيْنَ اٰمَنُوْا ۚ وَمَا يَخْدَعُوْنَ اِلَّاۤ اَنْفُسَهُمْ وَمَا يَشْعُرُوْنَ ۚ فِىْ قُلُوْبِهِمْ مَّرَضٌ ۙ فَزَادَهُمُ اللهُ مَرَضًا ۚ وَلَهُمْ عَذَابٌ اَلِيْمٌ ۢ بِمَا كَانُوْا يَكْذِبُوْنَ

98

This disease, as pinpointed here and in the following verses (2:10-15), is seen to result from a condition of dissociation*(nifāq)*,[2] caused by doubt*(shakk,* of oneself and of others, as well as of God) and envy*(hasad)*. Wanting to be accepted, there is an endeavour to deceive, in the desire for self-enhancement, that has as its goal pre-eminence or power, because there is no acknowledgement of a **Final Controller** of events. It is a self-deception that expresses itself in an easy conformity with the dominant group, plus a continual rationalisation by such persons of their inconsistencies. The result is that, as the **Qur'ān** puts it:

"they are bewildered in their arrogance." في طُغْيَانِهِمْ يَعْمَهُونَ

Consequently, there is a constant endeavour to maintain an impossible cycle of conflicting thoughts, to sustain the appearance of stability; what the Sufi Master Ashraf 'Alī Thānvī, described as *"circular thinking".* [4] Such instability inevitably leads to an obsession with security and an inability to accept change. Spontaneity and freedom of action are replaced by conformity, passivity and rigidity of habit. Idols of every kind, are grasped in order to secure stability amongst a confusion of feelings and motives. It is this state of affairs that Sufism addresses, believing that anything preventing a realisation of the Unity of Existence should be spurned and rejected.

Sufi disciplines reflect an holistic concern and approach to life, having as their aim the overcoming of this dualism,

99

achieved by sacrificing the ego- the sense of pride – or *'I'*, that reflects a limited self. Only by giving up cherished notions and orientations is progress towards a Unitary State possible. The inner dissonance that characterises the life of the disbeliever [5] – reflected by interpersonal conflict – represents a false self*(na's al-ammārah bi-s-sū')* that must be sacrificed.

Since relationships become for such people a matter of exploitation, in which their vanity and greed is inflated, one who becomes aware of having this disease withdraws from secular relations and turns the gaze inwards in order to shatter the false persona. This was expressed in a saying of Muhammad (with which we began this book) as quoted by the Sufi Master Rūmī:[6] *"Die before you are dead!"* meaning that the Unitary State and death are equivalent; for unless we sacrifice our limited self with all its preoccupations, fears, anxieties and limitations, God as the **Transcendent Reality** is veiled*(Hijāb)*. Acknowledging **Transcendence** and **Infinity**, necessarily means a loss of the finite and limited. All Sufi practices are directed towards this awareness, which is conceived as positive rather than negative; a continuous process taking place over the whole of life – an ongoing, rather than a temporary initiation.

This process – seen as purification – is not a straight path of development, but one which has ups and downs, highs and lows, in its progression. Sometimes, there can be states similar to depression*(qabd)*, while at other times,

100

there is the experience of developmental unfolding*(bast* - literally; expansion of light). The first can be understood as the grieving of the limited self*(nafs al-lawwāmah)* at its passing, while the latter is a movement towards a self at peace with itself*(nafs al-mutma'innah)* [7] (see table below).

Transcendent Self: *The Immanent Infinite*			
QUR'ĀNIC REFERENCE	ARABIC SUFI TERM	DEVELOPMENTAL STAGE	SELF TYPE
89:27	*Nafs al-mutma'innah*	Integrated Psyche	Realised self
75:2	*Nafs al-lawwāmah*	Accusing Psyche	Limited self
12:53	*Nafs al-ammārah bi-s-sū'*	Commanding Psyche	False self
Instinctual Animal State: *Nafs al-Haywāniyah*			

Sufi Master 'Abd al-Qādir al-Jīlānī (died 1166), described this process of self-liberation, or Transcendence, as going through three stages: "I-NESS" - *personification,* that is when the disciple becomes absorbed in the Teacher; "HE-NESS" - *deification;* when the Sufi becomes absorbed in God; "ONE-NESS" - when the realised Sufi*('Arīf)* has attained the stage of being at unity with all **Existence.** [8]

The final stage brings a certainty*(yaqīn)* [9] that ITSELF is a Unitary/Paradisical State. Having discarded limitations and illusions that trap the ego-bound self, the realised Sufi*('Arīf;* gnostic) knows experientially, a **Reality** that is not Time-bound;[10] an attainment in which all dichotomies disappear, ego and non-ego, subjective and objective; so that the **Transcendent** or Real Self, can be present in every aspect of life.[11] However, until this final stage is reached,

101

expansion is necessarily followed by contraction. [12]

Thus, there is a movement from an instinctual animal state *(nafs al-haywāniyah)*, in which there is a passive obedience to natural impulses; through the stage of being at the command of the ego's passions and whims – the commanding psyche *(nafs al-ammārah)*. Then to a state of awareness of imperfections and limitations – the accusing psyche *(nafs al-lawwāmah)* – that ultimately enables a stage of rest, reintegration and inner peace – the integrated psyche *(nafs al-mutma'innah)* – to be achieved. In the final stage there is participation in, and illumination of, the creative movement of the Immanent Infinite. The limited self of everyday experience has been transcended and the Transcendent Self realised.

Although human beings have been created in *"ahsan al-taqvīm"* (the best of patterns),[13] they also have a choice of doing evil and descending into a state of *"al-asfal al-sāfilīn"* (the lowest of the low).[14] As the best of creation, the human being has been given the ability to perceive the inner nature of the essence of things [15] – described in Sufi terms as the heart *(qalb)*. This knowledge brings with it the capacity to be influenced by the emotions in a negative as well as a positive way. It is a two-edged sword[16] by which the self can be known, through *mastering* [17] the emotions. Sufism is *tibb-i-rūhānī* (therapy of the spirit), [18] whereby the experience of knowing God – in a concrete sense – takes place through the experience of the Self.

Sufi Disciplines as a Means of Cognitive Reorientation

There is a resistance to accepting **Reality** on the part of those in duality. Since they are themselves divided, they are unable to accept the **Unitary nature of Existence**. The first symptom of this sickness is the alienation from their self/Self, which in turn leads to alienation from Nature, from society and from their fellow human beings, the result being that they are also alienated/cut-off from the remedy to their problems. Consequently, their supposed remedies – that is the elevation of the debased – prevents them from accepting their transcendent potentials.

This is epitomised by *Desacralisation* : the emphasizing of lower aspects of existence; so that anything pertaining to the sacred and transcendent is disregarded. There is a separation of processes and their inter-dependence into components that become *things*. Turning to what excites and titillates, perception is dulled. This is excused by dubious concepts such as Freud's repression, but for the Sufi, *it is not the repression of our animal nature that creates mental disturbance, but the suppression of our transcendent nature.* For the dualist, rather than inner life becoming the means for elevating the *psyche,* by the beautiful and aesthetic (emphasizing our transcendent nature), it becomes a mechanistic "stimulus and response". According to this view we are no more than animals, so that experiments applied to pigeons, rats, or chimpanzees, can, it is erroneously believed, tell us about *human* nature!

The end result of such an orientation is what René Guénon has called *dispersion into multiplicity*. [19] Unable to find or focus on a centre, the dualist is pulled in contrary directions at one and the same time, each new craze exerting a fascination and imprisoning their *psyche* in the process – what *Bābā* Dovid Yūsuf called *the prison of self*. [20] Life for such people becomes a chasing after wind; a circular process of thinking and acting – the only common aspect of which is the total lack of direction. Unable to find a way, they do not know who they are, creating an anxiety that can only be assuaged by the relentless assertion of a meaningless *'I'*. For without a system of moral values and beliefs, based upon a genuine inner certainty*(yaqīn)*, (not the clinging to an externalist hypocrisy)*'Me'*, the product of relationships, cannot exist.

In this sense, the Sufi engages in a genuine dialogue with **Existence**. Aware that conversation consisting of ceaseless questioning that has its basis in self-glorification, i.e., *"show me that I'm right"*, is in reality a monologue, a Master refrains from answering many of his disciples' questions;[21] so that when *Bābā* Dovid Yūsuf was asked several questions by an Indian Muslim scholar and professor who wished to become a disciple, the Master did not *immediately* answer them. Not that he could not do so, but because he realised that such questions can form a block to true understanding, so preventing progress on the path to genuine self-knowledge: spiritual growth is not possible if the mind is cluttered with empty words. Similarly, in other cases and with other individuals, unless such questions were rooted in the disciple's experience as related to spiritual development, the Master dismissed them. Such expressions of irrelevance are indicators of a frustrated spirituality, trying to be satisfied by ego-knowledge, resulting in a clouding of the mind. They arise because the confused *psyche* of the dualist finds it irksome to meditate on real problems, as these will necessarily involve action and change.

(The woolly-thinking of the dualist is a mark of self-pity and a seeking for love and attention) Sufi disciplines are a means for cognitive reorientation, in which the focus is on a primal, holistic integration with the **Transcendent**, immanent within us, rather than on a separatism that reduces all experience to its lowest common denominator, i.e., self-interest. This perspective is truly holistic, for it does not separate belief from action, matter from spirit:

> There shall be no impassable gulf dividing God from man, spirit from matter: They shall be the first and last links of a single chain.[22]

Therefore there is no tendency to dwell on the past as in Western psychology and therapy, for *one who dwells on the past, is driven to the past through regression.*[23] Spiritual transformation/cognitive reorientation, is centred on the *now !* Only by having the courage*(himmah)* to transcend the limited perspective of a past-orientated self, can the disciple realise the **True Self**. Wallowing in self-pity or self-devaluation, is in reality a form of self-indulgence, the real aim of which is self-glorification.

This does not mean there is no repentance, quite the contrary. Unless there is an acceptance of one's actual limited perspective - limiting actions - what is generally termed as sin (the real meaning of which is to miss the mark of completion/perfection/wholeness) no progress can be made. One must begin by admitting to oneself with sincerity *(ikhlās)*, [24] unhelpful habits, in order for change - a turning around, or repentance *(tawbah)* to take place. Reverence *(mākhāfa)* is the beginning of a process of purification that precedes and accompanies the development of love *(mahabba)*, leading ultimately to realisation *(ma'rifa)*. There must be an acceptance of limitations, that a feeling of awe *(taqwā:* fearful-awareness) for God's stupendous Power and Majesty, might develop. [25] This in turn leads to a desire for purification that expands into a love of God, through following the example *(sunna)* of the Master. From this, wisdom - as well as a realisation of **Truth***(Haqq)* - develops, leading to union with the Will of God *(ittihād)*.

This change in orientation is not one of despair, but of a desire for continuous redirection. There is no revelling in, or enjoying of, repentance. The reason for **Infinite Mercy** is because of the sincerity with which the disciple surrenders to that Mercy. From the Jewish or Muslim viewpoint, the most heinous sin is to ascribe partners to

106

God (as in the Trinity), whereas for the Sufi, it is the refusal to recognise that only One exists. It is towards the recognition of this ONE and only **Reality**, that the Sufi path is directed, and it is the whole purpose of repentance according to them. Rābi'ah al-'Adawiyya of Basra, Iraq (died 801), is reputed to have said to a Muslim who claimed he had not sinned for sometime:[26] "*Your existence is a sin* to which no other sin can be compared."

It is the conscience, the **accusing psyche**(*nafs al-lawwāmah)*, that aware of its limitations, has the capacity to move towards the Unitary State. To be a **Muwahhid** [27] or Sufi in the true sense, the *sālik* (seeker) must be resurrected – i.e., become a new person – just as at the time of Judgment, the bodies of the dead will rise. For this reason, the *Day of Resurrection* is linked with the **accusing psyche** in the *Qur'ān* (75:1-2):

I do testify by the Day of resurrection;

I do testify by the accusing psyche

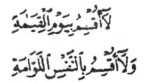

For the Sufi, this experience takes place outside of Time, as well as within it. For the *'Arīf* (realised Sufi) in attaining the Unitary State*(ittihād)* has negated the limited self*(fanā' fi-Llāh)* (see table in **chapter four**), together with its psychic developmental stages. By persisting*(baqā')* in this extinction*(fanā')* the self has been transformed, or resurrected and its **Transcendent** nature realised. Thus the

107

psychic stage of heightened conscience(*nafs al-lawwāmah* - **accusing psyche**) becomes the means through which transformation takes place. Viewed in this way, it can be seen that repentance is continuous/timeles; for ultimately it stands outside of Time(=realisation of **Transcendent Self**).

For this reason, Sufis of the *Chishtiyya Order* [28] have described three kinds of repentance, that when examined, can be seen to be one; for all elements of our Timebound existence are absorbed when approaching the **Timeless One**:

> *Repentance of the Present:* means one should be' penitent about one's errors (sins).
> *Repentance of the Past:* means reminding one of the need to give other people's rights to them. If one has reprimanded someone unduly, one should ask forgiveness from the victim of that hostility. If one has committed adultery, one should ask forgiveness from the One (God). [29]
> *Repentance of the Future:* means to decide not to commit any sin...[30]

In this cognitive reorientation, there is a movement away from neurotic, masochistic tendencies (self-persecution, or absorption); realising that in accordance with the principle of *Enantiodromia* enunciated by Heraclitus, to emphasize anything to an extreme, will produce the opposite effect. To affect repentance, the Sufi directs will and intention away from preoccupation with self - the opposite to the approaches of the externally religious, whose disciplinary efforts towards penitence are often self-orientated. Unlike these approaches, God's assistance is *invoked,* not pleaded for. By utilising Names of God in *Dhikr* (remembrance -

see **Appendix 1**), there is a reorientation away from the limitations of self - what sin actually IS - towards the **Transcendent**(God). A saying of Muhammad describes this:

> Those who invoke God so that their eyes overflow *(fādhat 'aynāhu)* with fearful-insight *(khashyah)*, that the earth might be watered *(yusību 'l-ardh)* by their tears; these He will not chastise on the Day of Resurrection.[31]

This symbolism refers to the ego, whose hardness and self-orientation is softened by remembrance (invocation or *dhikr*) of the inner and primal nature *(fitrah)*. During this penitential act, the outer *(zāhir)* - symbolically the earth - is dissolved as if by tears, by the inner *(bātin)*, so that resurrection has already taken place within the heart as well as in actions (potentially): God - both **The First***(al-Awwal)* and **The Last***(al-Akhir)*- becomes eternally Present in the NOW. It is said of the Sufi that they are *ibn al-waqt* (born of the moment);[32] meaning that through remembrance, they remains in the timeless instant.[33]

The eyes as organs of perception are two dimensions of the ego, past and future - what we are and what we want to be. The right eye corresponds to the sun - to activity and to the future, the left eye to the moon - to passivity and the past. These are dissolved, or transmuted, by a blinding flash of insight (awe/fear) obtained contemplating the **Transcendent** immanent within. It is the deepening of this process and its full realisation, that constitutes the Sufi experience. When it is enacted - known in a real sense

- the Sufi sees nought but God. God is seen everywhere, in everything, as all things are seen in Him. By learning to love God, the Sufi comes to know God and the self. Love consists of both an active and passive mode. In the active mode, there is a giving away of oneself – charitable acts of endeavour based on faith. In the passive mode, there is patience, calm and surrender. In both cases, agitation, self-centredness and all forms of self-deception (inward and outward) are remedied. This is achieved by changing the orientation from ego to love of God. This attitude, or orientation of being, has not been better expressed than by the aforementioned Sufi, Rābi'ah al-'Adawiyya who in poetic prayer exclaimed:

> Oh God! If I worship You out of fear of Hell,
> then burn me in it;
> If I worship You for hope of Paradise,
> exclude me from it;
> But if I worship You for Your sake alone,
> then deny me not a vision
> Of Your Everlasting Beauty.[26]

In this spiritual journey from the limited to the unlimited Self, the different levels of personality, are necessarily brought into conflict with one another, creating forces of resistance and protest, which make the smooth functioning of consciousness difficult. Impulsive actions and remorse are, together, part of the struggle to overcome the promptings of the commanding psyche(nafs al-ammārah bi-s-sū'). Turning the orison(dhikr) to God, through repetition of Divine Names[34] (Dhikr-Arabic/Zikr-

Persian/*Zeker*-Hebrew), transforms, replaces, converts passionate promptings, into divine invocations that chasten and purify consciousness, by remembrance*(dhikr)* of the love of God.[35] (Chanting Divine Names, the Sufi, through an act of conscious awareness, links all the worlds of existence, endeavouring to disperse the veils of illusion, in order to grasp that there IS ONLY GOD ! That the Sufi exists only when and inasmuch as s/he is a manifestation, a reflection, of the **Divine Essence**.

> In remembering God, God remembers the
> rememberer (fa'dhkurūnī) – **Qur'ān** 2:152.

Various **Qur'ānic** passages and sayings of Muhammad [36] indicate *Dhikr* as the supreme act of worship, inasmuch as that it is God who is invoking Herself. Its power arises from the identity of the Divine Name with Him who is invoked by means of Her own Act, His own Self-knowledge, and Her own Self-consciousness. (The act of invocation can be likened to that of Creation and Dissolution/Reabsorption, which takes place through the breath of God*(Hū),* who is the **Source** of the means of invocation, so that the greatest exponent of Sufism in its most traditional form,[37] wrote:

> When a man becomes familiar with *dhikr,* he separates himself (by his action inwardly) from all other things. Just as at death he is separated from all that is not God..So that what remains(at death) is the invocation*(dhikr)* alone. If this invocation is familiar to him, he rejoices that all things which have kept him from it have been removed. Thus does he find himself alone with his **Beloved**.

Dhikr is the supreme method for the unification of personality, by the very fact that it recalls its participant to the Original Primal State from which that person emerged and to which they will return. In Sufi cosmology existence is cyclical, so that the end is as the beginning, [38] a fact reflected in the root form of the word, which is also true of the Hebrew form *Zeker* (literally; a sign of what was once there), [39] betraying its common origin. [40] Thus consciousness is fixated upon what was, and what will be, in the timeless moment of NOW! There are no hang-ups or habituations, derived from expectations (the crutch of the past); nor desires or passions to imprison the self (sense of failure or frustration arising from attempting to control the future). A unitary state of being is achieved that becomes a basis and pattern for all of life's activities.

The Heavenly Ascent of the Prophet Muhammad as an Archetype of the Sufi's Development

While the Muslim sees Muhammad as the sole Exemplar, [41] the Sufi - whatever the outward divisional allegiance [42] - *traces out the mode* of Muhammad's spiritual ascent, as depicted in the traditional account of his heavenly journey. Unlike the externally religious, the Sufi's devotion to the Path*(Tariqa)*[43] is total, rather than being a token allegiance based upon place of birth or parental designation.

This ascent is referred to in the *Qur'ān* (17:1), where it simply refers to the *night journey (al-Isrā')* of Muhammad from the *Ka'aba* in Mecca, to the site of the temple remains in Jerusalem,[44] where, it is believed, he ascended to the highest heaven, or point *beyond which none may pass* (*Qur'ān* 53:14). While commentators have interpreted these passages differently – some believing it was a vision, while others have taken it literally – the event known as *Laylat al-isrā' wa-l-Mi'rāj* (Night of the journey and Ascent) is celebrated by Muslims on the 27th of Rajab, and is surrounded by traditional stories. For the Sufi, the stages of ascent are stages on the spiritual path in which the form(body) is absorbed by the inclination (*psyche*/soul/ self); the inclination by its vitality(spirit); and the vitality re-absorbed into its **Source** or origin (Divine Presence). The symbolism of the Ascent is for the Sufi a description of the ascent of the soul (the journey of self to **Self**) and is so described in Muhyī'd-Dīn ibn 'Arabī's *Kitab al-Isrā' ilā 'l-Maqām al-Asrā* , and Rūmī's *Mathnawī* (4:552).

These developmental stages can be linked to degrees of selflessness or purity, and another derivation of the word *Sūfī*: from the Arabic *Tasawwuf* (mysticism, esotericism) meaning purity – in concept as well as an etymological derivation - from the root *sfw* (to be pure). Rūmī often used the reed pipe to symbolise this, [45] and in Hebrew the word *sūf* means reed. Thus in Kabbalistic Judaism, which as we have seen shares a common origin with Sufism, the coming out of Egypt by the Israelites required them to pass through the sea of reeds*(yam sūf)* ; also symbolising

113

for the Kabbalist, the necessity for purity.

It should be realised, in passing, that the commonly accepted idea that *Sūfī* is an actual (rather than allegorical) name, based on the Arabic for wool *(sūf)* cannot be valid, because not all Sufis, in all periods, have worn wool. Nor did those who wore it do so at all times. The only evidence we have of Muhammad wearing wool (**Sahīh Al-Bukhārī** Vol.7; 11:691) indicates that it was not a common practice for him to do so (he could not get his woollen cloak off to perform ablutions before prayer). The wearing of wool as an *allegorical reference* to a particular kind of mystic, can be understood by examining the history of wool in its connection with religious rites. ____

The worshippers of *Isis*, dressed in linen *(Tibullus* 1, 3:30*)*, considered *the purest covering for divine things* by the ancients, with wool regarded as *unclean* by the followers of Orpheus and Pythagoras (Apuleius's **Apologia** 56). The Jewish prophets (**Leviticus** 6:10) and priests (**Leviticus** 16:4) also wore linen. The exception to this were the Romans, who generally wore wool in their religious rites. But even in this case it had uncanny associations (Pliny's **Naturalis Historia** 11, 56:147), and balls of wool at the 'Festival of the Lares of the Crossroads' represented slaves (Festus's **Pilae Effigies,** **Macrobius Saturnalia** 1,7:35). Wool was associated in this case with the notion of sacrifice(Ovid's **Fasti** IV:652-660). By using this term (in an allegorical sense) such persons

114

were showing a disregard for convention, or external form, just as the Hebrew slaves did in ancient Egypt, who when sacrificing the paschal lamb, showed their rejection of the Egyptian taboo against animal sacrifice and the eating of lamb, which was sacred as a symbol of the Egyptian god Osiris. The term *Sūfī* applies to the *sacrifice of self*, as in the mystical interpretation of the Jewish Passover (see **Exodus** 12:3-13).

In the case of Muhammad's and the Sufi's, Ascent, the developmental sequence is a reflection of the Arc of Existence. Muhammad's Ascent traces out the movement of the **Logos** through the prophetic cycles, beginning with Adam. Muhammad - speaking for all prophets - said:

> I was conceived when Adam was between water and clay. Whoever has seen me, has seen the Truth. [46]

meaning that the potential, or unfolding of the cycle, was present to begin with. The ascent of the Sufi occurs as the result of this dispensation through the Universal *Logos*, or **Spirit**, as was the case for Muhammad, his message containing all previous Revelations (as was true of Masters before him) and descending into his heart in its entirety on the **Night of Power***(Laylat al-Qadr).*[47] It is this night and not the "Night of Ascent" that begins the Sufi's spiritual journey. Just as Muhammad ascended to heaven because of the realisation (of his **Transcendent Self**) which permeated his being at the commencement of his mission, so too, is it the reception of that same timeless Revelation, within the

115

heart of the mystic, that allows ascent to occur.

For this reason, Sufis have been concerned to keep night vigils, following the example of Muhammad, who would often spend the night in prayer. This should not surprise us for the practice of **Salāh** (ritual prayer) depicts the Arc of Existence.[48] Suʾi prayer is a meditation that includes use of the body, voice, silence and stillness, as well as covering the whole day in periodic sessions. When held in congregation, it has individual elements within it; when performed individually, there are elements affording recognition of the group. This, because it is said, that it is not individuals as such who are praying, but *the whole of Creation,* through using the voice (the words) of the Universal Teacher*(Al-Insān al-Kāmīl),* Master, or "Lord of the Age", who echoes the first wo/man.[49] In another sense, those individuals that participate in **salawāt,** are engaging in THE eternal cycle of disintegration/renewal – eternal creation/dissolution – as depicted by its cyclical prostrations. It is holistic in conception and enactment.

As is the case for Australian Aboriginal rituals, the Sufi believe that participating in *Salāh* is akin to actually annulling Time. That is to say, the act resurrects, depicts, participates in, acknowledges and realises – our **Origin** as being outside of Time; that by the death of the ego *(anā'),* there is a rebirth into a timeless unified state: this is in fact what the Ascent of Muhammad is about. While for the Muslim, Muhammad's Ascent is an event in Time, for the

116

Sufi it is *both* inside and outside of Time. [50]

Therefore the Sufi, following Muhammad's example and that of all Masters, including his/her own, practices seclusion, fasting, invocation*(dhikr)* and night vigils. This same notion – returning, coming from, being in the **Source** – as depicted in prayer, is expressed in the words of the devoted female Sufi saint, Rābi'ah al-'Adawiyya:

> I have cut-off my heart from this world entirely, completely controlling my passions; so that for the last thirty years, every prayer I have made, I have performed it as if it were my last. I have broken my bonds to people for fear that they might distract me and imprison my heart; so that at the beginning of each day I pray:*" Master involve me entirely with serving your Self alone, that none may distract me from You."* [51]

It is in this light that the Sufi understands, comprehends in the fullest sense, and therefore seeks to follow and participate in, Muhammad's ascension to the *highest heaven* or Paradisical State of Unity*(Tawhid)*. Being beyond Time, *from pre-eternity (azal) into post-eternity (abad)* – words which reflect the rapture of Divine love – the Sufi is so taken up with serving the **Beloved** (God) that there is no room for self-concerns.

This process occurs as the result of the death of the ego, thus enabling the Sufi to participate in the return of Creation to its **Source**. In the traditional account, Muhammad ascends to heaven through riding a beast *(Burāq)*. This word is derived from the root *baraqa,* meaning "to shine like lightning", having reference to illumination or insight, as well as to the word for blessing, as in the Hebrew **Baruch**. If this is coupled with the fact that it is presented in iconography and sculptural form,[52] as having a human head, it can be understood to represent the embodiment of the Intellect*(al-'Aql)*. In Sufi terms, this corresponds to the Divine faculty of *Knowing,* as in the Platonic *Nous,* or the medieval *Intellectus.* It is a flash of recognition, a realisation, or revelation*(kashf),* a remembrance*(dhikr)* of our essential **Transcendent** nature. This is because the *'aql* is identified with the **Spirit***(ar-Rūh)* or active principle, as symbolised by Adam. In traditional representation, the *Burāq* is half-human and half-animal, reflecting the fact that it is Creation which returns with Muhammad (and the realised Sufi) to its **Source**. The face of the *Burāq* is female, symbolising the soul, or Eve: the feminine passive or *nafs,* which in order to ascend (fulfil its transcendent potential) must subdue its animal nature. Thus in graphic description, the *nafs* is "ridden" to Paradise, or the Unitary State.[53]

Just as the mystical state of Union*(ittihād)* is timeless, so too is it beyond the limitations of space and the limited self*(anā')*. It is a transcendence of the individual nature, as it realises, attains, and recognises its **Divine Source**. Consequently, one of the earliest of Sufis, Abū'l-Qāsim ibn Muhammad al-Junaydof Baghdad(died 910), defined Sufism as meaning that *"God should cause you to die to yourself,*

118

so as to live in Him," calling this process of dying to self *fanā',* deriving it from the **Qur'ān** (55:26-27):

Everything perishes (fānin) except His Face (Self) ;

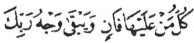

the *life in Him*, he called *baqā',* meaning continuance.

The meaning here is not that the individual *(dhāt-i bashariyyah)* ceases to exist, but that the individuality – a gift from God – becomes perfected, transmuted, by being eternalised in God. The Sufi no longer lives for self, but for God. This mystical experience of Union is terminated in order that the lover may return to the everyday world of existence. Thereafter, there is a continual yearning for reunion with God the **Beloved**, and the return to this life is a source of trial *(balā')*. Just as in Muhammad's case, who, when returning to earth the next morning, to continue life in this world, was taunted by the Quraysh,[54] who were to him a continual source of trial *(balā')*.

In the traditional account, Muhammad ascends through seven heavens, this representing the seven degrees of manifestation and the cycle of prophetic Revelations; Muhammad, praying with each of the different prophets in bodily form on Jerusalem's Temple Mount, before encountering them as spiritual realities; each in a different sphere, or heaven, as depictive of stations *(maqāmāt)* along the Sufi path. A station *(maqām:* literally standpoint) is to be contrasted to a state *(hāl)* which is transitory and impermanent; whereas a station as an aspect of the Divine

119

knowledge is a permanent realisation; just as a Master, though exhibiting numerous and varied qualities, is always characterised by a specific mode of being. Thus there is both flux*(talwīn)* as well as stability*(tamkīn)*. It is only when the ultimate station is reached - which according to the Sufi Master, Abū Sā'īd ibn Abī'l-Khayr (died 1049) in his *Maqāmāt-i-arba'īn* (the oldest text concerned with the subject) is *Sufism itself* - does this cease.[55] Abū'l-Hasan 'Alī al-Hujwīrī (died 1077), writing in his exposition on Sufism, **Kashf al-Mahjūb li-Arbāb al-Qulūb (Revelation of the Veiled for the Gate Masters of the Heart)** explained it: [56]

> A station is a standpoint on the Path *(Tarīqa)*. It refers to the perseverence required to fulfil what is inescapable during that period of life. One cannot proceed onwards from a station, without first accomplishing all that is required at that point. So that first there is the station of **Repentance**, followed by **Reform**, then **Sacrifice**, then **Trust** etc. You cannot pretend to **Reform** without first being completely **Repentant**, nor can there be **Trust** without there is first **Sacrifice**.
>
> Whereas a state*(hāl)* is something independent of this in being a gift from God that enters the heart ..... all who long for God have been given a particular station as indicated at the beginning of the journey, [57] and though benefit may be had from the other stations through which they may pass, finally there is one in which they stay. For each station and the journey to it, are not just a question of how to behave and what to do, but are indicators of purpose and destiny.[58]
>
> Adam's station*(maqām)* for example, was **Repentance**, Noah's was **Sacrifice**, and Abraham's **Obedience**. The station of Moses was **Submission**,

and that of David *Sorrow*. The station of Jesus
was *Hope*, and that of John the Baptist *Piety*.
Whilst our Prophet's (Muhammad) was *Praise*.
Each of these men - in turn - drew from other
sources in which they rested for a while, but in
the end they came back to their destined station.

Although the various Masters have emphasized different
characteristics of the Path, according to the needs of the
time, the capacities of those addressed, and/or the context
and manner of teaching employed,[59] it is still possible to
see an underlying pattern. In fact, these differences are in
themselves a part of the Teaching, just as according to the
traditional account, the number of times that God asked
the followers of Moses, and those of Muhammad, to pray,
differed. The reason for this is that in both cases, we are
talking not of the outward form, but of the inner spirit, or
motivation *(tasawwuf);* it is the spirit which precedes and
determines the form, the latter being its manifestation.[60]

Similarly, when Muhammad attained the summit of the
Ascent, he encountered the *Lote Tree of the Uttermost
Limit (sidrat al-muntahā)* as mentioned in the *Qur'ān* (53:
13-18),[61] this being symbolic of the bounds of knowledge
and spiritual attainment, beyond which neither human or
angel can pass. It represents heavenly bliss - or Divine
Union - for in the *Qur'ān* (56:28) Lote trees are connected
with such a state; while the *Qur'ān* (14:24-25) also links
the tree as a symbol with heavenly knowledge.

Thus, the Path is the means by which self-knowledge
and spiritual attainment, are linked: *"The revelation of Self*

is the Revelation of the Cosmos itself," is how *Bābā* Dovid Yūsuf explained it. Through recognition*(kashf)* of the **Unitary Nature of Existence***(Tawhīd),* the *psyche (nafs)* attains a unitary state*(nafs al-mutma'innah)* (see table in this chapter). It has come to a state of rest and repose *(tamkīn);* having annihilated*(fanā')* the lower self, or egotistical tendencies;*(anā')* it now subsists*(baqā')* in God (see table in **chapter four**). The seeker*(sālik),* having sought nothing but God, in sincerity *(ikhlās),* on the Path of purity*(Sūfism),* has become a *muwahhid* or Sufi proper. Abū Bakr al-Kalābādhī (died 995) in his **Kitāb at-Ta'arruf li-madhab ahl at-Tasawwuf** summated it: "Truth*(Haqīqah)* comes after states of ecstasy and takes their place."

Notes and References

1) This Arabic term, derived from the **Qur'ān** (2:10), expresses the notion of imbalance and disharmony, as well as illness.

2) This is aptly expressed in the Arabic term for hypocrite *(munāfiq,* one who practises *nifāq*(self-deception), which is related to *nafaqun,* meaning a tunnel: i.e., a place to hide, a lower place. The holistic concepts of Sufism, as expressed in the **Qur'ān** and Arabic, are not easily reduced to English.

3) This is the literal translation of *Illāh*, a Syriac term, which is the oldest known word for God, being the term from which the Hebrew *Elohīm*, and the Arabic *Allāh*, are derived.

4) From,"al-Basā'ir fi'l-Dawā'ir", in his **Bawādir - al- Nawādir** (Urdu), Pakistan Press, Lahore (undated).

5) In Arabic, *Kāfir:* literally meaning, to cover over or hide.

6) *"Mūtū qabla an tamūtū "* - **Mathnawī** 6:742.

7) These three stages from the **Qur'ān**, were later expanded to seven.

8) Sir Muhammad Iqbal, **The Development of Metaphysics in Persia**, Luzac, London, 1908, pp, 47 ff.

9) This word has reference not to dogmatism, but to understanding, as in the **Qur'ānic** *yaqilun* (16:67) - a verbal form of the word *'aql* - meaning the Divine faculty of *Knowing* - the **Creative Intellect**.

10) **Qur'ān** 103:1; 89:27-30.

11) Sufism is not a form of brainwashing as some have implied, but is rather an acknowledgement, or realisation, of the **Greater Self**, *in which all move and have their being*, achieved through attainment of a Unitary State (see **Mathnawī** 3:3669 on this point).

12) As pointed out by Sufi Master, Ahmad ibn Muhammad ibn 'Atā' Allāh (died 1309) in his **Kitāb al-Hikam** (9:80-83).

13) **Qur'ān** 95:4-5, also a saying of Prophet Muhammad.

14) This is the esoteric meaning of the *Garden of Eden* story in the Bible (**Genesis** 2:8-17) and the **Qur'ān** (2:35-38).

15) This is the esoteric meaning of Adam being given the ability to *name* things (see **Genesis** 2:19-20 & **Qur'ān** 2:31-34).

16) See notes 17 & 20 in **chapter three**.

17) The meaning of the epithet *Master*, given to Sufi Teachers.

18) A term which in the Islamic medicine of medieval times was as applicable to physical medicine as it was to Sufism.

19) See note 15 in **chapter four**.

20) See his beautiful prayer on this subject; "The Song of Love", in **Leaves from the Tree of Life: Sayings, Meditations & Prayers for a New Age**,, as spoken by **Bābā** Dovid Yusuf, compiled and edited by David Heinemann, Rainbow Trust Publications, Northampton, 1995, pp, 58-59.

21) While philosophers have supposedly hallowed the Socratic question & answer teaching method, they have in fact debased it. For the Master developed a method, in which by questioning, HE forced his

123

disciples, to see the inner implications of their claimed beliefs. In other words, their duality.

22) *Essays on Islam* by G.E.Sell, SPCK, Madras, 1901, p,10.

23) Muhammad Ajmal, *Muslim Contributions to Psychotherapy & Other Essays*, Psychology Research Monographs (5), National Institute Publications, Islamabad, 1986, p, 48.

24) Literally *of pure intent:* i.e., without duality. According to the Sufi – as is also the case in Judaism – there is no original sin inherited from Adam, for each person is responsible for their own actions and the results thereof. In Islam, which has a similar view, sin is divided into two categories: *dhanb* (inadvertent, unintentional, or misdirected actions, or shortcomings) and *ithm* (deliberate, wilful acts); so that, not just Jesus, but all Prophets, including Adam, were sinless *('ismah),* for though they may have committed *dhanb,* they did not practise *ithm.* The two are rarely distinguished in Sufi writings, where the word *khati'ah* is used to cover both categories, as sin is conceptualised differently by Sufis (see next note).

25) Not to be confused with a morbid fear of punishment, that Rūmī derisively calls the *attitude of the slave* (**Mathnawī** 5:2180). Nicholson (see **Bibliography** 1989 pp, 4-11) and other Orientalists have misunderstood this concept, because they have confused Sufi *taqwā* with the Christian's fear of God's punishment of an inherited sinful tendency. Writing in his monumental, *The Revelations of Mecca*, an encyclopaedia of Sufism of 566 chapters *(Al-Futūhāt al-Makkiyya* Cairo, 1329 A.H.), under the subject of **SIN,** Ibn 'Arabī describes it as: *bewilderment in a wrong action for which the doer must naturally suffer till ignorance is removed. As in disease (which can be an outward manifestation of sin) though one must suffer, eventually health will be recovered.* Sin's effects are not seen as a punishment requiring a ransom sacrifice, but as natural consequences of foolish acts. For this reason, Sufis are not afflicted with either fear or guilt over sin, what fear there is – if any – is of disapproval rather than of punishment.

26) Farīd ad-Dīn 'Attār, *Tadhkirāt al-Awliyā'.*

27) The word has both the meaning of being in unison with, as well as being a believer in God's Unity.

28) Followers of the Sufi saint, Muhammad Mu'īn ad-Dīn Chishti of Ajmer, India (died 1236).

29) Notice how in this holistic concept, the two categories of *sinning against others* and *sinning against God* - as defined by Talmudic Judaism - are both included and transcended.

30) Extracted in modified form, from the *Chishtiyya* dicipline manual, as in Ajmal above, 1986, p, 47.

31) This is a *tawatur hadīth* (see note 19 in **chapter four**).

32) **Mathnawī** 1:123.

33) Master *Bābā* Dovid Yūsuf said; *"we (Sufis) must continually invoke God in every moment and every act, with every breath as His own breath."*

34) According to a saying of Muhammad, *"To God belongs ninety-nine*

Names." These are described in the *Qur'ān* (7:179) as, *"the most beautiful Names."* Lists of Names which are traditional – the majority of them being derived from passages in the *Qur'ān* – may differ to some extent, but will always be no more than 99, a number which by implication means that God's Names are endless, as well as specific: i.e., God is both **Transcendent** and **Immanent** (see **Appendix 1**).

35) *Dhikr* is the central rite of Sufism, which, while it may vary from Order to Order (in some cases it involves dancing, and/or music, while in others it may be silent), has as its common elements: the repetitive chanting of Divine Names, use of the breath, and leadership under the direction of a recognised Master (more on this in later chapters).

36) *Qur'ān* 29:45; 63:9; 73:8 and the *Ahadīth* (sayings): *"the polish of the heart is remembrance of God"*; and *"those who remember God have the most excellent degree"*; and *"On the Day of Resurrection, the men and women who invoke God much, shall have the highest esteem"*, etc.

37) Abū Hāmid Muhammad al-Ghazālī, in *Kitāb Dhikr al-Mawt wa-māba'dahu*, Book 40 of *Ihyā 'Ulūm ad-Dīn*.

38) Rūmī, *Mathnawī* 1:1142, regarding the continuity of creation/dissolution; also Haeri 1987 (in **Bibliography**).

39) In Hebrew, *Zeker* is associated with a commemorative act*(azakarah)* and religious rites of worship*(minchah)*, giving it a broader meaning than "remembrance". It literally means, *fixing the mind upon*.

40) The similar Syriac term *dukhrānā*, as used by Eastern Christians for their rites, shows the common Semitic origin and meaning of the word, arguing against those who would see it as a derivation of Indian, Persian, or Central Asian rituals.

41) Which was true for the people of his time (see *Qur'ān* 33:21).

42) The Sufi are not concerned with external forms, but use whatever possible – including in some cases appearing to be heretics (e.g., Jesus the Nazarene, Mansur al-Hallaj) in others as ultra-orthodox – in order to achieve their purpose: so that the *Bektashī*, while outwardly *Sunni* Muslims, secretly venerate the *Shī'ah* Imams; while *Bābā* Dovid Yūsuf has authorised *Shaykh's* in both *Sunni* and *Shī'ah* branches of Islam, as well as being recognised as a Teacher in all of the world's religious traditions, including the tribal.

43) A word literally meaning 'Way', and that has reference to the Path as a whole, as well as to a specific Sufi Order.

44) *"for a night journey from the Sacred place of prostrations"* (masjid: i.e., place of prayer, the Ka'aba) *"to the furtherest place of prostrations"* (i.e., the temple site of Jerusalem).

45) *Mathnawī* 5:358. Though the word has many meanings, in his *Revelation of the Veiled*, Al-Hujwīrī (died 1077) states that the term *Sūfī* has no definite origin as a literal name (see Nicholson's translation 1911, p, 43). It must therefore be seen as an allegorical expression, rather than an actual name.

46) Rūmī, *Dīwān-i Shams-i Tabrīz*; 99. Note the parallels to Jesus's

125

reference to himself: **John** 8:58; 14:6; 1:1.

47) Though it was spoken over a 23-year-period, on specific occasions, according to questions asked and needs of the time, the Revelation is believed to have begun on either the 25th, 27th or 29th, night of the month of *Ramadan* (the exact day is uncertain) and is commemorated by traditional Muslims on these nights.

48) *Salāh* - the literal meaning of which is *Glory* - usually engaged in as part of a communal act*(salawāt)*, is distinguished from individual and personal prayer*(Du'ā)* as in the Christian, or Hindu sense.

49) In some senses this notion parallels that of the Primordial Man of Jewish mysticism, *Adam Kadmon*. According to the Sufi, there is in each Age, a Teacher who encapsulates the Universal elements, that where present in perfection in the first wo/man (Adam who also contained Eve). This Teacher can be seen as the *Grandshaykh*, or Chief - *Bābā* - of all Sufis, though he (or she) may not necessarily be recognised as such (see note 13 in **chapter one**).

50) God creates Time, so it does exist, but for the Creator and those who have realised their essence; i.e., the Sufi, there is no Time.

51) 'Attār's **Book of Divinity**. To completely understand the significance of this prayer, it is necessary to realise that Rābi'ah dwelt alone in poverty, resisting all offers of marriage, including that of the Emir of Baghdad.

52) Modelled forms exist, particularly in South East Asia (e.g.,Brunei, Malaysia, Philippines, Indonesia - a fine example exists in the **Cultural Garden Museum**, near Manila airport), while in the Indian subcontinent and Iran, it is usually depicted pictorially (e.g.,the **MS Khamseh**, of 1410, by Nizāmī, in Shiraz). Though representations differ, all have in common a combination of human and animal form, with a female face. Note similarities to the Sphinxs of Greece and Ancient Egypt (see note 16 in **chapter three**).

53) The self is not killed (Muhammad does not die in the *Mi'rāj*), only controlled, or tamed, for it is part of the means of ascent, just as Adam's *knowledge of good and evil* (**Genesis** 3:1-7) creates the possibility of a return to Paradise. It is the egotistical tendency *(anā')* which dies (see Rūmī's **Mathnawī** 4:3562 & 3:3669), not the individual personality.

54) An Arab tribal clan that controlled the economic affairs of Mecca through religious power, by claiming its superiority.

55) There is a translation and discussion of this, in S.H. Nasr's **Sufi Essays**, George Allen & Unwin, London, 1972, chapter 5.

56) This is my own rendering, but there is a translation of Hujwīrī's **Kashf al-Mahjūb**, by R.A. Nicholson, Luzac & Co, London, 1911.

57) By this is meant, that while striving on the Path is necessary for the attainment of any station, whatever station that is finally dwelt in, or primarily manifest, is already ordained.

58) That is, it requires God's action and not just our personal effort.

59) For example, Al-Qushayrī(died 1072) listed 10 stations; 'Attār, in his **Conference of the Birds**, depicted the Path as 7 valleys that are crossed in the following order: *Quest, Love, Mystical Perception,*

126

Detachment, Independence, Unity, Bewilderment, and the Realisation in Annihilation(Fanā'); Rūmī speaks of 700 degrees of sainthood, corresponding to 700 veils of light (**Mathnawī** 2:821); while An-Ansārī(died 1089) listed a 100. Similarly, extra stages of progress (as subdivisions, including after the attainment of *baqā*) are also added sometimes, so making the *nafs* ascend through 7 stages; see Spencer Trimingham (in **Bibliography**) 1971, pp, 152-157.

60) Though, as we have seen, they are interdependent. This provides a key to answering the question, so often asked; Are Sufis Muslims? If the foregoing has been comprehended, it will be relised that the question is not answerable in a reductionist way. See Yunus Emre *City of the Heart*, 153:2, Element, Shaftesbury, 1992, p, 117.

61) This passage and the other(17:1) concerning the *Night Journey*, are the sole references in the **Qur'ān** pertaining to the Ascent, the real meaning of which only the Sufi have preserved.

7

THE GUIDE TO THE PATH

"For there always exists among us, someone whose hearing, sight, sensibilities and faculties, are those of God. Who manifests these signs as did the Prophet (Muhammad) when he spoke his message."

Muhyī'd-Dīn ibn 'Arabī

The Master - Guide and Teacher on the Path of Spiritual Development

Sufi disciplines are a means for creating *interiorisation*, an awareness of the inner life and its motivations. However, such interiorisation can become introversion, fuelling ego-inflation and becoming in turn, a source of mental dualism, illusion and self-worship, the very opposite of what Sufism aims to achieve, that is surrender rather than vanity.[1] To prevent this the seeker *(sālik)* submits to someone who has already attained the Unitary State; the *Shaykh*(Arabic), *Pīr*(Persian), *Dede*(Turkish), *Bābā* (Central Asiatic) whose image, breaks through desires, frustrations, preoccupations and expectations, associated with the limitations of duality: love of self is replaced by love of the Master.[2]

The word *Shaykh* means Elder and has reference not to age but spiritual experience, even though the *Shaykh*, or *Shaykhna*(female) is likely to be older. It should be realised at this point, that Sufism does not discriminate against women who have been teachers and guides, hundreds of years before Christianity or Judaism, had seen the necessity - as yet to be recognised in Islam. Ibn 'Arabī and Rūmī saw woman in her beauty, human qualities and essential nature, as a *vision of God*.[3] Not only was God referred to as our Mother by Rūmī, but in the original languages of Sufism (Arabic, Persian, Urdu, Turkish), there is a deliberate use of the feminine gender, such as in *Shams* (Rūmī's teacher), or **Beloved** or **She**(Hiya) for God.

By entering into a relationship with a Master, cognitive reorientation can occur. The disciplines imposed are a means for creating an awareness of the **Transcendent**. The Master assists the courage, concentration and resolve *(himmah)* of the disciple, reinforcing efforts*(mujāhida)* in the struggle to overcome the impulsive tendencies of the animal nature*(nafs al-haywāniyah)*.

Dhikr (invocation of Divine Names) in whatever form it may be practised (it varies with the Master, and/or Order) changes the basis of orientation by causing a remembrance *(dhikr)* of the **Transcendent Self** (God), through focusing on the inner primordial nature*(fitrah)*. Maintaining a state of vigilant awareness*(Murāqaba)*, by continually examining conscience through meditation*(murāqiba)*, under guidance of a Master, healing takes place. Contemplating*(tafakkara)* with a view to eliminating moral weaknesses*(Takhliya)*, through strengthening virtues*(Tahliya)*, vices become weak and eventually die out. The two aspects*(Takhliya - Tahliya)* are linked through meditating on the remedy as well as the

129

imperfection at the same time, though the specific manner in which this is done, together with the practical exercises that will be linked with it, are likely to vary, not only according to the individual concerned, but also with different Masters and Orders.

The intimate relationship between Master and disciple [4] *(murīd)*, requires a commitment to confess all that is experienced during this struggle for purification, whether it be lust, anger, envy, jealousy, or obsessional and/or depressive thoughts. The disciple is also required to report the contents of dreams,[5] that are interpreted by drawing out the disciple's inner and unrecognised motivations, with the intention of overcoming dualities of thought or action.

The Master gives the disciple the whole of his/her attention *(tawajjuh)*,[6] with all of his/her being, a process that is described in alchemic language as *throwing fire*.[7] The result is that the disciple will pass through various developmental stages, that can be summarised as; a **unity of actions***(tawhīd-i-af'āti)* – followed in order that there might be a **unity of attributes/qualities***(tawhīd-i-sifātī)* – so that finally there can be a **unity of essence***(tawhīd-i-dhātī)*. This experience is achieved through devotion, as symbolised by fire, ultimately, to result in a state of wholeness that is both a communion with the **Divine** and **Creative Nature (Transcendent Self/God)** as well as being a state of mental and self-purification. This final stage was described by Master Jalāl ad-Dīn ar-Rūmī, as one in which

130

Divine knowledge is absorbed in the Sufi's knowledge (an indescribable state that it is beyond the
distinctions and similes of semantic thought, as is
God) how can people comprehend this statement? [8]

The fact the Master has limitations, is in itself a
difficulty to be transcended. It provides the basis for a
conflict over ambivalent attitudes towards the Teacher,
who ultimately ceases to be a reflection of the struggle
within the self; what the Sufi Master and poet, 'Abd ar-
Rahmān Nūr ad-Dīn Jāmī (died 1492), in his *Salmān and
Absāl*, analysed as the phenomenon of projection, pointing
out that Absāl(whom Salmān envied) was really a power in
Salmān's soul - within himself - that he was looking for
outside himself(in the external world).[9] By withdrawing that
power - seeing that person as they really are - not only
does the Master assume a rightful humble place in the
scheme of things, but the disciple is enabled thereby to
transcend immediate experience, so being drawn to a love
for all Masters, for all beings - for the **One and Whole** -
that is above and beyond all limited selves.[10]

The Qualifications of the Spiritual Master

There is a total submission on the part of the disciple to
the Master, which together with the mind-opening effect
of the exercises used, could lead to abuse and a total
destabilising (rather than growth) of the disciple's mental
state, were it not for the Master's spiritual qualifications.
The nature of these qualifications preclude this possibility,

[11] and though many will dabble with Sufism and leave its practice (or be considered unsuitable, as is often the case with *Bābā* Dovid Yūsuf's followers) these persons will be more stable, fulfilled, and contented, than previously.[12]

Although the requirements for being a Master, have been described in various ways, common elements are to be found in these different descriptions. The essential characteristics are to be found in the **Qur'ānic** story of Moses being initiated and instructed by a mysterious teacher known as **Khidr**, [13] a story which represents the limitations of all external religions (symbolised by Moses) that can only be transcended by esotericism - *al-Khidr* - the inner dimension which transcends form. These qualities - or the Master's stages of being - can be summarised: [14]

1) The Teacher's lifestyle will show wholehearted dedication to God, being free and independent of anything that could compromise a recognition of God as the only **Reality**.

2) There will be the capability of receiving directly, without any form of intermediary whatsoever, truths concerning the Nature of Existence.

3) An intimacy with God will be evident.

4) A knowledge of God will be shown that is independent of intellectual ability, or sensory perception.

5) Evidence will be shown of a knowledge of the essence, as well as of the actions, of the **Creative Reality**.

However, it should be realised that:

the hierarchy of stages and the various ranks of

religious leadership are not contained within limits and numbers. Being a *Shaykh* is not a question of personal appearance, that is, the contour of one's face or beard, by which people may discern that such-and-such is a *Shaykh*. To be a *Shaykh* is to experience great intimacy with God.... When a. .. novice perceives in his own heart the beauty of a *Shaykh,* he becomes enamoured of...his saintliness and draws peace and contentment from him ... [15]

It is the Master's devotion to God, which in turn causes the disciple to be devoted to the Master. The self-concern or vanity, which lies at the heart of mental confusion, is dissipated by love, resulting in the disciple achieving a unitary state that is a reflection of, or is engendered by, the Master's love. The purity of the Master's devotion to Oneness renders the heart of the disciple vulnerable, making duplicity unsustainable. The complete surrender of the Master to God is the example, means and image, by which the disciple's vicious circle of thoughts, painful memories, regrets, vast and empty dreams, and endless frustrations, are all overcome in a total surrender to God, through that Master. It is the Master's attitude rather than ability which makes progress in the disciple possible. The simplicity of the Master,[16] which has become legendary in the case of Jalāl ad-Dīn ar-Rūmī's Teacher/Master Shams ad-Dīn at-Tabrīzī(died 1247),[17] overshadows any of the disciple's attainments. This adds weight to what the Master does, or says, so reducing the resistance to change to a minimum. [18] This overshadowing caused Rūmī (already a

133

Muslim teacher of distinction, before Shams appearance changed him into the Sufi poet and Teacher we know of today) to attribute his *Dīwān-i-Shams-i-Tabrīzī* to his Teacher, as if Shams had written it himself.

Thus the Master becomes "The Perfected, or Complete, wo/man"*(Al-Insān al-Kāmīl)*, the Universal Teacher,[19] who though having human individuality as an external form, will also be in virtuality and principle, a possessor of all other forms and states of existence. This is because that Master's inward reality is identified with the whole Universe, so that in this connection, Rūmī wrote:

> Thou art not a single thou, but a hundred thousand men hidden in one man; a sun hidden in a mote; the sky and a deep sea which is a drowning place of a hundred thou's; a hundred thousand stacks in a handful; a hundred thousand Gabriels in the earthly frame of man, comprehending all realities, unifying all contraries. [20]

Not that the Perfect Master is God, but that the Teacher bears the imprint of God's attributes, even though not being that **Ultimate Reality**.[21] The Master is a spiritual shepherd who guides humanity according to God's commandments, providing food for all according to their need and capacity – limitations being within the recipient and not in the Master's dispensation. The Master is a medium through which God's lovers empty themselves of selfhood, so that God may unite them with Himself, becoming both lover and **Beloved**.[22] For this reason, Prophet Muhammad, was spoken of as "Beloved of God"

(Habību'llah), since he perfectly displayed the glory of Divine Love. This is the origin of the most common expression for God in Sufism – the **Beloved***(Habība)*.

The Master's capacity for reflecting back to the disciple what is in that disciple's soul is a result of the Master's extreme empathy, because of a connection with the diverse elements present within the Universe, as contained within that Master's self. This ability creates within the disciple an openness of being, that makes it possible to develop interiorisation. The manifestation of this effect can often be observed physically. We have the account of Rūmī's meeting with Shams of Tabriz, [23] of which Rūmī wrote:

> I was raw then I got cooked. Now I am burned....
> but it is this burning of the heart that I want, it
> is this burn which is to me as everything – more
> precious than any worldly kingdom – for because
> of it, God calls secretly in the night-time. [24]

In a contemporary Sufi circle*(halqah)*, it is not uncommon to observe seekers*(sālikūn)* break down and weep, shake uncontrollably, or even faint on approaching a Master, on either the first occasion, or in some cases later, when taking the initiation pledge *(bay'ah)*.

Together, an awareness is created that enables the participants to engage in a silent dialogue, a conversation of spirits. For the disciple, this leads to a realisation of inadequacies, that in other cases would be likely to create hostility, or defensive reactions,[25] but the spiritual context in which this takes place, together with the Master's deep empathy, does not allow this to occur. For the Master, it is a positive transmission of **Reality** *(hāl-Haqq),* [26] that opens the disciple to spiritual benedictions *(bāraka),* and a cleansing of the heart *(dil/qalb),* or orientation, from all false idols, or enslaving conditioning. The disciple becomes aware of another dimension of being within, reflected back by the Master, just as the mirror reflects the sun. Rūmī, referring to his own sun (the name *Shams* means sun) in describing this, wrote:

> The Beloved said: *'I am your own soul*
> > *and your own heart,*
> *Why are you so stricken with terror?'.* [27]

The spiritual Master's function, is to return the disciple to the Primal State of Unity *(Fitrat)* that existed before the descent into duality, symbolically depicted in the *Qur'ān* (2:35-38) by the story of the *Garden of Eden.* In order to do this, the Master must make the disciple aware of:

1) The state of being.

2) The level of knowledge and awareness of **Truth.** [28]

3) The degree of love, or state of union, with God.

Using the sun as a symbol of God, and likening the heart to a mirror, we can link these factors with developmental stages:

1) Is the realisation that the heart is a mirror that does not reflect the sun, which in turn leads to repentance.

2) The mirror of the heart begins to reflect the sun, being cleansed of the *rust of forgetfulness* that it may become established in peace and certainty.

136

3) There is acknowledgement that in reality only the sun exists (i.e., is permanent/unchanging/Source of all life), as shown by the fact that there is no desire to separate individual choice from Divine decree.

Connected with this is the symbolism of the moon (soul of the mystic) reflecting the sun's rays(Divine Knowledge), for without the sun, the moon's existence would not be known, while the sun's existence, though independent, is reflected by the moon. Describing this, Master Abū Bakr Sirāj ad-Dīn wrote in his *Book of Certainty*:

> Just as the rays of moonlight strike upon various material objects which reflect them according to their aptitude, so the intuitions strike upon the faculties of the mind, which if they have truly received the doctrine will flash back a light of recognition...this light means that a purely mental understanding of doctrinal teaching has been transferred into the knowledge of Certainty.[29]

This is illustrated by the Sufi concept of prayer, where the opening of the hands and the bowing of the head are to both receive and acknowledge, rather than to implore or beg, from a distant God, as when hands are held together. For the Sufi, prayer is not a monologue in which God is addressed, but a conversation, in the sense that the mystic devotee has the feeling of being talked to by God. It was from such conversations that the Bible, *Qur'ān*, and other mystic writings of the world were produced,[30] coming from an attitude of mind, that consisted of openness, a looking for direction, rather than confirmation of a selfish choice already made.

137

Discipleship, is a two-way conversation, in which the disciple first listens, then later replies, in the form of action (initiation and submission to the disciplines imposed by the Master) thereby showing devotion to God; thus acknowledging that the Master, as Exemplar, has attained this desirable state of being – that of unison of the heart, with God. The results of this conversation are that events are no longer experienced as meaningless and random, but as purposeful. The bare facts of existence become clothed with a meaning of which the disciple is a part. The desire to dominate Nature because of its seeming ruthlessness is replaced by the feeling that one is part of an ever-unfolding plan. There is a sense of communion, rather than helplessness; of harmony, rather than disorientation; of significance, rather than absurdity; of infinity, rather than mortality.

Relationship with a Master manifests that Master's qualities, for his/her qualifications, rest upon the ability to create interiorisation, to engender an awareness that in love, external and internal are one. Wine(devotion to God) must necessarily be contained within a vessel(devotional form), but in becoming drunk *(sukr)* the inebriate empties the vessel. If, as the Sufi Master, Dr. Javad Nurbakhsh, once said, *"Sufism is a way to God through love"*, [31] then as the late Sufi Master, *Shaykh* Muzaffer Ozak said, *"The Shaykhs are the pourers of the wine, the dervish (Sufi) is the glass and Love is the wine."* [32]

138

Becoming a Disciple – the Meaning of Initiation

Sufism asserts its message of Unity actively as well as implicitly; both the manner of teaching, the Teacher and what is taught, are treated as inseparable. To quote a contemporary Sufi Master; *"What the Teacher does is as much a part of the teaching as what he says."* [33] Therefore, every action, gesture or symbol, has an inner as well as an outer significance. The *Bay'ah* (initial pledge of loyalty taken as a first stage in the initiation process) should be understood in this way. It is modelled on the oath of allegiance (*bay'at ar-ridwān:* literally, pact of felicity) taken by Muhammad's followers under a tree at Hudaybiyyah, 10 miles from Mecca, when his enemies prevented him from returning to that city.[34]

The coming together of hands – that regardless of what form that particular Sufi Order's *(tarīqat)* [35] initiation ceremony may take,[36] will be its central component – is akin to the placing of the child's hand in that of the parent. Such an action indicates the desire to be led, instructed and protected. It is a symbol of humility before the *wise old wo/man*, who is a Universal figure of guidance in all folklore traditions. Similarly, it requires acceptance of that desire by a Master. From the Master's perspective, such a commitment entails an obligation of affection and kindness *(shafaqat)*, while from the disciple's viewpoint, it requires the observance of correct standards of behaviour and etiquette *(ādāb)*.

The first is a spontaneous response, elicited because the disciple has through the correct attitude, demonstrated humility. It signifies that a relationship has begun upon given terms. It is more than a pledge*(bay'at)*, it is also a contractual covenant*(bay'ah)*, that entails obligations, has requirements to fulfil, and confers benefits. From the disciple's, as well as from a psychological point of view – unlike Western therapies, including psychiatry – it is a demonstration of a genuine desire for change, plus a readiness to accept counsel that is given, unconditionally.

This relationship has obvious emotional and intellectual connotations, and opens up to its participants the possibilities of enormous transformation. That such does occur can be witnessed by anyone who has observed the members of a Sufi circle over several years. Such changes can occur at a physical or mental, as much as at the spiritual, level, from the curing of neuroses, crippling illnesses, and impediments of speech and vision, to the remission of cancer. This should not surprise us, for initiation – of which the *bay'at* is the first stage[37] – symbolises death and rebirth, by means of a covenant with God – it is this power that the *bay'at* confers. All genuine Sufi Orders are only able to initiate others into these mysteries, because in some way or another, they trace *their teachings* back through a line of transmission (*silsila:* literally; a chain or series of links),[38] ultimately leading to God. Rūmī tells us:

140

..... it is the same with the Sufi *Shaykhs* - from external appearance they are of many kinds, varying greatly in their spiritual states, as well as in what they say, or do - but viewed in terms of their goal they are one, for all are engaged in the search for (the Transcendent) God.[39]

The *bay'at* is therefore a first step towards God, initiated by invoking His Presence through the authority *(bāraka* [40]*)* of the Master. It is the opening of a door by means of the major virtues of humility *(khushū'),* charity *(karāmat)* and truthfulness *(sidq),*[41] which at their highest level, are internalised by the Sufi, as signified by the *bay'at.*

Humility is a recognition that the disciple is nothing in him/herself, and an acknowledgement that only God exists inasmuch that S/He is both Source and Completion. Only God is truly Great *('Azza wa Jall)* and according to the most oft-repeated Sufi invocation; *"there is no god but THE God"('lā ilāha illā 'Llāh')* which for a Sufi, means that ONLY God exists. *Bay'at* - first step in the initiation process - is a recognition of this.

Charity means to give, to sacrifice - so that the supreme act of charity is the giving of one's life. It is a step which naturally evolves from the first step, as above, in that it is a realisation that everything we have comes from and belongs to, God. It is the giving-up of self, in order to attain recognition of *the* Self. The *bay'at* is a commencement to following the path of selflessness, for Sufism is nothing other than this.

141

Truthfulness means seeing things as they really are, recognising that the **Ultimate Reality** is that God alone is the **Origin** of all knowledge – including that of one'self – for God is the **Source** of everything. Such a realisation necessitates submission; it is a desire to be totally open to Direction – this is what *bay'ah* signifies.

For the Sufi, these qualities are inseparable from each other, and their implementation, beyond an external and limited manifestation of them as in religion. Yet, in practising them as a Sufi, one will inevitably also practise them in their limited external form. Similarly, humility, charity and truthfulness are all desired qualities for the happy and healthy-minded individual, as well as requisites for overcoming duplicity, self-deception and all forms of mental dualism (neuroticism).

It is with this in mind that the disciple will be asked to conform to a canon of behaviour – *Adab* – that will reinforce these qualities. But these matters of etiquette *(ādāb)* are not in themselves a sufficient means for transformation. Rather, they are a precondition for taking the pledge, after which the disciple agrees to (a)report everything experienced and to (b)obey all the Master's instructions,[42] that the disciple may be purified of weaknesses *(takhliya)* and strengthened in virtues *(tahliya)*. This is assisted by the Master either conferring upon the disciple a new name and/or giving the disciple an exercise to perform*(wird)* in connection with a Divine Name, or use

142

of a litany or formula containing such. The form this takes varies, but what is common to all Orders is the use of a Divine Name (sometimes *Allāh* itself, pronounced in a specific way) that is to be repeatedly invoked at particular times (often in connection with a meditative exercise), prescribed in accordance with the disciple's temperament.

The use of the **wird** (invoking prayer, formula, or litany to orientate the mind towards God) has the effect of breaking through the cycle of self-indulgent thinking, paradoxically – through interiorisation – causing the disciple to be more outgoing, rather then self-obsessed. This, together with the admission of all problems, as well as agreeing to follow all counsel unreservedly, has the effect of breaking down the eg*(anā'),* which from a Sufi perspective, is THE source of all mental conflict. This is contrary to Western philosophy, whose explanations for social problems – including its psychiatry and therapies – are all designed to strengthen the ego, by the dubious method of decreasing internal stresses, through excusing, vindicating, or seeing the cause of such conflicts as inevitable (i.e., the self-satisfaction of our base desires is necessary). The Sufi Master removes such conflicts at source; false humility, ulterior motives, duplicity and manipulative behaviour are rooted out, rather than being explained away.[43]

The reason for this difference lies in the acceptance of the category of Sacred, which has little, if any, meaning to

Western psychology and society. The *Bay'ah* creates an awareness of this category within the disciple, and all subsequent activities reinforce it. The operative word is *respect* (for the Master, Life, its **Source** and one's **True Self**), the lack of which lies at the heart of social and mental conflict.[44] The canon of conduct that the initiate will subsequently observe (see **Appendix 3**) is a way of recognising, fostering and creating, an awareness of the necessity for respect. The holistic approach of Sufism precludes any separation between thought and action, so that speaking when the Master is present, failing to stand up when he enters the room, sitting in his seat, using his cup, or any other such infringement of *ādāb*, belies the claim to see the Master as a Master. By insisting on an awareness of actions, an awareness of thinking is created and a Unity of Being is exercised. Initiation – of which the pledge is the first step – is the creation of this consciousness within the disciple.

The Relationship between the Master and the Disciple

Devotion, which in turn leads to an emptying of the vessel of self, arises because of the unique relationship existing between Master and disciple, a relationship equivalent to that between parent and child, described in Sufi terms as *wilādat 'l-ma'nawiyya* (spiritual-begetting). What has been written by Western psychologists, psychotherapists and psychoanalysts, on the therapist acting out the role of the

144

parent in the therapeutic relationship is not what concerns us here, for Sufism's methodology and philosophical basis predates Western psychology by over a thousand years. [45] It is obvious that a learning relationship, in which a teacher is treated with special respect, and in which love is engendered, will be likely to cause the pupil to assume the child role.[46] However, it is not this, but the effect of that role on the disciple in the Greater Therapy (total existence), that primarily concerns the Sufi Teacher.

In Sufi literature, the child has a special symbolic role to play, because of its primal capacity to be aware of the **Unitary Nature of Existence.** Mothers will testify, how very young children seem to have telepathic abilities and precognitive powers. Only later do these fade and die out, as the child learns to see itself as separate and distinct. Therefore, to take on the child role is to assume a state in accordance with our truest nature. It is in this light, that we can begin to understand attitudes towards children in Sufism, that parallel those portrayed in stories of the *yanuka,* or wonder child, in Jewish and 13th century general Spanish literature, exemplifying the common origin of these diverse traditions.[47]

Master Rūmī [48] portrays the world as a nursemaid (not our real Mother) whose services have been utilised for a few days, but beseeches our true **Mother**(God) to take care of us without an intermediary (a return to the Unitary State), for the saints (Perfected Masters) are as children in

145

exile. He tells a story of a *Shaykh* who plays with children in preference to mixing with adults, yet, when asked a question concerning marriage, shows himself to be very wise.[49] This story appears to be abstruse, until one understands Rūmī is showing that attaining the Unitary State, is not a question of acquiring intellectual knowledge, but rather of returning to the primal childlike state – discovering the forgotten, true and inner nature *(fitrah).*

Most adults follows a rigid pattern of life, endeavouring to hide the fact that nothing but change is constant, whereas the child approaches each day, ever ready to learn afresh, looking for change. The child is by nature creative and playful, but the adult is conforming and fearful. Consequently, the child in both Jewish and Islamic culture is a symbol of renewal, continuity and hope. It is the childlike personality that sustains and renews culture: the artist, the poet, the dreamer, as, for example, Joseph, the youngest child of Jacob/Israel, who, with his outlandish coat of many colours, sustains and enables the rebirth of his people, not by war, but by the *living out* of dreams, a story, which though told extensively in the Bible (25 percent of **Genesis** – chapters 37 to 50), is also in the *Qur'ān (sūra* 12), indicating its importance.

The Master is a Joseph, pointing out the significance of the disciple's dreams, that the disciple may be retrieved from the angst world of dissociation. Just as a child needs to be understood, loved and accepted, so, too, does the

146

Master induce within the disciple trust, based upon the ability to understand that disciple; an ability arising from his/her empathy, as in the *Shaykh* in Rūmī's story, who rides upon a hobby-horse when playing with children. It is the Master's openness, lack of desire for reward, and total disregard of what others might think, that enables the disciple to also forget acceptance, overcome envy, and defeat duplicity. In both accounts, Joseph, son of the Patriarch, desires prison rather than sacrificing his **True Self** for the sake of being accepted by the Egyptian elite. Joseph is for the Sufi, a symbol of **Divine Beauty** that so enraptures the soul, that it pays no regard to physical well-being, just as in the *Qur'ān* (12:30-35) women cut their hands with fruit-knives in distraction, whilst gazing upon Joseph's beauty. It is the ability to induce such a response in the disciple that characterises the true Master. It is the child role of the disciple that opens up the possibility to being so enraptured. Rūmī explains:

> When your spirit (disciple's) recognises my spirit
> (the Teacher's) completely, then both spirits will
> recollect that they were only One in the past.[50]

In this therapeutic relationship, the rigidity, conformity, anxiety and fear, that afflicts the dualist, and which is typical of the materially centred life, is defeated. There is an acceptance on the part of the disciple to change. And since there is no fear of loving, things are not taken too seriously. An attitude reflected in the lives of many of the genuine mystics of all the traditions: the antics of Christianity's St.Francis of Assisi, of Judaism's Yehuda Halevi, are repeated in the life of the contemporary Sufi Master, *Bābā* Dovid Yūsuf, who often has his disciples in stitches. There is a realisation that all is but a pastime; that death renders us all vulnerable to decay. The child knows it is playing, but the so- called "realist" cultivates a pretence that fools even himself. It is the acceptance of our total dependence on the Mother, on God, that is engendered in the disciple, by creation of the child role.

It is in this context that the attitude of Prophet Muhammad can be understood. Mālik (died 795), in his collection of sayings – *Ahadīth* – records that whilst out walking, Muhammad saw some children, whom he greeted before greeting the adults. In another saying, Muhammad was reported to have said, *"Love for children is equivalent to having God's Mercy in one's heart."* Or again: *"One who does not treat children affectionately is not one of us."* In a similar vein, the Sufi Master *Bābā* Dovid Yūsuf, speaks with respect to children, often giving them preference over adults in greeting and teaching.

Change – the essence of the Sufi teaching relationship – can only occur when there is a total acceptance of self. Children are openly "naughty" – to use a phrase – and it is only with time, that they learn deception and duplicity. The disciple is encouraged to be childlike, to discover the degree to which there is spiritual impoverishment. Not by

148

the Master lecturing the disciple on faults, but through an open dialogue of friendship and honesty. The use of the story, of verse, or dance, are all Sufi teaching methods that foster the child spirit; ways of inducing change indirectly through inner motivation, rather than through open confrontation and attack. The childlike purity of the Master, and its induction within the disciple by teaching etiquette*(ādāb)*, correct attitudes and respect, creates for that disciple, a **Unity** of Perception, Will and Being. This is the true trinity of the Sufi, for whom the so-called "Christ child" is a symbol of *the Jesus of the heart*. A phrase that has been used by many Masters, such as Sanā'ī, 'Attār and Rūmī.[51] It represents Master and disciple in a purified state – one in which both persons, plus the manner of seeking/teaching are together a **Unity**:

> The Christ child symbolises a divine message; an infusion from the spiritual realm, that overwhelms the heart, intellect and soul, filling them with blessings and occupying them with that spirit, so the self may be freed from its dispersion.[52]

Seeing the Sufi Master as a parent or role model does not mean that Sufism subscribes to Western psychological notions that mental distress is the result of a disturbed childhood. The use of a role model is not confined to Western psychology, for it finds a much earlier expression in the attitude of the traditional Muslim towards Prophet Muhammad. The major division of Islam – the *Sunnī* – derives its name from its supposed following of the ways

149

customs and example*(sunna)*, of Muhammad. Even the *Shī'ah*, though their emphasis is different, [53] do not deny this, for its justification is found in the *Qur'ān* (33:21).

The Sufi emphasize a *living way*, not a traditional religion that is past-orientated, therefore the link to Muhammad is the dispensation (not transmission) [54] of the same authoritative power*(Bāraka)*. That both *Sunnī* and *Shī'ah* sects should require an Exemplar, testifies to the fact that there is within the human *psyche*, a sublime need to identify with something beyond the limited self. We do not need to posit a disturbed childhood, or deficient parents - nor do we need to deny this if it was the case. [55] Instead, we can acknowledge that there is within us, an implicit realisation, that we can be truer, greater than in practise we generally are. Immanent within the human *psyche* is a **Transcendent Self**. It is the awareness of this fact in its fullness, that constitutes the culmination of the Path as a realised Sufi (*'Arīf* - see table in **chapter four**).

The picture of the human being as presented in the **Qur'ān** (20:122) is that of a representative - reflecting the Grandeur and Glory of **Divinity** (2:30; 6:165). For as it says in the Bible (**Genesis** 1:26-27), we are made in *God's image*. This, despite the fact that we might err, from time to time, which happens because we are given the choice to use or abuse this capacity(33:72). This elevated description of the human being was aptly expressed by the great Sufi martyr(see **chapter one**), Husayn ibn Mansūr al-Hallāj:

I am He whom I love, and He whom I love is I -
... If thou seest me, thou seest Him,
And if thou seest Him, thou seest us both.. [56]

Al-Hallāj was not speaking of the ego*(anā')* - for this passes away - but of the **True**, permanent, undying **Self**: the **Immanent Transcendent**. This realisation is a passing away of all limited self desires*(fanā' al-fanā':* literally; the extinction of the extinction, see table in **chapter four**) into a recognition that God alone exists*(fanā' fī-Llāh:* literally; extinction in God), ultimately, to remain in this condition eternally*(baqā')*. Such a state is not the destruction of self (how can it be if all is said to exist in God?), but one of self-purification. Master *Bābā* Dovid Yūsuf, explained this:

> To subdue one's lower self, means to transform that self, so that its qualities are of a transcendent and enduring - an eternal nature. It does not mean that the self is entirely extinguished, for the basis of the capacity to ascend is the ego. Like the tiger, the seeker must struggle with it, until it can be mastered and tamed - made submissive like the cat. Then the seeker having become a Sufi, has no of it, but can ride it to Paradise! [57]

The root of such a union*(ittihād)* is love. The *'Arīf*, or realised Sufi is so much entranced by the **Beloved**(God), that *kindness and affliction - roses and thorns* are all experienced as expressions of love. Everything is seen as existing within, and as coming from the **Beloved**. Good and evil, beauty and ugliness, are all recognised as being from the **Universal Lover**, and as a lover of the Universal, the Sufi in coming to know Self, also knows God. All that

151

exists is loved equally as attributes of the Beloved reflected within the self.[58]

It is in such terms, that Rūmī describes the *union with God's Light(ittihād-i-nūr)*; [59] such a union occurring as a result of knowing oneself through contact with the Universal wo/man*(Al-Insān al-Kāmīl)* – the Master,[60] so that one can declare – as did Rūmī – that though he could not find his Teacher – when Shams disappeared and Rūmī went to look for him in Damascus – that he and his Teacher were One:

> He and I are the same Light, you can see him, or you can see me, whatever you wish... Why do I say me, or him, when he is myself and I am him? ...I am him now – I am speaking of myself! It was nothing other than myself that I was seeking.[61]

The Master, as the ideal parent and perfect role model, fulfils that disciple's inner needs. Through the example of selfless love, it is learnt that since divisions, differences and disputes, are all in the service of the ego, then Truth and Love are identical. In a natural way – as experiences in living cause past events and their learned response to arise in the disciple's life – the twin pillars of reward (Heaven/Paradise) and punishment(Hell/Alienation)[62] are transcended, for all events are seen as expressions of the Beloved's (God's) Love.

The Master as a Means for Transcending the Limited Self

As there is no institutionalisation in Sufism, the Master is of prime importance in its transmission. In fact, it could be said that the Master is the institution. What forms of organisation that do exist, exist for temporary purposes only - usually for a specific purpose. The setting up of *Takiyyah* (meeting-places for Sufis) [63] as religious edifices - as opposed to communal meeting places [64] - is a mark of deterioration and has little to do with genuine Sufism. For this reason, a Master's position must be consistently upheld and reinforced by the disciple's humility and trust.[65] Sufism stresses that the attitude of the disciple is as important as the manner of teaching. Unless the disciple comes as a *sālik* (seeker) prepared to be taught, then no progress will be made and difficulties will be created for others in the group *(halqah)*. There is a necessity to believe in the Master, who must be considered as a physician of the soul. There must be a surrendering of that *psyche*/soul for treatment in the same way that one trusts one's life to a surgeon. As Rūmī put it:

> If someone is sick, they will give up sweet pleasures and drink the bitterest of medicine, but if they have no hope of being restored to health, how will they be able to endure this?...You must become as if you were totally ignorant and then trust completely that you will be released from your ignorance....Reason is what brings the sick man to the physician - but after that it is of no use to him - and he must surrender himself completely to that physician.[8]

Despite this, the Master is not considered a god, as is the case with the Hindu *Guru,* but as an instructor, [66] whose

153

purpose is to take the disciple to the point where a Master is no longer needed, or ideally, to the stage at which the disciple can become a teacher.[67] It is a relationship in which both Master and disciple are subservient to God; a recognition that whatever station is attained, is only so because God ordained it. It is a mutual dependence on God alone, in which all activities and disciplines are designed to acknowledge (in the case of the Master) and to attain awareness of (in the case of the disciple), the **Unitary Nature of Existence**. Sufi Master, Ja'far as-Sādiq (died 765), reported that God had told Muhammad:

> the best way of seeking closeness to Me, is *in the performance* of what I have prescribed for My servants. If anyone performs even more than is required, I love them for it more also. When I love that person, I become the eyes with which they see; the ears with which they hear; the tongue with which they speak; and the hands with which they hold. If they call to Me, I respond; If they ask Me, I give to them.[68]

It is in this light that we can begin to understand Ibn 'Arabī's words, as quoted at the beginning of this chapter, which have reference not just to the Teacher of the Age, whom the Sufi believe appears by Divine Providence every hundred years, or so,[69] but also to the Sufi Master. This is because the Master's relationship to the disciple reflects that Master's relationship to God. The whole aim of fostering such a relationship is to deepen devotion on the part of the disciple-- first to the Master, then through that

154

love, ultimately and independently, to God. Devotion (religion would call it piety) is the means by which the animal nature *(nafs al-haywāniyah)* is transcended, and self-orientation and worship overcome. That is why, regardless of what means and methods are used (they will vary according to time, circumstance, and individual differences and needs of the disciple) there will be a common core throughout.[70] As Abū 'Alī Husayn ibn 'Abd Allāh ibn Sīnā (Avicenna, died 1037) wrote, in chapter nine of his book *Isharāt* (**Illuminations**):

> To realised Sufis, worship means exercising of the mental faculties of thinking and imagination, so that they may be diverted from a preoccupation with material concerns to Divine ones. Thus by constant practise, these faculties are brought into harmony with their true human nature – that is devotion to God – so that when the inner *psyche* desires illlumination, they do not prevent it. [71]

The rigorous disciplines imposed on a disciple by a Master are for this purpose. They are part of *Adab* – a word that in its root refers not only to courtesy and politeness, but also to morals – and which is continually stressed by the Sufi. Although specific and customary guidelines will vary with different Orders and Masters, behind them lies a deeper inner meaning, not accessible to the uninitiated.[72] These have as their purpose, the breaking-through of external perceptions(called *mental sets* in Western Cognitive Psychology) in order to acquire Unitary Vision. It is for this reason that, while different

Sufi Masters and Orders are part of a singular tradition their teachings may vary - even on occasions seeming to contradict one another. There are no standard textbooks (these are produced according to the needs of the time), no time-scale for the learning process, and one cannot "join" - in the usual sense of the term. Monetary payment is also discouraged, since it encourages the belief that Sufi knowledge - **gnosis** - can be purchased.[73] What the Sufi Master conveys to the disciple is not something that has been learned from books - nor even from other people's experiences - but what has been learnt by that Master's experience, the aim being to induce within the disciple, the same sort of experience. What is taught differs according to the disciple's needs and potential; not according to the preferences of the Teacher. Time-honoured principles are adapted according to prevailing circumstances. The same question may be answered differently by different Masters, and even by the same Master, differently at different times. It may not be answered at all (in the direct sense) for as explained by Master *Bābā* Dovid Yūsuf:

> We are not so much concerned with the question as we are with what lies behind it. It's the question that's not asked, which is the one which we attempt to answer; paying due regard to the fact that if it is answered too directly, the ego will be hardened, rather than softened.

St. Francis of Assisi (1181-1226), the Christian mystic, wearing a pure wool cloak typical of Sufis of the Maghrib (sketched from the earliest known painting of him, at St.Gregory's chapel, Subiaco). Returning after a *meeting with Islamic mystics* at Damietta, Egypt, he was given an ivory horn (worn by members of some Orders) which he always carried with him. His famous *Canticle of the Creatures* is a Tuscany variant of a prayer by the Egyptian Sufi, Dhū n-Nūn Misrī (died 859).

Notes and References

1) *Islam,* literally means achieving reconciliation/peace by surrendering to God, i.e., acknowledging the Universal **Will** and **Direction**, in all - and every facet of - life.

2) For this reason, it is common for a seeker to dream of dying, or of the death of a relative, or someone close to them.

3) *Mathnawī* 1:2431;5:372. Wherever I have used the masculine as in the repetitive use of Master, or in translation, it should not be interpreted as giving a priority to men. English, in attempting to be neutral, has in practice become male orientated, as in the American expression *guys.*

4) The literal meaning of the word 'disciple' is one who is subject, by their choice, to a discipline.

5) In order to avoid reinforcing the ego, dreams or their interpretation are only discussed with the Master.

6) The word has the same root as *tawbah;* used in the **Qur'ān** (110:3) to mean a change of heart, and also as a figure of speech for God's willingness to turn to those who turn to Him/Her.

7) This is based on an esoteric understanding of the meaning of *hell-fire* as found in the **Qur'ān** (104:6-7) and in all the scriptures of the world without exception. It was elucidated by the Persian Sufi 'Ayn al-Qudāt al-Hamadhānī (see **chapter one**) in his *Tamhidāt* (see **Bibliography** 1992, pp, 51-52) and will be explained further in a later chapter.

8) *Fīhi mā fīhī* (**In it what is in it),** Tehran and Azamgarh, 1928 (in brackets mine).

9) Sufi writers pointed out that infatuation is an externalisation of your own power. Conversely, criticism is a projection of your weakness, (see e.g., **Mathnawī** 1:1306).

10) Ultimately, as Abū Bakr al-Kalābādhī said in his *Kitāb at-Ta'arruf li-madhab ahl at-Tasawwuf:*"The Sufi are in agreement that the only Guide to God, is God!"

11) Sexual abuse; deliberately prolonging therapy for money; a creation of (medicinal) drug dependency; the substitution of one form of neuroticism for another; mental and physical abuse- even suicide - are commonplace in Western psychotherapy, as well as amongst the followers of the new cults, mushrooming in an attempt to fill the vacuum created by secularism. Genuine Sufism, encourages none of these things.

12) The fully initiated core of *Bābā* Dovid Yūsuf's followers are few. Yet, despite this, he has influenced many people from all walks of life: academics, medical practitioners, conservationists, even royalty, as well as the poor and the uneducated - including other *Shaykhs.* Numerous individuals experience a complete change in their lives - plus mental and physical healing - as the result of his teachings, despite the fact that he remains "hidden" or unknown.

13) See notes 13 and 14 in **chapter two.**

158

14) These five elements can be found in a variety of forms: see e.g., Manerī 1980, pp,30-33; Nurbakhsh 1978, pp,115-116 & Ajmal 1986, p,32 (full details in the **Bibliography**).

15) *Sharafuddin Manerī: the Hundred Letters*, as translated by Paul Jackson, SPCK, London, 1980, pp, 31-32 (italics mine).

16) Simplicity – in the sense of purity of intention – rather than the multiplicity of motivations that characterises so-called sophisticates. It may, or may not, be accompanied by an actual lack of literary learning. Certainly, in the case of Rūmī's Teacher, Hajjī Bektāsh Velī (a renowned Sufi *Shaykh* who was a contemporary of Rūmī, though the two never met), Yunus Emre(died c 1339) and many others, their spiritual stature was not accompanied by literary knowledge, even though Yunus Emre's reputation as a folk poet was considerable.

17) Despite coming from a generation of renowned scholars, it was not until Rūmī met his Teacher, that he became the great poet, dancer, and musician that we know of today. His son refers to this change brought about by Shams ad-Dīn: "Never... did he cease from music and dancing...He had been a *muftī:* he *became* a poet" (translated by Nicholson 1950, p, 20).

18) Whether it be psychiatry, psychoanalysis, or one of the new type of therapies on offer, as every therapist knows – it is the avoidance of real change, that bedevils therapeutic practice.

19) See note 49 in **chapter six**.

20) *The Mathnawi of Jalalu'd-Din Rumi*, translated by R.A. Nicholson, Gibb Memorial Trust and Luzac & Co, London, in 8 Vols, 1925-1940: III, 1302-3 & VI, 4578.

21) This should be borne in mind, for Rūmī, like many Sufis, has often wrongly been accused of Pantheism - **Mathnawī** 2:1170.

22) *Mathnawī* 3:3611-3612 & 1895-1896; 1:1740.

23) Although the accounts vary (see Eva de Vitray-Meyerovitch's 1987 compilation of the various accounts, pp,23-29), they all agreee that Rūmī was physically shaken.

24) *Mathnawī* 3:203.

25) Much of Western psychotherapy, especially psychoanalysis, is about dealing with these reactions; whatever jargon that may be used such as: "reaction formation"; "secondary elaboration"; "rationalisation"; "hostile behaviour"; "social inadequacy", etc.

26) "State of truth"; from which *Haqīqah* (esoteric truth), the name for Sufi teaching is derived. The word *Haqq* means Reality or Absolute, and is as equally applicable to God as to exact knowledge/Truth.

27) *Mystic Odes* 1022 (a partial translation of Rūmī's *Dīwān-i-Shams-Tabrizī* by Vitray-Meyerovitch, 1973).

28) Knowledge is here used in an active rather than a passive sense: i.e, as in *"Adam knew his wife and she conceived a son" (Bereshit/Genesis 4:1 in Hebrew Bible).

29) Abū Bakr Sirāj ad-Dīn's *Book of Certainty*, London, 1952, in Bakhtiar (see **Bibliography**), 1976, p,59.

159

30) All the world's major religions developed from such conversations. Much later, the living mystic experiences on which these faiths were based, were externalised to become the formal religions that we know of today.

31) See note 34 in **chapter four**.

32) *'Love is the Wine': Talks of a Sufi Master in America*, edited by Ragip Frager, Threshold Books, Putney, Vermont, 1987, p, 95.

33) *Bābā* Dovid Yūsuf, replying to the question as to why he should stand on his chair and begin to change a light bulb in the middle of a discourse. At the time he was speaking of seeing the Teachers as spokesmen for the **Eternal Spirit**, not as individual Masters, who as bodily forms, pass away.

34) *Qur'ān* 48:18. The term *ridwān* used here is also used in *Qur'ān* 9:72, where it signifies the removal of the veil of separation from God, and final acceptance of that soul into a state of union (Paradise). For traditional Muslims this takes place after death, but for the Sufi, it has a much broader meaning.

35) See note 43 in **chapter six**.

36) This may involve a shaving of the head, answering of questions, exercises demonstrating the group's acceptance of the new member, the use of an axe, bag, mat, bowl, turban, or whatever is specific to that particular Order.

37) A probation period - usually 3 years - may be followed by several initiation stages, sometimes as many as 7, as in the *Khalwatī*. The whole process can take several years, as in the *Ni'matu'llāhī* where it takes 12 years. In some cases, as in the *Bābā'iyya* (**Fraternity of the Universal Way**) there are various degrees and forms of initiation. Where there is only one stage, or initiation is easy and encouraged, what we are talking of is a folk/cult-group and not a genuine Sufi Order (see **Appendix 4**).

38) All Orders trace their origins to Prophet Muhammad, except four - three of them able to authorise *Shaykh*s -with their founders having received their teachings in a different way. The *Tijāniyya* claim their founder, Abū'l-'Abbās Ahmad at-Tījani (died 1815), received it in a vision from Muhammad. The *Khādiriyya* claim authorisation not from Muhammmad but from *al-Khidr* (see note 13), while the *Uwaysī* trace it to a spiritual experience - independent of any connection with a live Teacher, being named after Uways al-Qarāni from Yemen, a contemporary of Muhammad, who never met him. The *Uwaysī* do not generally initiate others, unless as in some cases, they become members of other Orders. Finally, the *Bābā'iyya*, uniquely, claim authority on the basis that their founder, being an *Uwaysī* and having direct knowledge, was later instructed by Muhammad in vision, to seek *bay'ah* with other Orders for the purpose of unity. He was initiated into, and/or recognised by all major *Sunni* & *Shiah* Orders, including the aforementioned(over 40).

39) *Fīhi ma fīhī* (**In it what is in it**), Tehran and Azamgarh, 1928.

40) A word literally meaning, "to settle"; that refers to God's Grace and Blessings. Sufi Masters generally have a charisma (as Weber,

the founding father of the sociology of religion, described it) and a sense of presence which attracts others, and assists them in exercising authority over their disciples. Referring to *A Sufi Saint of the 20th century*, Lings (1971,p.84) said,"*His presence was such that when he went out he was liable to draw men irresistibly after him down the street.*"

41) As part of initiation procedures, members of the *Bābā'iyya* wear a cord with three knots, to symbolise internalisation of these qualities (see **Appendix 4**).

42) The disciple is expected to discuss weaknesses and difficulties in following the Order's disciplines, plus asking permission and advice on marriage, employment and place of residence. Refusal to agree to follow this direction constitutes a violation of the disciple's pledge *(bay'at)*, and teaching will, as a consequence, be terminated.

43) As a psychotherapist, it took me some years before I realised that Western psychotherapeutic systems (of whatever school, including psychiatry) operate as theoretical rationalisations, rather than as actual changers of personality and behaviour.

44) The lack of this quality, perhaps more than any other, is what characterises our society with its endemic level of violence.

45) Sufism, as a continuation of the esoteric tradition, goes back for at least 6,000 years. But in its setting-out of an exact psychology in a form comparable to the Western reductionist kind, we are talking of the development of Sufi philosophy in response to the interaction between Christians, Jews and Muslims, that occurred at the height of the Islamic Era.

46) It could be argued that Sufism has special value in its deliberate creation of the parental relationship, and is therefore more likely to be successful than waiting for this to develop in a transference procedure, or whatever.

47) Jones, J., *From Abraham to Andrenio*, 1969, pp, 69-73.

48) *Mathnawī* 5:698-702 & 3:81.

49) *Mathnawī* 2:2338-2430.

50) *Mathnawī* 2:3137 (in brackets mine).

51) See e.g., Rūmī's *Discourses*, translated by A.J.Arberry, John Murray, London, 1961, p, 33.

52) Abū'l-Mufākher Bākhrazī's *Aurād al-ahbāb wa Fusūs al-ādāb*, edited by Iraj Afshār, Tehran, 1975, p, 245.

53) The *Shī'ah*, see 'Alī, son-in-law and cousin of Prophet Muhammad, as the Exemplar of their faith.

54) Where there is an emphasis on this chain of authorisation, we can guarantee that this is not a genuine Sufi group, but a pseudo-one (Muslim cult) - see **chapter ten**.

55) I have yet to find anyone who could honestly claim their parents were ideal, or whose childhood has not been disturbed in some way or another. One frequently finds individuals who have had the most difficult childhood, yet who have grown up to become stable and responsible adults.

56) Quoted by R.A. Nicholson, in *The Mystics of Islam*, Arkana, London 1989, p,51.

57) A similar point is made in a letter of Sharafuddin Manerī; see *The Hundred Letters*, as translated by Paul Jackson, SPCK, London, 1980, p, 344.

58) *Mathnawī* 1:1570-1574.

59) This Light is everywhere, but it is only visible to those whose vision has been purified. It is not a literal union with God, in the sense of an incarnation*(hulūl)* as in the doctrine of the Trinity; an impossibility for Rūmī (see *Mathnawī* 5:4139-4147 & 2038).

60) *Mathnawī* 5:2114.

61) *Walad-Nāma* by Sultan Walad, Homaī edition, Tehran, p,60.

62) A symbolism that is to be found in many esoteric traditions, e.g., Kabbalistic Judaism, Freemasonry, Medieval Rosicrucians.

63) *Tekke* is the Turkish form of the word, *Zāwiyah* the name used in the Arab West, and in Iran, *Khānaqah*. For a historical perspective on the use and change of these terms, see J. Spencer Trimingham's *The Sufi Orders in Islam*, Clarendon Press, Oxford, 1971, chap 3.

64) *Bābā* Dovid Yūsuf encourages the creation of sacred gardens, that include wildlife conservation areas, together with the growing of medicinal herbs and medicine houses attached. These are not considered as religious edifices, but educational centres, that are community owned and managed, rather than investment projects as in Church property.

65) That this can lead to a misuse of power is discussed later.

66) The word often used for a Sufi teacher is *Murshid*, which can be applied to any kind of teacher. Though *Shaykh*, or Master, can be used interchangeably with *Murshid*, the former terms are generally reserved for a senior Teacher, i.e., one who has several *muqaddam* (male) *muqaddama* (female) under him/her, or who is the head of a Sufi Order.

67) Becoming a Master is not the aim of Sufism. Few attain this stage or privilege, and those who desire it are quickly eliminated. Not all *'Arif* (realised Sufis) teach, and there have been several Saints *(Awaliyā)* who have not done so. Furthermore, being given the title *Shaykh* (Elder) does not necessarily mean that, that person, is a teacher in the fullest sense of the word.

68) See note 31 in chapter six.

69) The word used to describe this is *Al-Qutb*, meaning axis. It refers to the spiritual centre, that is thought to be located in/around/through/with/at a given moment in time, *as well as* outside of it, of the Teacher of the Age. There is a story explaining this, in which the Master *Shaykh Mulay'* 1-'Arabī ad-Darqāwī (died 1823), while walking through the market of Fez in Morocco, crossed paths with an angel, who at the precise moment that they met shoulder to shoulder, proclaimed *"Al-Qutb!"* - indicating the holistic nature of the role (time, place, event, person) as a Transcendent reality, though the individual functions as, or through that, only when they are given the capacity to do so (see *Mathnawī* 5:2339).

162

70) Sufis explain different practices of Prophet Muhammad at different times in this way; as also the different requirements of the various Great Teachers of all the world's religious traditions, who are seen as essentially having One message.

71) Ibn Sīnā provides a good example of understanding Sufi practice from an inner (esoteric, informed), rather than an outer (exoteric, rigid, formalised, naive) perspective, in that, although he was attacked by that most traditional of Sufis, Al-Ghazālī, for his philosophy, he was at the end of his life (in contrast to his early life which was hedonistic) pious. Yet he had always been a Sufi (in spirit), for to use a Sufi saying; *"Two things though opposed may actually be working together."*

72) For example, a disciple may be instructed not to allow his shadow to fall on the Master, or not to step on the Teacher's prayer mat – all of which have an inner as well as an external meaning (see **Appendix 3**).

73) Any group taking money for teaching can be discounted as a Sufi group, excluding many of the fashionable cult-groups who use this label. However, dependant personalities are also discouraged, so that prospective initiates must be employed, and are required to contribute in other ways, including time (see **Appendices 2 - 4**).

8

PRACTISING TRANSCENDENCE - SUFI DISCIPLINES

"Low in the earth
I lived in realms of ore and stone;
And then I smiled in many-tinted flowers;
Then roving with the wild and wandering hours,
O'er earth and air and ocean's zone
In a new birth
I dived and flew,
And crept and ran.
And all the secret of my essence drew
Within a force that brought them all to view
And lo, a man!
And then my goal.
Beyond the clouds, beyond the sky,
In realms where none may change or die -
In angel form; and then away
Beyond the bounds of night and day,
And Life and Death, unseen or seen,
Where all that is hath ever been,
As One and Whole." [1]

Mevlana, Jalāl ad-Dīn ar-Rūmī.

Sufism and the Creation of a Transcendent Consciousness
The purification of thought takes place by sustained effort
(mujāhada), subordinating one's desires - as they appear
as thought impulses - to those of God's Will and Direction
(ikhtiyār, meaning: to choose what is chosen by God). A
process primarily achieved by reflecting on Divine Names,
through their invocation*(Dhikr)*. For to remember*(dhikra)*
God is to recall/recollect the Primal Unitary State*(Tawhīd)*,
that, if persevered with, will ultimately enable this unitary

164

state*(ittihād)*, to be attained permanently*(baqā')*. *Dhikr/Zikr/Zeker* enables all transitory and fleeting pleasures to be seen as illusory, for they are limited and finite, whereas God as the only persisting **Reality***(Wujūd)*, is endless Bliss. Thus the *Qur'ān* (13:28-29) describes *Dhikr* as a source of satisfaction, through which *Tūbā* (blessedness, joyfulness in all situations) is attained, despite external conditions.

Muhammad said: *"My eyes sleep but my heart remains awake"*, meaning that he was the Master of his thoughts, able to control them, being never overpowered by them, because his heart's orientation was always towards God. In describing how discursive thought causes *the heart of a man to be subject to more commotion than a boiling kettle,*[2] the Prophet, on another occasion said:

> The heart is influenced by the imagination, in the same way that a feather hung on a tree in the desert, is continually being turned topsy-turvy by the wind.[3]

To attain a mastery of thought and consequently of feelings, in conjunction with *Dhikr*, the Sufi utilises fasting and regular prayer. The aim of all these practices is to purify thoughts and actions, by concentrating on God. It is not an asceticism in which the body is controlled, but one in which the mind is subject to discipline; so having more similarities to Buddhism, than Hinduism. However, in contradistinction to Buddhism, it does not seek to attain this by insight alone, for anything that strengthens the ego fosters the illusion of self. Rather, it is *self*-renunciation.

165

As we have seen, knowing - in the Sufi sense - cannot occur without the perceptive faculty, the *eye of the heart.* This expression refers to the **Spirit's** effect - as the organ of transcendent vision - upon the innermost being, and is symbolised by the moon(the heart) and the sun(the **Spirit**). The moon reflects the sun, and the light that passes between them is this organ of transcendent vision. The heart is the point at which the human and limited self ends and the **Transcendent Self** begins. The **Spirit** is the centre of one's consciousness and the night is symbolic of the soul. Hence the mystic expression, *the dark night of the soul,* meaning the time when the moon has no effect, being obscured by *self*-produced clouds that obscure its light.

The effect of repetitively repeating Names of God is to cause a temporary loss of individual limited consciousness, so inducing a transcendent awareness, or ecstasy. We should not confuse this transcendent consciousness with non-linear thinking, or similar terms coined by Western psychologists, in their attempt to explain non-rational intellectual processes. It is not a mental activity in the usual sense of the word at all, being neither rational or irrational. Similairly, while Sufi stories have the effect of inducing a sense of multiple-perspective - of seeing things in new ways - that is not their real purpose. Rather, like Zen *kōans,* their aim is to produce a transcendence of rational thinking by statements that, at first sight, appear to be contradictory. This weakens the control factor, that

166

in being exercised through arid intellectualism, has strengthened the ego or conditioned self. For this reason, their is no engagement in arguments over religious questions, for *he who knows the Truth cannot dispute it.* [4] The Sufi views questioning and discussion as a sign that understanding has decreased, or is even non-existent. Writing in his *Dīwān-i-Shams-i-Tabrīz*, Rūmī said: *"The man of God is not a book learned scholar."*

Despite the many Sufis of academic bent, such as Al-Ghazālī, Frithjof Schuon, Titus Burckhardt, René Guénon and others, the Sufi quest is not an intellectual one. Not that it is anti-intellectual, or even non-intellectual, but in using approaches which transcend the intellect, as well as the emotions, it could be termed intellectually neutral. Ibn 'Arabī, writing in his *Fusūs al-Hikam* following Socrates, claimed that knowledge was not gained in the intellectual sense of being personally acquired through mental effort, but was *discovered*. It is there in the mind all the time, but is hidden by *veils* which have to be dissolved – it is this to which Sufi practices are directed.

Sufism cannot be learnt from books, although reading may be helpful as an introduction to its practice, nor can it be learnt through history (someone else's experience). It can only be *experienced* as the result of one's own practice. It is in this light that Sufi injunctions against intellectualism can be understood. It uses methods which overcome bias and preconceived ideas, not by intellectual

167

assault, but by avoiding, going around, and transcending such objections. The Sufi calls these barriers *ego-traps*. To *ego-traps,* can be added the problem of commercial brainwashing in present-day society, which acts so as to inhibit learning, by inducing a passivity and readiness to succumb to materialism, sensationalism, cynicism and depravity. Rather than appealing to intellectual processes – usually self-defeating, in that it strengthens ego-control mechanisms– or directly arousing emotions, as in radical types of psychotherapy, like: Primal, Rebirthing, or Encounter groups, – that can have disastrous effects, either literally, or in attachment to the process itself – there is a subtle and indirect approach. This bypasses rationalisation and similar ego-defence mechanisms. It is not that there is a complete disregard for intellectual, or emotional approaches –both may be employed occasionally – but that what use is made of either, is subservient to the usual transcendent mode of communication.

Sufi Practices

In order to achieve such transcendence, certain preliminary procedures must be strictly followed. This is the reason that rules of etiquette*(ādāb)* are enforced, for unless preparation is made, no learning will take place. The Sufi experience requires the setting aside of mental blocks and habitual ego-defence mechanisms, that arise from the conditioned and limited self. Only when this has been done

168

- what is called *riding the ego* [5]- is it possible to perceive, clearly and directly, the true nature of **Reality***(Haqq)*. The expectation of a reward – something not only encouraged by Western society's commercial orientation, but also by the adherents of religious externalism – mitigates, what we shall here call *receiving* Sufism.[6] Only when the thought of personal reward has been completely disregarded – when there is no expectation whatsoever – can Sufi development begin. Discussion is discouraged for it simply reinforces existing opinions, and encourages the erroneous belief that it is nesessary in order to learn. Transcendent knowledge cannot be obtained by this method, for it encourages the intellectual (in the Western sense) mode of perception, at the expense and exclusion of other forms of learning.

The Story

The most favoured vehicle for instruction is the story; for stories can put across feelings, intuitive patterns, and material that otherwise would be difficult to convey because of it not conforming to the logistics of analytical thought. Stories can also focus on items that people usually dismiss, such as e.g., the unpleasantness of death, the vulnerability of human beings, or the ridiculousness, pomposity and irrelevance, of much of what is considered as essential in life. By the use of humour, and/or verbal shocks, fixed patterns of thinking can be circumnavigated and an element of awareness introduced into a jaded and lethargic temperament. As *Bābā* Dovid Yūsuf put it:

169

*It's the ideas that you disagree with most strongly,
which are the most important ideas for you.*

Humour

The use of humour can be illustrated by the following
story found in Rūmī's, **In it what is in it** *(Fīhi mā fīhī):* [7]

> There was a jester who wished to restore a king's
> sense of humour. The king had offered money to
> anyone who could make him laugh. Now it so
> happened, that when the king was walking along
> the bank of a river and in a rage, that the jester
> was walking along on the other side. But the king
> paid no attention to the jester, but just kept
> looking into the water. The jester, desiring to
> gain the king's attention, said: *"What is it that you
> are staring at, that you look into the water so?"*
> The king replied nonchalantly: *"I see a fool !"* The
> jester replied: *" Your Master - I am not blind !"*

Repetition

In order to develop sensitivity (that has become dulled by
the creation of a thirst for new and different experiences –
i.e., forever harsher, always different, ever increasing in
intensity) the Sufi Master employs the use of repetition.
Rather than becoming bored, this cultivates concentration,
self-discipline and application, and has the effect of
implanting in the mind, every facet of meaning, of the
phrase or word repeated. The effect is that the seeker may
suddenly appreciate what something ACTUALLY means,
rather than its obvious meaning.

Poetry and the Oral Emphasis

The Sufi emphasis on sound [8] – certain things must be
oral even when written down, the verbal story, and the

170

chanting of Names of God– just some examples – are ways to break through the limitations of reductionist thinking and the brain's semantic censor. This is why the Sufi have often used poetry to express their concepts,[9] for poetry can be assimilated by the mind on several levels at once, thus inducing a holistic perspective. There is the aesthetic appreciation of the beauty of the word arrangement, the sensual perception of the rhythmic sound, as well as the contemplation of its meaning. In poetry, the ego is not permitted to select, opinionate, dismiss, or analyse in a dissective way. Material that might otherwise be rejected, because its acceptance would entail a change in attitude and way of life, can be assimilated on a different level, for sensory input comes through a mode other than the semantic one; consequently it can remain dormant at the preconscious level, until experience allows its absorption.

Reformulation

There is also a constant reformulation of the way that Sufism is presented, making it more accessible to the culture in which it is expressed. While other teaching methods concentrate on the outward form of the material, the Sufi Master aims to get across the inner meaning. As this is not a passive process and requires effort from both parties, the Master is selective in his choice of disciples, and there is usually a probationary period for eliminating those whose ego - and consequently resistance - is too great to benefit from it. The reason for this is, that when

171

the Sufi talks about knowledge, it is about transcendent knowledge*(ma'rifa)*, not academic or intellectual knowledge. Only by purification*(mākhāfa)* of the self through the love of God*(mahabba)*,[10] can this transcendent knowledge be realised. The Sufi consider academic learning an inferior mode of perception, so that the accomplished academic and Sufi saint, Abū Hāmid Muhammad al-Ghazālī, who came to see these limitations in his own life - despite immense intellectual achievement - wrote in his 40 volume compendium *Ihyā 'Ulum ad-Dīn* (**Revival of the Religious Sciences**):[11]

> The child cannot have knowledge to the extent of an adult, and the everyday person cannot understand what the educated scholar has grasped. In the same manner, even the educated scholar cannot understand what the saint who is enlightened - the Sufi - has realised.... How could it be otherwise? [12]

For the Sufi, understanding inner clear perception, an innate ability to recognise what is true - is not an intellectual activity in the usual sense of the term. The belief that all learning can be contained in books, is a sickness, and an example of how conditioned the average person is. Like the happily married grandfather, who, when asked why he was reading a 'Masters and Johnson' sex manual, replied, *"You are never too old to learn!"*

It is not simply a question of finding the right answers, but also of finding the right questions; this is what according to a contemporary Sufi Master, constitutes the

172

basis of Sufi knowledge [13] It can be understood - to use my own terms - *as a form of deconditioning; a means of overcoming self-induced, self-centred and self-motivated, brainwashing. The Sufi experience is an holistic one, in which the search for self and the search for God, are part of the same journey.*

Dance

In this light, we can understand the use of dance, which Arberry (1950, p,62) pointed out, has like poetry, always been a part of Sufi practise. The **Hadrah**, *'Imārah*, or other Sufi dances, are ways to produce within their participants, altered states of consciousness, and so are called *Dhikr as-sadr* (Remembrance in the breast). The state*(hāl)* that is induced is described as ecstasy*(wajd)*, although strictly speaking, it is believed that these psycho-gnostic states *(ahwāl)* are ones over which the mystic has no control, since they are *gifts* (from God) rather than attainments.

That this is not a psychotic condition can be discerned from the description given of a lunatic as one *without his hāl(bila' hāl)*. It corresponds roughly to what is described in psychological literature as the 'somnambulistic state', and is equivalent to a stage of (not the same as) hypnosis. In essence, it is a state during which identity is held in abeyance and in which subconscious impulses are brought to the surface. This does not mean that normal positive impulses and inhibitory restraints that make up the under-lying moral code are removed, as is the case with some

173

types of frenzied dancing observed elsewhere.[14] It can be considered as a deconditioning process, in which the ego is restrained and processes of intellectual control withheld, as is perfectly described by the common expression used for entering into such a state – *"kharj al-ahwāl,"* meaning, out of conditions.

It is while in a state *(hāl)* of ecstasy *(wajd)*, that those who engage in the *Hadrah,* or other practices which have the same effect, can enter into *jadhb* (Divine attraction), a mystic state of emotional detachment. Characterised by a cataclysmic discharge of nervous tension that remains unaffected by the emotional background, it is equivalent to the trance state described by Belo,[15] which comes *from too deep a level to be influenced by custom, or idiosyncratic trends in the personality.* I would describe this state myself, as a suspension of ego or self-effacement It should be mentioned at this point, that it is while in this intermediate state – during ecstasy *(wajd)* and before absorption *(jadhb)* in God[16] has been reached – that participants can be distracted from reaching the goal, and consequently, become engaged in aberrant practices such as head-slashing, or the making of animal sounds, as can be observed amongst the members of healing cults.[17]

The Use of Music

It is because of this danger that the *general use* of music is discouraged in Sufism.[18] Hujwīrī(died 1077) quotes Ibn Hamadān – an early Sufi(date unknown) – in his exposition

174

on Sufism (the first in Persian): [19]

> Be certain you do not become engrossed in music,
> for it will hold you back from higher perceptions.

Although music has been used by the Sufi, often as a response to the rigidity of externalist Islam - one example being sung *Ghazal* [20] - this is done with caution. It is realised that *some music* can stir up animal passions,[21] for all music can influence the emotions. Unless it is used with discrimination, it can block, rather than assist in the development of higher awareness by blunting sensitivity. Therefore, the Sufi Master, Mu'īn ad-Dīn Muhammad Chisti(died 1236), who *used music* to teach Sufism, wrote about Sufis who disregarded this fact,[22] because they believed that the emotional states, which they experienced, were equivalent to spiritual states. Consequently, they became fixated on these emotional states and did not attain the spiritual ones.

In other words, if the vehicle becomes an end in itself, then the end is not achieved - as in use of carved figures to represent the unrepresentable. They do not assist in awareness of spiritual realities, but actually make it more difficult by fostering the illusion that such realities can be seen with material vision. We must beware of assuming that the ends and the means of Sufi practice are the same, as is often the case with religious developmental systems, some of whom exhibit external similarities to Sufism (e.g., Yoga, Buddhism, Taoism, etc).[23]

Visual Imagery

Sufi practices have given rise to, and/or influenced, other systems, who in the process have changed the nature and meaning of the original practices.[24] For example, diagrams used for teaching, as in the designs on mosques or ancient synagogues, with their stylised calligraphy, have cryptic meanings which only Sufis can decode.[25] Similarly, many of the emblems used on medieval Cathedrals, have like Freemasonry symbolism, Sufi origins.[26] The purpose of these designs are not to hide things from the non-initiated, but rather to inculcate that obvious and external meanings are not the same as inner experienced truths.

Other practices, have as their aim, the development of concentration and clear perception, by stilling the *hiss* that arises through subvocal entrapment*(hadīth al-nafs)*. This is achieved by fully occupying the rational faculty*(nafs-i-nātiqah)* – so avoiding subvocal discourse and circular thinking – while at the same time quietening the mind, so that the **Transcendent Reality** may be perceived; practices varying with different Orders.[27]   For example, sometimes there is the use of an *internal* visual image, employed in conjunction with *Dhikr* and movements of the body and head. Or there may be multiple vocal invocations of one of the Divine Names at the same time as they are counted-off on prayer beads*(misbahah/subhah/tasbīh)*.[28] These rosaries usually contain 100 or 109 beads, including the *Alif* or finger-shaped bead, used to indicate the beginning and end

176

of a count, facilitating the number of times a Divine Name, or invocatory phrase of a litany *(wird)*, is recited.[29] The practice of using prayer beads is based upon that of an early "Companion" (intimate disciple of Muhammad): Abū Hurayrah ('Abd ar-Rahmān ad-Dawsi, died 59 A.H./678 C.E.), [30] who used a cord with a thousand knots. Others used date-stones and pebbles, while Muhammad used his fingers. There is therefore no ground for assuming that this is an example of a later introduction of a Christian, or one of the other religion's practices, for Muhammad in comparing Christian practice with his own, is reported to have said about the Christian rosary: *"How excellent a remembrancer is a rosary."* [31]

The Use and Meaning of Rhythm

Anyone observing *a Dhikr/Zikr/Zeker* session, regardless of the method used, will immediately be aware of the constant rhythm which runs throughout. Though musical instruments, such as drums, tambourines, or flutes may be used – a practice known as *Samā'* – this is not the general rule. Nevertheless, the rhythm will be apparent and natural rather than forced, and never encouraged as an end in itself.[18] It is the breathing that causes this rhythm, and it represents a change from the ordinary breathing of the individual, to the Unitary, Universal breathing of the Cosmos. The sacrifice of individual rhythms – whether in dancing, or repetitive invocations of Divine Names, using prayer beads - is a mode of repentance. It signifies that

177

forgiveness and purification has occurred, and proceeds to a prayer of unison, invoked through blessing the 'Teacher of the Age', or Universal Teacher. The expiration of the breath and sinking of dancers to the ground at the end of the dance, symbolises the death of the limited self and the attainment of Peace in God. The dance, or the invoking of Divine Names with prayer beads, corresponds to the gasping breath of the dying, as they become reabsorbed into the **Cosmos** from which they came; an enactment of death,[32] an anticipation of dying, a recognition that death is nothing but extinction of the conditioned self into a **Greater & Transcendent Self.** Breathing in represents absorption(*Istighrāq*) into the Oneness of the Essence; breathing out the manifestation of that **Essence** in Divine Names and Qualities.[33]

The Retreat

Repetitive invocations of Divine Names, in conjunction with solitude and fasting, is for the Sufi disciple, the most important method for realisation of **The Transcendent.** Called *Khalwah,* the name has reference to the practice as well as to where it takes place, and will be participated in after the probationary period,[34] according to the differing approaches of the Sufi Order concerned as well as the disciple's needs.[35] As explained by the Sufi Master, Abū 'l-'Abbās Ahmad ibn Mustafā al-'Alawī (died 1934):

> The *khalwah* is a cell in which I put the novice after he has sworn to me not to leave it for forty days if need be. In this oratory he must do nothing but

178

repeat ceaselessly, day and night, the Divine Name
(*Allāh*), drawing out at each invocation the syllable
āh until he has no more breath. Previously he must
have recited the *Shahādah(la ilāha illa'Llāh*, there is
no god but God)seventy five thousand times. During
the *khalwah* he fasts strictly by day, only breaking
his fast between sunset and dawn....some *fuqarā*
obtain the sudden illumination after a few minutes,
some after only several days, and some only after
several weeks. I know one *faqīr* who waited eight
months. Each morning he would say to me: *'My heart
is still too hard'*, and would continue his *Khalwah.* In
the end his efforts were rewarded.[36]

Travelling, Fasting and Renunciation

In addition to the primary practice of *khalwah*, there is
that of journeying - from which the word *dervish* is
derived [37] - being one of the oldest of Sufi practices.
Listed by Abū' Hasan Muhammad ibn Ahmad al-Fārisī
(date unknown), an early Persian Sufi, as one of the
essential elements of Sufism, its justification is found in
the **Qur'ān** (30:9; 29:20). Significantly, it can also be seen
as an indirect reference to Abraham (father to both Arab
and Jew), and the Jewish pariarchs and their descendants,
for whom the expression "sojourner" or traveller, is
continuously used (**Genesis** 12:1,10; 17:8; 32:5; 15:13, 1
Chronicles 29:15,etc) in the Bible. Like the *khalwah,* it has
as its aim *jalwah* (being filled by God)[38] in order to realise
a **Greater Self** through a divesting of worldly attachments
(tajrīd) - home, country, permanent abode - that peace
and rest*(tamkīn)* may only be found in God. Considered as
essential for early Sufis, nearly all of the Great Masters

179

travelled extensively during their lives, either in search of a Master, or because of being sent to find another Master (sometimes named, sometimes not), or simply as part of the spiritual development process.[39] Other practices, such as a giving away of earnings, voluntary hunger, or similar disciplines *(Inkār al-kasb* [40]*)*have the purpose of decreasing reliance on the limited self (ego/*anā'),* so increasing trust in, and awareness*(tawakkul)* of, the **Greater Self.**

Apart from the activites which disrupt normal routine, the disciple is generally encouraged to continue living – what for want of a better phrase – we could call a normal way of life. The process of self purification*(nafī)* continues side-by-side with everyday responsibilites, rather than as with some traditions, whose practices often constitute no more than a removal from one cultural context to another. A change in outward form does not necessarily mean inner change, so unless there is a specific reason for doing so, the public wearing of distinctive clothes, the eating of special foods, or adoption of alien customs, is avoided. This is one way in which genuine Sufi groups can be marked out from pseudo-ones, who show by their desire to stand out from the crowd, an attachment to ego, rather than a lack of it.[18] The Sufi say:*"If Sufi teaching cannot be applied to everyday life, then how can it be applied to any other situation? What value does it have if it only works in unusual surroundings?"* So taking part in activities generally termed ascetic is not done on a permanent basis.

180

Sufi Master, Ahmad ibn Muhammad ibn 'Atā' Allāh (died 1309), explained in his **Kitāb al-Hikam** :

> Devout persons and ascetics who cut themselves off from things, do so because these things cut them off from God. However if they could see God in all things they would not need to cut themselves off.

Abasement

Following general principles and established methods, adapting them according to individual needs, the Master will, by his/her attitude towards the disciple, reveal that disciple's duality, the aim being to expose – and so negate *(nafī)* – the ego, or the sense of I *(anā')*. This is done in a manner applicable to the disciple, rather than as a general procedure for all. Sufi Master, Al-'Arabī ad-Darqāwī related how, when he was a disciple, his Master snatched off his turban, winding it around his neck, humiliating him, so as to expose to him, his latent anger.[41]

Other unhelpful qualities, such as pride (demonstrated by a false humility) will be revealed, so that they can be reflected *(tafakkara)* upon. Subliminal pride *(kibr-i-azīm)* is a common trait for those who pursue spiritual endeavours, for quite often behind the aspirations of the disciple (of whatever tradition) lies the desire for self-glory.[42] This has long been realised in Sufism, and as in Zen Buddhism and Taoism, confrontation is used to challenge, and so reveal, latent attitudes. Statements like, *"I am an ignorant man"*, or *"I know nothing"*, by a disciple, are likely to be confirmed by the Master, so revealing *(kashf)* inconsistent

181

intentions, arising from a dualism created by the disciple hiding things from self, as well as from others.

Confession

Another way in which negative qualities or attitudes are overcome is by deliberate encouragement of the opposite quality. For example, if a disciple feels envious, resentful or jealous the Master will encourage the disciple to express positive feelings about that person, both, directly - by letter or verbally - as well as thinking positively of the person, and saying so in public. It is believed that a positive quality can overcome a negative one, as part of the human ability to transcend our animal characteristics. By correct use of the rational faculty *(nafs-i-nātiqah)* the lower selves *(nafas:haywāniyah, ammārah, lawwāmah)* can be outgrown, and their characteristics, eventually recede.

Instead of openly discussing a disciple's problems, the Master may draw attention to parallel cases, so that the disciple can become aware of deficiencies, and also draw encouragement from the example of someone else who is similarly struggling. By a positive use of what Freud called projection-introjection, the problem is both revealed and decreased. As in the Old saying: *"A problem shared is a problem halved."*

For this reason, disciples are required to admit *(ittilā')* their difficulties(not their sins), that the Master may give guidance and encouragement. This cannot be compared to Christian confession for the Master discourages feelings of

182

guilt. Instructions given are not conceived as commands, but as an acceptance of the disciple's difficulties, with a resolve by the Master, to both encourage and guide.[43]

The disciple will be asked to engage in a dialogue with **Creative Reality** before sleeping. This dialogue is not an unwholesome wallowing in guilt, but an open admission of problems, and the fact that there are difficulties in overcoming them. Instead of making false promises – that only undermines resolve when not fulfilled – there is frank admission of the fact that weaknesses may be repeated. In this way difficulties are not ignored or pushed out of consciousness, but accepted and outgrown. Persistence in such a dialogue makes the disciple aware of a **Greater Self**, so finding a greater resolve. Weaknesses are therefore transcended, rather than ignored or fought with.

Dream Interpretation

With this in mind, dream-interpretation *(ta'bīr ar-ru'yā)* is used, for according to Prophet Muhammad: *"Every dream is a true dream, but Evil changes it."* [44] The meaning here is, that a person though guided in sleep, with reflection, can change what is **Transcendent** in nature into something carnal, so as to satisfy desire. For this reason, Sufi dream interpretations are based upon spiritual and transcendent meanings of symbols, rather than being reduced to sexual, egotistical or profane interpretations. Dreams, it is believed, arise not from the base instinctual animal level, but rather from above (the **Transcendent** level), and it is worth noting that symbols *are by nature* transcendent.[45] Sufi dream interpretations are much more straightforward than those derived from analytical schools of thought, and are elevating, encouraging, positively revealing - rather than being negatively disturbing.[46] For an example of this, see the following dream and its interpretation by the Sufi Master of our Age, *Bābā* Dovid Yūsuf:

> I dreamt I was in a valley in the countryside out-side the city. People were brought to me suffering from incurable diseases. Many needed surgery for tumours and the like, and all were dying. There were some nurses and doctors among them. I felt great sympathy for these people, but realised that since I was not a surgeon, there was nothing I could do for them. However, out of compassion, I prayed for them. Then a doctor present said; *"I can give them surgery, but I cannot give them hope and that is what they need!"*
> At this point I woke up, but the dream was so vivid, that I could not forget it.

The Master replied:

> The **Beloved** has shown you that He is the sole **Master of Destiny**. The valley you are in is one of trial. The difficulties you encounter on the Path are so great that they threaten to overwhelm you, but since He is the **Beloved**, He does not ask you more than you are capable of. He has shown you, that even were He to cure your material difficulties, it would not remedy your spiritual needs. For though the world has many remedies, it cannot treat its spiritual ills without the **Great Physician**. You are on the Path; you have - by the Mercy of the **Compassionate** - been given the remedy. This remedy is spiritual - moral, ethical - it lies within yourself. You must not be distracted from the Path for many are watching

184

your progress - even the angels - therefore keep on till the end of the road for He will not fail you. But you must never at anytime rely on your limited self, your ego, for if you do, these difficulties will overwhelm you. The **Beloved**, will take you through, but you must accept His Wise Guidance and Love.

It should be realised, that the interpretatition given here considered the *individual* needs of the disciple *within* a transcendent framework; had it been a different disciple the interpretation would have been different, even if the ingredients were the same. Notice the Master's intuition *(kashf)* and understanding of the disciple's situation (he had just lost his job and was threatened with eviction from his house, and two of his closest friends - also disciples - had abandoned the Path). The temptation to interpret the dream so as to reinforce the disciple's ego is resisted,[47] yet at the same time it is not discouraging, negative or trivial. It appeals to transcendent values which strengthen the resolve and the person as a whole. While public interpretation is not usually given (as this only reinforces the limited self/*anā'*), in this case, the Master was making others in the group aware of the disciple's personal needs -- including encouragement. The guiding factor, as in all Sufi methods, was -

Empathy

Not only is empathy the basis of the Master's methods, but the Master uses empathy as a method in itself. By encouraging the disciple to see another persons difficulties,

185

by relating parallel situations and – in addition – showing empathy with the disciple, an awareness is created that transcends difficulties. This is in contrast to Western psychotherapeutic methods, where the so-called insight is often disturbing, reinforcing masochistic tendencies and self-preoccupation.

While this gives some idea of the major methods employed by a Sufi Master, it is only a part thereof, for just as Sufism believes in the reality of a **Transcendent Being** and inculcates the notion of transcendent values, so too does it employ transcendent methods, that go beyond what may be written.

Notes and References

1) Sir M. Iqbāl's beautiful rendering of Rūmī's text, in his *The Reconstruction of Religious Thought in Islam*, Ashraf Press, Lahore, 1962, p,187 (see *Mathnawī* 3:3901; 4:3637 & *Dīwān-i Shams-i Tabrīz;* 12). This Monist conception is not be confused with metempsychosis, as Glassé (1989, p, 204) has done and which Rūmī rejects *(Dīwān-i Shams-i Tabrīz;* 199).

2) Rūmī, *Mathnawī* 5:3221 & 1:123.

3) Badī' al-Zamān Furūzanfarr provides four versions of this saying; see **No 219**, in his 1982 compilation.

4) *Qur'ān* 53:28.

5) A reference to Muhammad's Ascent on the *Burāq.*

6) See note 7 to chapter five.

7) There is a partial translation by Arberry, entitled *Discourses of Rumi*, John Murray, London, 1961.

8) This emphasis, which exists in tribal societies, argues for Sufism's antiquity as an expression of the esoteric tradition, in contrast to the visual emphasis that is found in Jewish and Indian mysticism, that results from a written rather than an oral language.

9) Sufism has had many poets, and Sufi poetry is of the highest order As far as Persian poetry is concerned, Classical Persian poetry is largely Sufi in content, inspiration, style and form. In Turkey, their greatest folk poet was the Sufi, Yunus Emre, while in Arabia, the *Hanīf* (member of the *Hunafā')* Sufi Umayyah ibn Abī's-Salt was a poet of renown before Islam's advent. In our own time, Master *Bābā* Dovid Yūsuf produces poetry extemporaneously in the manner of the Bard.

10) For the Sufi, these 3 elements are inseparable, constituting a triad by which Sufi development takes place: i.e.,*mākhāfa* = purification, *mahabba* = expansion, *ma'rifa* = union.

11) Book 2(**Marvels of the Mind**), Mustafā al-Halabī, Cairo,1347 A.H.

12) The proof of this statement is the continual reference by Muslim academics to the superiority of Al-Ghazālī's writings, while they themselves reject the Sufi perspective.

13) *Bābā* Dovid Yūsuf. Similar points were made by the late Idries Shah; see his 1966 & 1977 works in the **Bibliography**.

14) A person under hypnosis will not contravene their moral code. For example, a hypnotist cannot hypnotise someone to commit a murder or adultery, against their will.

15) See Belo.J, *Trance in Bali*, Columbia University Press, New York, 1960, pp, 212-213, for an explanation of this point. It should be realised that Belo is not talking of Sufi dancing, but the parallels are exact.

16) While *wajd* is temporary, *jadhb* can be permanent, or long-lasting, those who experience it as such are spoken of as being *majdhūb* - a fool of God!

17) The difference between genuine Sufi and pseudo–Sufis, or Muslim cults, will be examined in chapter ten.

18) Muslah ad-Dīn Sa'adī (died 692/1292), *Gūlistān* (**Rose Garden**), Edition by Khalil Khatib Rahbar, Tehran, 1969, in the section *'Manner of the Dervishes'* (Persian). There is also an excellent French translation by Omar Ali-Shah, 1966.

19) 'Alī ibn 'Uthmān Hujwīrī's, *Kashf al-Mahjūb li-Arbāb al-Qulūb* (**Revelation of the Veiled for the Gate Masters of the Heart**), Persian Edition, V.A.Zhukovsky, Leningrad, 1926, p.126.

20) Indian, Sufi *Qawwālī* singers and poet-musicians, convey their message by shocking their rigid Muslim audience.

21) Witness, for example, how some forms of Western popular music have contributed to a a violent drug culture.

22) *Risalat* (**Epistle to Disciples**). See Shah: London, 1966, p.16.

23) If one witnesses a Buddhist paying homage to the Buddha, one will see the same prostrations as are made in Islam, yet the meaning and result are very different. Similarly, the same exercise performed by a Sufi and a Muslim*(Salāh)*, while corresponding, has a totally different meaning and effect for the Sufi, than for a Muslim.

24) Shah claimed (1966, pp. 18 & 32) that mandalas and other magical inscriptions are deteriorated forms of what were originally Sufi teaching diagrams.

25) See Shah 1964, pp. 182-191, 382-383, 393 & 399.

26) See note 32 in chapter two.

27) The *Naqshbandiyya* use silent *Dhikr* (personal intonation), dwelling continuously on a Name of God in all activity, so that its adherents must intone the Name *Allāh* at least 5,000 times in 24 hours. Awareness is maintained by a variety of practices employed in addition to this, such as keeping the eyes downcast when walking, whilst looking at a spot about 3 ft ahead and counting the footsteps. (Those familiar with Buddhist walking meditation will notice some similarities.)

28) This is the origin of the so-called *worry-beads,* found in Greece and other Balkan countries.

29) Sufi prayer beads have many symbolic meanings that can only be taught orally. In short, they represent the cyclical nature of existence, with God - **The One***(Alif)* - as the **Source** from whom we come and to whom we return. It should be noted that not all Masters at all times have used prayer beads.

30) Significantly, he is the primary transmitter of Muhammad's sayings in the compilations of the *Sunnī* division of Islam.

31) Quoted by Martin Lings in his 1971 work, p, 100.

32) Like the Mass, it is a participation by representation. But it does not represent the death of Christ, but that of the participant - in an holistic sense(ego, spiritual, physical), as the participant engages in the continuous cycle of Creation.

33) Breathing out into the hands during devotions is used by Sufis and Muslims alike, but the latter do not generally understand either its meaning or its significance.

34) See note 37 in chapter seven.

35) In some Orders the retreat is in stages, in others, it is kept alive, so to speak, by yearly retreats that in some cases correspond to the Islamic *Ramadān*. However, even when this is not the case, it is likely that there will be a particular occasion, associated in the mind of the disciple, with the attainment of the goal *(jalwah)*. The *Khalwah* may take place in any secluded spot (wood, mountain) or building used for the purpose. One *Naqshbandī Shaykh* relates how he was lowered down a well, while the Master of the *Bābā'iyya* **(Fraternity of the Universal Way)** found himself left alone in the desert with the minimum of food and water. The word *khalwah*, literally means withdrawal/emptiness.

36) In Martin Lings, as above, 1971, p, 85.

37) From *Dār'wīsh* (literally; "without an abode", i.e., traveller). Also one without territory (beyond territorial distinctions), a traveller on the Path, for whom God is the only resting place.

38) This word describing the spiritual experience that marks the end or culmination of *kalwah* is derived from the word *tajalli* - that means "illumination; coming into the light."

39) The decrease of this practice, the travelling by aeroplane to go on pilgrimage to Mecca *(Hajj)*, or the reluctance of so-called *Shaykhs* to let go of their disciples, is a mark of psuedo-Sufi cults, and the deterioration of genuine Sufism.

40) These vary with different Orders, and also with *Shaykhs* within the same Order. The *Khalwatiyya* (so named because their founder practised frequent retreats) use voluntary hunger and silence as well as retreats. The *Shādhiliyya*, who abstain for the most part from ascetic practices, feed the poor and contribute profusely to charitable projects, while the *Bābā'iyya* practise anonymous giving, including regularly giving away the best of what they have (rather than what they do not want) in addition to journeying without means, and regular fasting and retreats. Many Sufi - from all Orders - also practise weekly, and periodic fasts, in addition to, or in place of, *Ramadān*.

41) *Letters of a Sufi Master*, translated by Titus Burckhardt, Perennial Books, Middlesex (undated), pp, 33-34.

42) Sometimes this is encouraged within the tradition concerned by the power derived from the respect given to such people. Witness, for example, attitudes towards Catholic nuns in Eire, Buddhist monks in Thailand, or Ayatollahs in Iran.

43) Confessing sins to someone other than God is forbidden in Sufism as in Islam (see Rūmī's, **Mathnawī** 5:3257, 3277).

44) Regarding dreams as messages from God and revealers of our true nature, see **Mathnawī** 3:1286; 4:3637 & 1:388.

45) Examining various schools of thought regarding symbols, will lead to the conclusion that no satisfactory theory for them in Western

189

psychological thought exists. This is because their transcendent nature is ignored, and there is a persistent - we might say absurd endeavour - to reduce them to semantic levels. In this connection, see Dan Sperber, *Rethinking Symbolism*, University Press, Cambridge, 1975.

46) For examples of Sufi interpretations of dreams, see Abd-al-Azīz Dabbāgh *Al-Ibrīz: Khazā'in-i-Ma'rifa*, Mehtab Publishers, Lahore (undated). For the meaning of specific symbols, see Nurbakhsh's six Volumes, in the **Bibliography**.

47) In analytical and similar interpretations, ego-enforcement goes both ways: the patient says what he is expected to say and the therapist says what the patient wants to hear.

9

TRANSCENDING RELIGION AND ITS DIVISIONS

"The religion of love is apart from all religions. The lovers of God have no religion but God alone."

Mevlana, Jalāl ad-Dīn ar-Rūmī

The Contrast between Sufi Practices and Those of Religion

It is often forgotten by researchers who attempt to see Sufism as either an outgrowth of Islam, or alternatively as an offshoot or syncretist movement derived from other religions, that from a Sufi perspective, such attempts are meaningless. We can find in Sufism, parallels with many religions, just as we can also discover elements which are distinctively Islamic. This can be understood, if it is realised that all religious systems, including Islam, are incomplete or deteriorated forms of the One Universal Religion which has many varied manifestations.[1]

For the Sufi, behind the illusory veil*(Hijāb)* which causes us to see creation in a multitude of forms, lies a central **Unity***(Tawhīd)*, for the only **Truth**, or **Reality***(al-Haqq)* is God. Whilst the Hindu will see Creation as illusory*(māyā)*, to the Sufi, it is the heart that is veiled, arising from a duality within the self*(shirk)*. The Sufi aspires to attain *baqā'* (that which remains, or subsists beyond all forms) by the process of *fanā'* (extinction, dissolution of ego, or conditioned self), just as the Hindu, seeks deliverance*(moksa)* from the cycle of life and death,

191

and the Buddhist, by attaining *nibbāna* (to be cooled, without passion or desire) – an analogous concept to *al-fanā'* – escapes *Samsāra* (cycle of rebirth). In reality, it is not the mysticism – the transcendent experience – that is different, but the context in which it finds itself. Religions as external systems are by nature diverse and conflicting. Artificial attempts to syncretise their disparities (as in Bahā'īsm, Theosophy and other similar groups), is to confuse the Unitary Basis upon which all religion has been founded, with the timebound exoteric forms that have developed from it. This, because, religions are institutions, whereas the transcendent experience is living and timeless, going beyond ANY formal system.

Those who attain perfection or completeness on the Sufi Path, neither hope for anything nor are they in fear of anything, for they are in a state of equanimity *(mawāfaqa)*. This is the same goal for the Hindu devotee, the Buddhist monk, and the Taoist sage, but is in complete contrast to the Muslim, who is instructed, like the Orthodox or Catholic Christian, to desire Paradise/Heaven and to fear Hell.[2] The route that each group takes to their respective goal is however somewhat different. The Hindu endeavours to find the **True Self** by focusing attention on the inner being. The Buddhist rejects the notion of self, believing in *anatta* (no-self), while the Muslim strictly follows an external code of law *(Sharī'ah)*, to obtain a personal *self-reward*. This is also done by the Orthodox Jew, but in the

192

latter case focus is on a group reward(Israel as a people).

In contrast to all these, the Sufi believes, as the poet Shams ad-Dīn Muhammad Hāfiz (died 1391) stated in his *Dīwān;"concentration on the self is the greatest of all veils between humanity and the Beloved,"* for:

Who will gain a reward from union with a
beautiful woman
Who is always busy playing at love with her
self-adoration.[3]

If one wishes to attain awareness of God's Presence *(Hudūr),* then it is necessary to be absent *(Ghaybah)* from everything else, including one's individuality, which does in fact exist, for though its outer and conditioned form may change, its inner essence is of God. It is in this light that the expressions of the Persian Sufi martyr, 'Ayn al-Qudāt al Hamadhānī, can be understood:

For as long as the wayfarer is *conscious of him-self* and is still some *'thing'* to himself, he will not be liberated.....On this path there is no more distressing adversity than your being, and no poison more deadly than the disciple's desires.[4]

The Sufi would agree with Buddhism that there is no self (other than God), for the notion of *an independent* self is an illusion, so that *Shaykh* Ahmad al-Alawī said:

Think it not me thou seest here clad in human qualities.[5]

For this reason, as we have seen (**chapter six**), Al-Junayd, coined the term *fanā',* derived from the **Qur'ānic** passage (55:26) referring to God's **Eternal Nature** – *"Everything* *perishes (fānin) except His Face(Self)"* - combining it with the word for the conditioned self or ego*(anā')* - whilst the *life in Him* he named *baqā'* (continuance). The meaning of these terms is not that the individual ceases to exist, but that the individual (real)ity is perfected, transmuted, and transformed by becoming eternalised in God. Being beyond form, the **Transcendent** is not a limited person, but something more than that, however, since that experience is personal, it is perceived as a personality, i.e., God. This mystical experience of Union is terminated, that the *Lover* may return to this limited world of existence. Thereafter, there is continual yearning for reunion with the **Beloved**, the return to continued existence being a source of trial*(balā')*. It is this which as we have seen (in **chapter six**) is depicted in Muhammad's Ascent to Heaven*(al-Mi'rāj)*, and return to earth, and is in some ways, reminiscent of a **Bodhisattvas'** (of Buddhism) return to wordly life in order to teach others.[6] For the Sufi, there is no self - in a permanent sense - other than the **Transcendent**, a concept to be found in the ***Qur'ān*** (24:39), where the self is:

a desert mirage that a thirsty man thinks is water, until coming to it he finds there is nothing - where he thought it was, God is....

حَتَّىٰٓ جَآءَهُۥ لَمۡ يَجِدۡهُ شَيۡـًٔا وَوَجَدَ ٱللَّهَ عِندَ

ٱلَّذِي بِقِيعَةٍ يَحۡسَبُهُ ٱلظَّمۡـَٔانُ مَآءً إِذَا

However, unlike Buddhism, suffering is not seen as unnecessary, or unsatisfactory *(dukkha)*, [7] but as having an intrinsic meaning. Rūmī states in his *Fīhi mā fīhī:*

> When everything is right the unbeliever forgets the Creator – by suffering there is a reminder... when the pain comes forgetfulness is torn away like a veil, for the sufferer acknowledges God, crying-out: *"Oh my Lord; Oh Compassionate One; Oh God!"* But after healing, then the veil of forgetfulness returns, and again he says: *"Where is God?"*...suffering has been created to overcome you, so that you may remember God... Believers, however, do not need to suffer, for when they are well they are not unaware of that suffering, but see that it is constantly present.

This does not mean that suffering is ignored, or that the element of desire that is present as an aspect of it, is not realised, for Rūmī again states:

> All pain arises from the fact that you desire something which is not attainable. When you no longer desire, the pain no longer remains.

In contrast to Indian religious thought, such desires are not considered to be the source of all suffering, nor is it believed that the individual has, through such desires, become trapped in the vicious cycle of birth and death *(Saṃsāra)*, for as Rūmī argues:

> It is ridiculous to believe that anyone would make a shackle to bind himself, for if one is seeking freedom it is ridiculous to believe that one would seek to be shackled. Therefore it follows that someone else has made this shackle. For example, if one seeks to be healthy, he would not make himself sick, for it would be ridiculous to seek

195

both health and sickness together ! [8]

In other words, desires give pain when they are not satisfied, which as the Buddha showed, they can never be,[9] for Nature is such that desires are insatiable. Desires arise because the things desired and the capacity for desire are already present; the human being does not create the desired object, nor the physical nature that desires the satisfaction of a need. These are created in order to show the futility of seeking ultimate satisfaction in anything other than the **Transcendent**, as expressed in the litany *(wird)* of a contemporary Sufi Master: [10]

> Say God suffices
> All things above all things;
> Nothing in the heavens
> Or on the earth, but God, suffices.
> Verily, He is in Himself,
> The Knower,
> The Doer,
> The Purposer,
> The Sustainer,
> The Omnipotent.

Buddhism's, Hinduism's and Jainism's failure to see that desires are not self-creations, but an inseparable part of the nature of **Reality** (i.e.,they are also needs),[11] leads to asceticism and a total disregard for physical health. This is in fact a hatred of the physical, rather than a recognition that all Life is One. Desires not only show our dependence on All, but they can lead to an attitude of thankfulness, gratitude and praise; hence the dissatisfaction that results from greed. Rūmī explains life as a seeking after origins,

196

our **Source**, of the place from which we came and to which we shall return. Our needs are questions, and whether satisfied or not, we receive an answer: all is dependent on **The One**:

> Hunger is a question from Nature: *In the house of the body why a crevice?* Give a brick, give clay – eating is the answer – *Take!* Not eating is also an answer; *There is now no need!* (death has ensued). Doctor comes to take the pulse, that's a question, and the veins pulsing an answer. To examine the urine is also a question and answer.

Rūmī explains that although God does not approve of, or create evil-*good does not exist without evil; you cannot show me good without evil* – nevertheless, the conditions in which it occurs, including its prerequisites, are created:

> this headstrong self in us, by its nature longs for evil for it runs away from good..... (he uses the illustration of the doctor). The doctor desires that people should be ill, since he desires to practise medicine and unless people are ill he cannot demonstrate his medical skill. But that does not mean that he approves of people being ill, for if that were the case he would not treat them and attend to their needs.... So it should be realised that God wills evil in one sense, but in another sense He does not will it. [8]

To desire something is not evil in itself, for not only has the capacity for desires been created, but the root of all desires is the desire to attain the Divine Presence/Realise the Ultimate Self. They are a means through which we can become aware of our utter dependence on **Reality**, and so realise the Unity of Existence*(Tawhīd)*.

For these reasons, as in Islam and Judaism, asceticism is rejected as a means of self-knowledge *in itself*. [12] While Sufis might live in seclusion, they are rarely celibate. One of the most celebrated of saints, 'Abd al-Qādir al-Jīlānī, is known to have fathered a large number of children.[13] Where celibacy has been the case, it has occurred in protest at the moral laxity of society - more specifically its political and religious leaders - than being a rejection of marriage as such.[14] The notion, often perpetuated by Muslims, that the political authorities encourage Sufism when they wish to divert the common people's interest away from thoughts of revolution, can therefore be refuted. In fact, Sufis have often been persecuted and martyred, because they have propagated and practised a worldview, that, if widely embraced, would have seriously disrupted the society in question.[15]

It is this involvement of the Sufi in the whole of life that distinguishes it from other paths of self-knowledge. Hinduism consists of two main paths: the "Path of Gnosis" *(jnāna-marga)* and the "Path of Love"*(bhakti-marga)*. Christianity is essentially a "Path of Love", i.e., following Christ's example of suffering and desiring to emulate him, whereas Sufism, whilst sometimes described as a "Path of Love", or a "Path of Gnosis", is in fact neither, for its aim is to transcend both distinctions. Hasan al-Basrī (died 110 A.H./728 C.E.), an early Islamic and prominent Sufi,[16] described it: *He that knows God, loves God.* Another Sufi

198

(unknown), and referred to by Abū Sā'īd Ahmad ibn 'Īsā'l-Kharrāz (died 899), in his *Kitāb as-Sidq*, said: *Intimacy with God is finer and sweeter than longing.*[17]

This intimacy with God creates an awareness of the **Unitary Nature of Existence**; it results in only THAT *(Huwa)* [18] being seen and known. The dual aspects of this world - perceived in night and day, life and death, etc., and constantly referred to in the *Qur'ān* [19] - are for the Sufi facets of **One Reality**. Multiplicity is possible because there is Unity *(Wahda)*, possible only because there is multiplicity *(kathra)*.[20] Those who do not know see only duality, whereas those who know - through the experience of intimacy - see only **The One**. In this sense, the nearest form of mysticism to Sufism is Jewish mysticism. In the Bible, to *know* a woman was to experience her sexually (*Bereshit* 4:1) and the symbols of *Lover* and *Beloved*, are to be found throughout the **Tanakh**. This is epitomised in the *Song of Solomon*, an anlogue of **Yahweh's** Love for His people, Israel, such spiritual experience being spoken of as a betrothal of knowledge (**Hosea** 2:19-20).[21]

This mystical sense of Union *(ittihād)* with the **Beloved** is simply a return to the original Primal State of Nature as contained within us *(fitrah)*, so it is not surprising that such concepts should be found universally. Consequently, the Sufi has no need of an intermediary for contact with **Ultimate Reality** (for the Sufi IS THAT!); whether it be a god-man, ritual object, sacred text, saint or prophet all of

199

which are examples and teachers, rather than mediators. [22]
As the *Sultan of the lovers* - 'Umar ibn al-Fārid - wrote
in his **Khamriyya** (**Wine Ode**):

> Since I was seeking myself by means of myself, I
> directed myself to myself, and my soul was shown
> the way to me by means of me.

Although this rejection of a mediator marks a distinction
from Christianity, there are still many similarities between
Christian mysticism and Sufism; this despite the fact that
Sufis do not believe in the notion of Christ as the supreme
sacrifice. [23] Christianity in its true sense(esoteric, *haqīqah*),
is mentioned in the **Qur'ān** (5:85-86) with great respect.
One of the greatest and earliest of Islamic Sufis, Ibrāhīm
ibn Adham(died 166 A.H./783C.E.) obtained his first
experience of mystical knowledge from a Christian
Anchorite monk called Simeon.[24] From a psychological and
religious developmental points of view, both understand
the necessity of sacrificing the ego. According to Sufis this
is the supreme sacrifice that all must eventually make in
order to attain union with God's Will and Purpose.

In Christian mysticism, contemplative prayer (the Sufi
would say *Dhikr*) is the means by which the aspirant frees
the self from all imagery and discursive thought (in Sufi
terminology **Hadīth al-nafs)**, a process made possible, not
by a simple discarding of forms, but rather by a reaching
out towards God in love. As in Sufism, God becomes the
sole object of attraction - the **Beloved** - loved for His own

sake and without thought of reward. Thomas Gallus, in his commentary on *De Mystica Theologia,* by the pseudo-Dionysius the Areopagite – a Christian Neoplatonist and Syrian ecclesiastic, living at the beginning of the sixth century – called this supreme mystical sense of God, *principalis affectio* and set it above the normal cognitive faculties of imagination, reason and intellect.[25] Gallus, put love, not the intellect, as the highest cognitive faculty; in agreement with Sufism, knowing and loving are aspects of one **Transcendent** capacity.[26] According to *The Cloud of Unknowing*, an early 15th century manuscript of unknown authorship, but whose influence has been central to many Christian mystics, especially the late Thomas Merton:[27]

> the plunge into the darkness of unknowing (as in contemplative prayer) is only a vivid image of the decision of faith *to love* and press towards a God whom the understanding cannot comprehend.[28]

Here as in Sufism, the contemplative's experience of Union is not to be confused with Pantheism.[29] This act of love is necessary because a clear vision of God is not possible to the mind, or accessible by reason, which again is in general agreement with Sufism. Similarly, like Sufism, in the topology of Richard of St.Victor [30] and in agreement with the major figures of the Western Mystical Tradition, "Imagination" and "Sensuality" are subsidiary faculties below the two chief powers of "Reason" and "Affection".

It is not only in the monastic tradition of Christianity that we find similarities regarding personal development as

201

are to be found in Sufism. The idea that difficulties are a way of bringing a person to God, as indicators of His interest, was also a belief of the Puritans in the latter half of the 16th century.[31]

Sufism and Islam

Similarities, as we have seen above, can be understood not by the notions of diffusion, or of syncretism, but by acknowledging, that despite external differences, there is a common core to all religions.[1] Like psychology, it is a concern with the self; in both cases with its boundaries and definitions, *but in the case of religion with its mortality.* What characterises Sufism, in contrast to external religious developmental systems, is its ability to transcend the definitions of finite self, Infinite Self.

It is this capacity that, despite having much in common with Islam, marks it out as different from that religion. Yet, by adhering to fundamental principles that lie *at the basis* of both Sufism and Islam, a common distinction is made between Sufism and Islam, and other religions. This basic similarity lies in the attitude of both towards events. There is no endeavour on the part of either to control things, to ask God/**Reality** to change what is. The idea of surrendering to God is the basis of the meaning of the word Islam(from *is-salām*, to surrender), and despite the persecution of Sufis by Muslims, this basic Islamic attitude epitomises Sufism. While the Buddhist seeks escape from

202

suffering by following the *Dhamma*, or the Christian endevours to overcome it by accepting the example of Christ, who is believed to have undergone suffering for his followers; in Sufism, there is an acceptance of **Reality** – a submission to, or Union with, its **Creative** capacity.

In submitting to that **Creative Reality**, all external limitations – including tradition, creed, national and ethnic distinctions – are abandoned; a step followed by all the Great Teachers, as in the case of Abraham, Moses, Muhammad and the Buddha, who in addition also left their homes. This, Al-Ghazālī, though called the *Proof of Islam*, was also obliged to do. Having achieved a reputation as an Islamic jurist and theologian, he turned away from formal learning and abandoned his home and post as a lecturer, to declare himself a Sufi. In his autobiography, *'Al-Munqidh min ad-Dalāl* (That which Saves from Error), he writes:

> I began learning their doctrines from books and sayings of their *Shaykhs,* until I acquired as much of their Way as is possible by learning and listening. I saw clearly that what is most unusual about them cannot be so learned, but can only be attained by direct experience, through ecstasy and inward transformation.[32]

Therefore, *in practice*, Al-Ghazālī distinguished between being a Sufi and a pious Sunni Muslim. He acknowledged, by his actions, that the first step towards Sufism is not professing Islam, but the abandonment of a worldy life in devoting oneself to God. Ironically, the Sufi by following Muhammad's command to: *"Die before you are dead..weep,*

and if you weep not, then try to weep," [33] finds himself/
herself in a position that transcends distinctions of creed,
and in opposition to the Muslim with limiting definitions
and attachment to the finite world, and for whom the Sufi
is a psychological threat. It was to this paradox, that the
afore-mentioned Al-Hamadhānī (died 1131) - who was
roughly contemporary with Al-Ghazālī (died 1111) [34] -
addressed himself. Writing concerning his own mystical
experience of death, he tells us that what distinguishes the
followers*(muqtasedon)*,[35] from those who have attained *the
Realm of Annihilation (fanā' fi't-tawhīd, fi'l-Haqq*,[36] i.e.,
the pious Muslim from the realised Sufi) is the latter's own
experience of mystical death and resurrection:

> The experience of this mystical state, enables the
> traveller(on the Path of self-annihilation)to realise
> the significance of *"Every soul will have a taste of
> death"* [37] and the meaning of death on the mystical
> Path. Then it is that the truth of *"all that is upon
> the earth will perish"* [38] is revealed to him, and he
> passes beyond when *"the earth will be changed to
> another earth"* [39] and reaches the realm of
> annihilation...It is at this point that the reality of
> the Resurrection is shown to him...for all the
> worlds lie within the human heart...for the lover's
> religion is the Love of God, his Paradise nearness,
> and Hell-fire farness from the Beloved...

Speaking to the externalist Muslim, he says:

> I know these words do not come from your world
> of religious convention, which is but the worship
> of hollow rituals and the adoration of tradition.
> Until you abandon spiritual conventionalism(all but
> God) you can never minister to the Real Truth.[40]

According to Al-Hamadhānī, all the grave's torments as described in the *Qur'ān* are a result of humanity's general condition and can be found in this present life. Torments of the after-life, as experienced by those who have not attained *fanā'* (annihilation) and *baqā'* (resurrection), are the result of being subject to the passions and lusts of the body, which is itself a tomb:

> Don't you realise that death (in the usual sense) is not real death. True death is annihilation *(fanā')*. Whoever does not realise *this death* has no life. Do you understand what I say? I say that as long as you are *'you'* and attached to your (limited) self, you do not really exist. When you cease to be *'you'* and (truly) become yourself....According to us, death is to die to everything except the **Beloved**, so that life can be found in and through the **Beloved**. When this is realised within yourself, then you will realise death (what it really is).[41]

This understanding of mystical death and resurrection takes Sufism beyond the bounds of Islam, for, once the limited self has been transcended, so have the limitations of creed; externals has become subsumed within the reality of a living faith. Although Islam stresses God's Oneness, proclaiming that God begets nothing, it does not make this connection, for it cannot make the connection without the experience, an experience that is based upon the *received* perception, that God is both **Immanent** and **Transcendent**. Though Sufi Al-Hallāj, was cruelly executed for claiming he was *al-Haqq* (**Truth/Reality** – by *implication* God) it was not Al-Hallāj, but his executors who were guilty of *hulūl* (localising God).[42] Since God is the only **Reality**, there can be nothing other than God. Put in another way, we can say that since God is by definition **The Infinite**, if there is anything else other than God, then that thing must either be **Infinite**, in which case it *is God* and there cannot be a separation, or it must be in addition to God, and therefore no longer **Infinite** and consequently not God. Al-Hallāj himself, explained it thus:

> It is You who has filled all *'where'* as well as beyond *'where'* too. Where are You then? (*Dīwān* 1:4)

Whilst all religions have as their aim the overcoming of problems associated with the human condition, including and especially that of death, Sufism attacks the problem head-on, so to speak, *by seeing that Reality* ! It does not ignore the limitations of the cultural frame, individual, or physical experience, or even of thought itself; but acknowledges - as do tribal peoples - that the individual reality is subsumed within a **Greater Reality**.[43] For this reason Sufism transcends all religious systems.

The Orphics, Pythagoreans and Buddhists, all believed in a Circle of Existence. Though each developed this notion in their own way, all believed in the eventual liberation of souls/self. Sufism, like Islam, believes that the ultimate destiny of Creation is for it to rejoin its **Source** (*Qur'ān* 96:8; 53:42; 42:53), just as the Pythagoreans believed that at the end of the *Great Year,* all will be restored to primal purity in the *Golden Age.* However this is interpreted, the

206

final destination of all creatures is their **realisation of Divinity**; for the Sufi, it is the consciousness of this eventual return *in the here and now*, that marks it out as the primal experience !

Baruch(Benedictus) **Spinoza**(1632–77), a Jewish mystic and philosopher, who for expounding a system with similarities to Sufism, was excommunicated by his fellow Jews and ostracised by his Christian associates. Yet after his death, his major work *Ethics*, influenced both these traditions.

Notes and References

1) Nicholson writes: "Since mysticism in all ages and countries is fundamentally the same, however it may be modified by its peculiar environment and by the positive religion to which it clings for support, we find remote and unrelated systems showing an extraordinary close likeness and even coinciding in many features of verbal expression... Many writers on Sufism have disregarded this principle; hence the confusion which has long prevailed" (in Lings, 1971, p, 121). The *Qur'ān* (4:150-152; 6:159) sees this as the result of a common Origin.

2) *Islam the Religion of Truth*, by Prof Abdul Rahman Ben Hammad Al Omar, issued by The Supreme Head-Office for Religious Guidance, Saudi Arabia, p, 59, states:
"A Muslim...will attain eternal bliss and happiness in the Hereafter. This is a call to every wise person who wants to deliver himself from the torment of Hell-Fire in the Hereafter, as well as the torment of the grave after death. Dear Reader, hurry up to rescue yourself and gain salvation."

3) No 487, in a version by Paul Smith, *Hafiz: Tongue of the Hidden*, New Humanity Books, Melbourne, 1988, p, 81.

4) *Tamhīdāt* (pp 49-50 in the 1962 Edition).

5) Martin Lings *A Sufi Saint of the Twentieth Century: Shaikh Ahmad al-Alawī his spiritual heritage and legacy*, George Allen & Unwin, London, 1971, p, 169.

6) *Buddhist Scriptures*, translated E. Conze, Penguin, 1959, pp, 30-33.

7) Why we find Al-Hallāj, and Al-Hamadhānī, accepting martyrdom.

8) *Fīhi mā fīhī*, Tehran & Azamgarh 1928, pp, 139,143,159,187&223.

9) The Buddhist has ignored the real essence of their Master's teaching.

10) *Bābā* Dovid Yūsuf, *Leaves from the Tree of Life: Sayings, Meditations & Prayers for a New Age* edited by D.Heinemann, Rainbow Trust Publications, Northampton, 1995, p, 70.

11) Even wants are based on indirect, or misunderstood needs.

12) *Qur'ān* 57:27, and Rūmī, *Mathnawī* 5:574.

13) Al-Jīlānī, born at Nif, South of the Caspian Sea, was known as the *Rose of Baghdad* (spending most of his life and being buried in that place) because of his development of Sufi exercises (see **Glossary** under **Wird**). His terminology was to find its way into the later European Rosicrucian Order. Estimates vary as to the number of his children, but according to *Shaykh* Nāzim al-Qubrusī (himself an initiate of the *Qādiriyya)*, were over a hundred.

14) See 'Abd al-Atī' Hammūdah's *The Family Structure in Islam*, American Trust Publications, 1977, for further details.

15) Political authorities tolerated, even encouraged, Sufis who seemed harmless, or pacifistic; whilst in the case of Sufis who actively and publicly, denounced moral laxity and injustice, they took action.

16) Most of the Sufi initiatic chains *(silsilahs)* pass through him; see J. Spencer Trimingham, *The Sufi Orders in Islam*, Clarendon Press, Oxford, 1971, especially, pp, 261-262.

17) Arberry's translation, *The Book of Truthfulness*, Oxford University Press, London, 1937, p, 46.

18) A word often invoked by Sufis, it refers to what is beyond being *(Hāhūt)*, equivalent to *the One who is One* of Plato's *Parmenides* and the Biblical description of God by himself to Moses (**Genesis** 3:14) as *I AM That I AM*. The Sufi say: *"la ana wa lā anta Huwā"*; neither *I nor you* but THAT ! (see note 33 in **chapter four**).

19) e.g.,*Qur'ān* 6:1; 3:156; 25:47,62; 27:12; 36:36-37; 89:1-5, etc.

20) *"Kathra fi'l-wahda wa wahada fi 'l-kathra"* (Multiplicity in unity and unity in multiplicity). The final stage of the perfected soul, as depicted in the Qādirī, Sufi manual: *Al-Fuyūdāt ar-Rabbāniyya*, by Muhammad Sä'īd ibn Ismā'īl, Cairo 1353 A.H., pp, 34 & 163.

21) Commemoration of Rūmī's death is *"Sheb-al-arus"* (The Wedding Night) and his tomb his marriage bed. Jewish and Muslim Sufis in Turkey, have mutually influenced each others concepts and music.

22) See note 15 in **chapter three**.

23) That Jesus died on the cross as a sacrifice for Adam's sin. is an idea that Sufis find repugnant and unhistorical. While Muslims have conjectured about the event, even to the extent of suggesting that someone else died in Jesus's place, to the Sufi, the passage in the *Qur'ān* (4:157) which states that he did not die, must be understood in the light of other passages (2:154; 3:169). These indicate that whilst the martyr seems to die, his eternal reality does not. According to Sufis, Christ (not Jesus) is alive in a principal state (4:158). In this sense we can understand Mansūr al-Hallāj(died 922) making similar remarks to Jesus at his death; or of *Shaykh* Ahmad al-Alawī(died 1353/1934) identifying with the Christ spirit (see Lings 1971, in **Bibliography**).

24) C. Glassé, *The Concise Encyclopaedia of Islam*, Stacey International, London, 1989, p,178, also Arberry 1950, p,37.

25) The Oxford manuscript, MS:69,f.131b, states the following: "Putauit summam vim cognitiuam esse intellectum cum sit alia que non minus excedit intellectum quam intellectus racionem vel racio ymaginacionem, scilicet *principalis affecio*. Et ipsa est scintilla sinderisis que sola uniblis est spiritui diuino."

26) However, as we saw in previous chapters, **The Intellect** *(Knowing)* - of Divine origin in Sufism - is used more in the sense of recollection than logical analysis, being distinguished from the rational faculty. Consequently, knowledge in Sufism is not a blind leap of faith as is the case here.

27) See the numerous references to it in his *Contemplative Prayer*, Darton, Longman & Todd, London, 1973.

28) Cloud 21:14-15, in *The Cloud of Unknowing and the Book of Privy Counselling*, editor Phyllis Hodgson, Oxford University Press, Early English Texts Society, London, 1944, p, LXIX.

29) See above, p, LVI.

30) Richard of St Victor, *Benjamin Major and Benjamin Minor*, Paris MS: P.L., t.cxcvi; Benjamin Minor Cap iii(col. 3) - Cap v(col.4-5): "The two chief powers of the soul are Reason and Affection."

Imagination and Sensuality are described as:
"disobedient servants, who minister to disordered and fantastic images and evil feelings"...

31) Downame. J, (1612) *The Christian Warfare*, 3rd Edition, pp, 204-205, in Thomas. K, *Religion and the Decline of Magic*, Peregrine, Harmondsworth, 1978, p, 95.

32) Damascus Edition, 1358/1939, pp, 124-125.

33) This is a saying of Muhammad, as conveyed by the Sufi (*tawatur hadīth*); see *Mathnawī* 6:742.

34) Despite the outward differences between the conformity, *Sharī'ah* stressing Al-Ghazālī, and the ecstatic heretical pronouncements of Al-Hamadhānī, there is an actual link between them. Al-Hamadhānī and Al-Ghazālī's brother Ahmad (died 1126) – who despite being younger, greatly influenced the former – shared a common teacher – *Shaykh* Abū Bakr an-Nassaj (died 1094). Al-Hamadhānī, through Nassaj's disciple, Abū'l-Husain al-Bustī.

35) Al-Hamadhānī (*Tamhīdāt* 1962 edition) bases this distinction on a *Qur'ānic* passage (35:32) in which the *muqtasedon* – *those who follow a middle path* – are distinguished from those who are exemplary or lead*(muqtadā)* and *are foremost in good deeds*. He understands the term *muqtasedon* as *lukewarm* (p,48), which while it conveys the sense of the *Qur'ānic* passage, is not strictly accurate, but probably used in order to contrast with those whose *hearts have been overwhelmed* by the *Fire which God kindled* within them (*Qur'ān* 104:6-7). It is important to realise that Al-Hamadhānī includes within the *lukewarm*, not simply the half-hearted, but also pious Muslims, and many considered as Sufis (pp, 41-42). This passage referring to the *Fire of God* in the *Qur'ān* (104:6), is interpreted by Muslims as a punishment; i.e., Hell-fire!

36) *Dying to self, in union with the Unity, by realising the Real.*

37) *Qur'ān* 29:57; 21:35; 3:185.

38) *Qur'ān* 55:26.

39) *Qur'ān* 14:48.

40) *Tamhīdāt* 1962, pp, 51,291-292 (in brackets mine).

41) *Tamhīdāt* 1962, pp, 287-289 (italics and in brackets mine).

42) For the Sufi an impossibility, consequently *hulūl* has a different meaning for the Sufi(see **Glossary**) than for the Muslim, who interprets it in the sense of an incarnation. Therefore, Rūmī commends Hallāj *(Mathnawī* 2:1346*)*.

43) For example, the Australian Aboriginal believes in what we shall here call, "real-time" (what we perceive and measure) and what they call the *Dream-time*; the ongoing background to all experience, which is at one and the same time cyclical and perpetual, a timeless state that exists both before origins and after physical death, and which can be entered into in the NOW by means of ritual (see James Cowan's, *Letters from a Wild State: An Aboriginal Perspective*, Element Books, Shaftesbury, 1991, pp, 91-95).

10

PSEUDO-SUFISM AND ISLAMIC CULTS

*"We quaffed upon the Remembrance of the Beloved
a wine wherewith we were drunk,
before ever the vine was created"*

'Umar Ibn al Fārid.[1]

The Institutionalisation of Sufism

Now that we have seen how Sufism differs from religious
systems, how its central component and basis of approach
to the mystical experience, lies in its concept of the self –
a concept in its realisation that creates a *Sūfī*, as distinct
from a Muslim, Christian, Jew, Buddhist, etc.,[2] – we need
to see how this in turn distinguishes genuine Sufism from
pseudo-Sufism and Islamic cults, which it is sometimes
mistakenly associated with, for, even in the time of 'Ayn
al-Qudāt al-Hamadhānī, such a division existed. This is
even more important today, because syncretist groups and
Islamic sects are proliferating, including some bearing the
name of Sufi. In the Islamic world, this is to a large extent
due to the resurgence of traditional Islam. *Wahhābī'ism*
throughout the *Sunnī* world and the *Shī'ah* revival in Iran
have both – though in different ways – contributed to the
demise of genuine Sufism. By stressing externalism and
negating the mystic experience, groundwork was laid for
secularism in both cases. Elsewhere, Protestantism has
helped create a materialist philosophy. This result, is an

211

example of what happens when a vibrant living experience is reduced to a dead worship of form and the past.

We are not concerned here, with Sufism's social-psychological, or anthropological role,[3] but with how it operates at the individual spiritual/psychological level. To do this, it is necessary to isolate what we shall here call *real-Sufism,* from pseudo-Sufism, which, though it may cater for certain social and psychological needs, should not be confused with it. The confusing of cult groups with Sufi one's leads to erroneous conclusions, especially to that of seeing the Sufi as a product of Islam.

Sufism is a path of contemplative mysticism based upon transcendent experience, rather than a philosophical system – though it has developed such a system – therefore, it has no need for the usual trappings associated with religion. The first Sufis were not concerned with theorising, but with *experiencing,* which is why there are very few writings that can be definitely attributed to them. Much of what we know is derivative, having been written by later figures during the period when Sufism had developed a philosophical system. The early Masters were Guides, who showed, exemplified and encouraged, those who sought them out, in the "Way of purification"*(Tarīq al-mujāhada),* in which there is a divesting of worldly attachments*(tajrīd).*[4] The development of Orders*(turuq),* and later of organisational associations*(tawā'if)* embodying methods employed by the original Master, were for the

212

purpose of disseminating their *particular* way amongst the people. However, this created difficulties, for attachment to externals, necessarily discourages interiorisation.[5]

To begin with, most Masters were migrants *(dār'wīsh)*, who formed around themselves groups of like-minded individuals. The bonds to the Master were highly personal and any associations formed, broke up after death. There is little evidence that any of these early Masters set up Orders, though clearly their methods and teachings were passed on.[6] When these associations began (as a practical expression of their mystic experience) to care for the sick, accommodate travellers and the unfortunate,[7] the nature of such groups also changed. This was assisted by disciples staying in the vicinity of their deceased Master's tomb, giving rise to the idea that the inherent virtue and holiness of such a person*(bāraka)*, could be transmitted even after death. It was but a short step from there, to seeing such virtue as a magical power*(bāraka)* that could be passed on (hereditarily, or otherwise), and people were not slow to utilise this notion to their personal advantage.[8]

Since becoming a Sufi is the result of an intimate personal Transcendent experience, such notions, however they might be disguised,[9] should not be confused with it. The difficulty of discovering the meaning of the word *Sūfī* arises from this – the fact that such groups were not formally constituted organisations as such – and from the earliest times, the origin of the word has been disputed.[10]

213

The first historical mention of it as a word referring to an organised body is to a loosely constituted group in Alexandria in 200 A.H.[11] that went by the name of *as-Sūfiyya'*.[12] A term that by its etymology is more likely to have reference to charity recipients than to mystics.[13]

The disparate nature of Sufis (that has led to them being confused with cult groups) is reflected in the various terms they have used to describe themselves. As we discovered, seeing the name *Sūfī* as an actual name (rather than as an allegorical reference to a mystic experience) is untenable.[14] One of the earliest of terms was the"Friends" derived from the *Qur'ān* (10:62-63). Later references used were: the **"Pure Ones"** *(safwa);* the **"Brethren"** *(ikhwān);* [15] the **"Renouncers"** *(zuhhād);* the **"Folk, or mystic people"** *(qawm);* the **"Companions"** *(suhba);* the **"People"** *(ashāb);* the **"Fraternity"** *(akhawiyya);* the **"Gnostics"** *('irfān);* the **"Travellers"** *(darāwīsh);* the **"Poor Ones"** *(fuqarā');* the **"Masters"** *(Khawājagān);* the **"Accused"** *(malāmati);* the **"Disregarders"** *(qalandarī);* and the **"Elect or Chosen Ones"** *(as-Sūfiyya),* etc. [16]

Al-Hamadhānī, writing in prison before his martyrdom, argued that it was this failure to understand precisely what a Sufi is, that had condemned him. It cannot be disputed about in terms of theological differences, he stated, because it has its own terminology based on experience, [17] and it is this experience - not philosophical similarities - that constitutes one being a Sufi.[18]

The Sufis have their own exclusive terms whose meanings they alone know. I mean by Sufis those persons who have directed their aspirations wholly towards God and are dedicated to following the Way to him.[19]

Sufism (a modern word used in an attempt to categorise), is a way of devotion*(mahabba)*, in which God becomes the **Beloved***(Mahbūb)*. Though this path produces knowledge*(ma'rifa)*, it does so *only as the result of experience* and not by other means. Ibn 'Arabī explained the difference, arguing that Sufi knowledge was beyond formal theology or philosophical speculation:

God is known only by means of God...a scholastic theologian says:*"I know God by that which He created"*, and takes as his guide something that has no real relation to the object sought. He who knows God by means of phenomena, (as opposed to the Noumenal experience) knows as much as these phenomena give to him and no more. [20]

This intense and highly personal experience cannot be institutionalised, for it is a *gift from God,*[21] that no amount of scholastic or theological learning can obtain.[22] For this reason, we find no definite evidence of organised *tarīqa*, nor recorded *silsila*, before about 500 years after Muhammad's death.[23] A full consideration of the history of (what is now called) Sufism, is beyond the bounds of this book, sufficient has been shown to demonstrate that formal organisation is not its basis, and that where there is an emphasis on this, deterioration has occurred.

This deterioration changed Sufism's outward nature. The

establishment of *Tawā'if*, in order to protect Muhammad's *method*, in the turbulent times during which such Orders multiplied, also provided the means for the charlatan to obtain power.[24] Sufis have been at their strongest during times of cultural interaction (Mongol invasion, Crusades, Colonialism) and it was then that the major Orders were established. Muhammad's internationalism (his intimate companions included an Abyssinian, a Persian, and several Jewish followers) and the "eternal" mystic experience, provided a means of relief at such times, as well as the conditions for the proliferation of charlatans. As the notion of inherent holiness and virtue *(bāraka)* came to be seen as a power, transmitted by touch, spittle or the breath, [25] so were superstitious concepts accommodated, such as astrology, divination, magic bracelets, talisman and the use of words from the *Qur'ān* in magical healing formulae – many of which are used by pseudo-Sufis today.

With institutionalisation, there was a movement away from experience to an increasing emphasis on intellectual knowledge, all of which made it easier for the pseudo-Sufi (characterised by an emphasis on externals) to proliferate. Submission to God, was replaced by subjection to the *Shaykh/Pīr/Dede*,[26] and cults of saint veneration and tomb worship began to develop alongside it. The narrative of Abū 'Abd Allāh Muhammad ibn Battūta (died 1378), shows clearly that tomb veneration and the concept of *bāraka* as a magical power associated with it, was not confined to so-

216

called Sufis, or even Muslims, but was an ethnic practice pre-dating Islam.[27]

In addition, other practices crept, in as with the spread of the Islamic Empire, contact was made with Indian and South East Asian cultures. Pseudo-Sufis adopted some of the extreme ascetic tendencies of the Yogis, including in some cases an imposed celibacy and vegetarianism; both of which are matters of choice and personal development, rather than being essential ingredients of the Sufi Path.[28]

While all this was going on, a further deterioration occurred in the opposite direction, other Sufis not wishing to be seen as members of syncretist cults, stressed their allegiance to legalistic Islam and conformity to *Sharī'ah*. The result was, that where before a characteristic of the *'Arīf* had been a living and creative spirit transcending externalism,[30] innovation *(bid'a)* was now seen as blameworthy. The full, inner, holistic interpretation of the teachings of Muhammad and the *Qur'ān (istinbāt)*, were stifled – to be kept secret for all but the initiated. What had been deep interior knowledge *(bātin)* – only accessible through interiorisation (the Sufi method) – now became secret mystical doctrine *(bātinī)*; from a literalist Muslim's point of view a cause for reproach; from that of the power seeking pseudo-Sufi, a jealously guarded secret. Pseudo-Sufism grew as the power of its proponents grew. Where in the beginning (still true of the genuine Masters of our time) a *Shaykh* was essentially a Guide in spiritual matters

217

- and as a Teacher, the only form of institution that existed - now large monastic-type establishments began to appear. A hierarchy developed in which the *Shaykh* was the attraction, replacing absorption*(istighrāq)* in God. Attraction to God *(jadhb)* was supplanted with physically-induced ecstatic states that maintained a fascination for the Master. Personality cults had replaced devotion to God. [30]

Islamic Cults and Magic

The desire to obtain power that characterises cult-groups is true of all magical systems and is contrary to Sufi teaching, where the opposite is desired*(nafī)*. Interestingly, there are more parallels between religions (including Islam) and magic, than there are between the latter and the Sufi Path;[31] where there is an acceptance of the uncontrollable elements of existence, such as sickness and death, which are seen, not as evils to be controlled or avoided at all all costs, but rather as reminders of God. Consider, for example, *Shaykh* Sidi Muhammad al-Būzīdī (died 1909), who, awaking one night and finding that one of his legs and arms were paralysed, touched his arm with the hand that could move. Believing that the immobilised limbs were a snake in the bed, he called for a light. When his mistake was discovered, instead of bewailing his plight, he said:

> *Glory be to God! This is an example of the illusion that befalleth the seeker ere he hath attained unto Gnosis* (By this he meant the error of believing that there is anything other than God). [32]

218

This lack of fear and natural humility (he was in reality a Guide and not a seeker) is to be contrasted to the pseudo-Sufi *Shaykh,* or cult leader, who encourages obeisance for its own sake. The Sufi aims to achieve detachment*(tajrīd)* from a concern with earthly things, and to identify with the **Supreme Will***(ikhtiyār)*, to the extent that the ego or conditioned self, loses its power*(fana')=* selflessness. This in stark contrast to the magician, cult leader, or pseudo-Sufi, who desires power.

For this reason, the outward similarity between *Dhikr* and the magician's use of 'words of power' is misleading. While pseudo-Sufis, in common with Muslims in general, use Names of God, or texts from the *Qur'ān* in this way, believing in the efficacy of words being pronounced in a specific way, this is not true of the Sufi. One of the characteristics of a genuine Master is a living and creative spirit that will generally have produced by inspiration *(ilhām)*, litanies *(wird)*, consisting of prayers and the like, often in the vernacular. Some Sufis have even performed *Dhikr* - including the *Qur'ānic* Arabic, Names of God - entirely in their own language,[33] in contrast to Muslims, who magically insist on using Arabic in every ritual situation.[34] *Dhikr* and the use of *Qur'ānic* passages are for the Sufi a reminder or remembrance*(dhikr)* of the One Eternal message of Unity, rather than being a means for gaining power, or asserting superiority over others. This is why the so-called *Whirling Dervishes* (**Mawlawiyya**), can

219

perform in public, believing that observers cannot be affected by actions or words not understood.[35] This is not like the magician, cult leader, or pseudo-Sufi, who believes in the power to control events, phenomena, or people, by actions or words, regardless of whether or not they are understood. The use of *Dhikr* as a form of *remembrance* (by its definition this implies understanding) characterises genuine Sufism, marking it out as different from pseudo-Sufism and Muslims in general, who believe in the power of the words, i.e., the Arabic and the way it is recited – rather than its meaning.[36] Significantly, this magical belief is what separated the *Qur'ān* – literally 'Recitation'- (of the One Eternal Message), spoken by Muhammad to the Arabian people; from the rhythmic chants(*saj'*) of the *kāhin*(soothsayer/diviner)[37] of pre-Islamic Arabia.

In the Biblical interpretation of magic, that has come down to us via the conclusions of Rabbi Akiba ben Joseph (died c135 C.E.), it is linked with divination[38] and astrology.[39] Since the Sufi believe that it is impossible to change **Reality**, such practices are not genuine Sufism, but can be attributed to its deterioration.

The charismatic influences(*karāmāt*) of Sufi saints are a result of their inherent virtue(*bāraka*) or spiritual radiance arising from their inner state(*tūbā*), and is distinguishable from the activities of magicians(*kāhin*), cult leaders, or pseudo-Sufis, who are believed to be deceivers by the *'Arifīn*. This is in contrast to general Muslims, or certain

220

classes of pseudo-Sufis*(muqtasedon)* – who, along with folk cults, that have often wrongly been labelled Sufi – may not only practise magic, but also believe in its efficacy. That there is a difference between genuine Sufism and folk cults that go by this name can be seen in the life of a *Sufi saint of the twentieth century,* Abū'l-'Abbās Ahmad ibn Mustafā al-'Alawī(died 1934). Having belonged to such a cult*(Īsāwīyya),* from whom he learnt the ability to perform conjuring tricks such as fire-eating and snake-handling, he renounced such activities, ultimately becoming a genuine Sufi Master in his own right.[40]

Pseudo-Sufism and Healing Cults

Orientalists, as well as anthropologists, have often mistakenly identified Sufis with syncretism. Ethnographers have equated them with the mystery cults of the Graeco-Roman world, or claimed that various folk, or healing cults, with tenuous links to Sufis, are representative of them generally.[41] In all these cases, it has been assumed that Sufi origins are quivalent to its later varied, and often aberrant manifestations. While it is undoubtedly correct, that cultural confusion and other anxieties surrounded the formation of Sufism in its organisational stages, it did not create the same response as in syncretism. In both cases there is regression, as is characteristic of anxiety, but instead of an escape into fantasy (a possible but not a necessary response) there is a reassertion of former values

221

in a new and transcendent form. This can be defined as **Reintegration**.

Examination will show there are three possible responses to socially engendered anxiety:

1)**Escapism**: mystery cults/syncretism=*pseudo-Sufism and Islamic folk cults.*

2)**Reactionism**:hostility/dogmatism/fanaticism=*Wahhābī'ism the Iranian revolution and muqtasedon-Sufis.*

3)**Reintegration**: reassertion of former values in a new and transcendent form= *Sufism in the real sense.*

The outward similarity between Sufis and Sufi-derived folk, or healing cults, arises from the fact that both occur in their most prolific stage, during times of cultural confusion. They involve a process of regression, in which former elements and/or previous archaic manifestations connected with our primal nature*(fitrah)*, reappear, or are duplicated in a deteriorated form. In a sense, folk cults – like Shamanism and Sufism – are endeavours to replicate what once occurred in a natural and spontaneous way. All are based upon a belief (conscious, or implied) in an original archaic primal state of integration*(Tawhīd)*, that can be either regained or accessed,[42] whether that state/place/time be defined as the "Dream-time", the "Garden of Eden", "Paradise", "Heaven", the "N.D.E." (Near Death Experience of surgically revived patients), or the "Golden Age" of the Greeks.

The Sufi aims to re-establish that primal state, or more

222

correctly to recollect, or remember*(dhikra)* it. Practices, like archaic rituals, are a means for experiencing the out of time experience. Or more exactly, they are a re-enactment - by acknowledgement - of previous states, that are present internally; such as, for example, the Sufi use/concept/realisation of worship/prayer(*salāh*), when it is believed that the Sufi participates in the prayer of all Masters, including one's own (even when the Master is not present) if it is performed in the prescribed manner.

However, like Shamanism, which Eliade has described as a *deteriorated* archaic technique of ecstasy,[43] Sufi-derived folk cults - to use my own definition - *represent the ability to utilise certain gains, obtained while pursuing the path of self-effacement, at the expense of reaching its goal.* Healing, discharge of emotional tension*(catharsis)*, resolving of traumas, the ability to defy pain and heat, all these are side-effects or natural developments, arising from using Sufi techniques, while ignoring its ultimate goal.

It should be mentioned at this point, that it is in the intermediate states*(ahwāl)* - that is, during ecstasy*(wajd)* and *before* reaching absorption in God*(jadhb)* - that participants involved in Sufi practices are liable to become distracted[44] and engage in aberrant practices, such as head-slashing, making animal sounds and the like, as well as being oblivious to pain, or overcoming physical, and/or mental disorders. There can also be manifestations of -to

223

use the Western term – psychic phenomena,[45] in addition to a general discharge of nervous tension; characteristics of Shamanism, as well as of Sufi-derived folk, or healing cults.[46] Numerous Western scholars have made erroneous conclusions about Sufism, through confusing it with such groups, including Shamanism,[47] because it has not been realised[48] that genuine Sufism – in contradistinction to pseudo-Sufism and other mystic systems – does not seek ecstasy as an end in itself. This point, discussed even in ancient times,[49] was formulated best by Abū'l-Qāsim ibn Muhammad al-Junayd(died 910) who said, *when Truth comes, ecstasy itself is dispossessed.*

Although mystic mythologies are used in Sufi practice, they are not deliberately abstruse. Their purpose is to break through mundane conceptions and evaluations, in order to destroy mechanical thought patterns (in religious language, idols). They are mystical in the sense that modern scientific theories relating to the New Physics are, that is to say, they are only capable of being formulated in symbolic terms. Similar to parapsychological concepts, it is not possible to understand them by conventional modes of thought, analysis or investigation; and what might be mysterious to the uninitiated becomes explicable to the initiated. This explanation is in fact not mine, but draws upon that of Ibn 'Arabī (though he does not of course mention the New Physics), who in turn was drawing on the writings and inspiration of Abū 'Īsā Muhammad al-*Hakīm*

224

at-Tirmidhi (died 892), who as a collector of the sayings of Muhammad, drew his concepts from that source.[50]

The difference between groups promoting ecstasy and abilities that derive from it to Sufism, is that the Sufi does not stress such activities, as the aim or purpose, but discourages them. In contrast to these systems, the Sufi encourages self-effacement, rather than activities which promote the limited self or ego. Cults quite often provide alternative sources of status for their members, reinforced by the humiliation these members encounter (and therefore encourage) outside the group, whereas the Sufi endeavours to avoid producing attention to self.

An additional important factor that must be considered when comparing such cults with genuine Sufism, is that the procedures used by these cults do not promote understanding (in the broadest sense of the term). No attempt is made to gain insight into problems. As is the case with problems in preliterate societies, the patient is provided with an explanation for the condition, which if accepted, will amount to the solution. In other words problems, difficulties, even physical cures, are a question of belief, and techniques used are designed to heighten suggestibility.

The difference between this and Sufism is that the Sufi is encouraged to understand self. Sufism is a path of self-negation through self-awareness. The Sufi is encouraged to accept responsibility for actions and to perceive their

225

relationship to other facets of life. It is this continual and consistent knowledge of the interdependent network of events, and consciousness of them, that characterises the Sufi more than anything else. Where the Christian might talk of *chance* or *accident;* the Hindu of *fate* or *karma;* and the Muslim of *Shaytān* (meaning the Devil) – the Sufi sees all as part of **One** *interdependent* **Reality**.

For this reason, Sufism, unlike Shamanism and folk, or healing cults, does not countenance the idea of ill-health arising from possession by an evil spirit. In Sufism, evil rather than being seen as a distinct power in itself, is thought of as being the result of ignorance. Since the Sufi considers that there is only **One Reality** (God in colloquial terms), sorrow and pain have their roots in the idea of the self as a distinct entity. An independent self is an illusion, therefore, possession is not possible.

Furthermore, healing in Sufism does not necessarily mean cure. We have the account of Muhammad's servant Bilāl, who, when dying prayed to God, whereupon Muhammad, answering God's call, sought him out. It was sufficient for Bilāl to see the Prophet before expiring. This was for him an act of mercy and his healing. We should note that Muhammad did not in any way attempt to cure him.[51] Therefore, healing in this instance was not equated with cure. The Sufi approach to illness is not to blame someone else, but rather to accept one's own responsibilty within a framework in which the **Interdependent Reality**

226

(God) is the real and final Decider. We have the example of the Sufi saint, Rābi'ah al-'Adawiyya, who, once when she was ill, said to a visitor who asked her what the cause of her sickness might be:

> By God, I know of no cause for my illness except that Paradise was displayed to me, and I yearned after it in my heart; and I think that my Lord was jealous for me, and so reproached me; for only He can make me happy.[52]

Sufism and Medicine

Rather than engaging in superstitious practices, the Sufi have often been involved in medicine – either as physicians or scientists, – and their influence has been enormous. A complete list of such figures is beyond the bounds of this book, but includes the following figures: 'Alī ibn Sahl Rabban at-Tabarī (died 861), Ya'qūb ibn Ishāq al-Kindī (died 873), Abū Zayd Hunayn ibn Ishāq al-'Ibādī (died 873), Abū Bakr Muhammad ibn Zakariyyā ar-Rāzī (died 925), 'Alī ibn 'Abbās al-Majūsī (died 994), and his contemporary, Ahmad ibn Muhammad at-Tabarī, and Abū'l-Walīd Muhammad ibn Ahmad ibn Muhammad ibn Rushd.[53] In addition, they have often been apothecaries, like the Sufi, Farīd ad-Dīn 'Attār (died 1229), or medical herbalists, such as Muhammad ibn Muhammad ibn Ahmad ibn 'Abd Allāh Radī ad-Dīn al-Ghazzī ad-Dināshqī al-'Amīrī al-Qurashī ash-Shāfi'ī (1457-1529 C.E.).[54]

This latter figure took a truly holistic approach, linking

227

medicine with agriculture and religion, claiming that the Sufi line of medical herbalists could be traced back through:

> Daniel, Hermes Trismegistos, Suqrit (Socrates)....
> Hiyusad of Babylon..al–Hākim(Plato?)..Hippocrates,
> Balinus(Appolonius), Ga en and Paulus of Aeginata
> (a 7th century physician).[55]

This holistic stance was also demonstrated in his own life by knowledge of agriculture, astronomy, logic, calligraphy, Islamic jurisprudence, chemistry, history, and various other fields apart from medicine, an attitude typical of the Sufi, who even if not of academic bent, will necessarily be open to all knowledge rather than being superstitious, or reductionist. The Sufi says, as did Muhammad, in a well known saying of his to be found in all compilations: *"Seek for knowledge even if you must go to China."*

One further aspect that must be considered when comparing Sufism with Shamanism and healing cults, is the prevalence of sexuality in the latter. Eliade has listed the sexual elements of the healing practitioner in his book on Shamanism.[56] That this is a characteristic of healing cults, who may utilise sexual energies,[57] is illustrated in the case of India, and European witchcraft.[58] However, despite the links between Sufism and both these traditions [59] – either as a genuine original link, or as a result of deterioration of some forms of Sufism – this cannot be claimed for the real Sufi, who neither encourages sexual licence, or sexual asceticism. There is little in Sufism that is suggestive of

228

sex, except the deliberate use of metaphors like "Beloved" as a term for God. This, as we have seen, is of conscious and deliberate use, having the meaning that all pleasure is a search for God, and, therefore, unsatisfactory until S/He is found. Hardly conducive to sexual repression or sexual licence.

Distinguishing Genuine Sufism from Pseudo-Sufism

Sufism has often been confused with cults because it has not been realised that the Sufi Teacher, as Ibn 'Arabī, explained:

> must act and speak in a manner which takes into consideration the understanding, limitations and dominant concealed prejudices of his audience.[60]

Specific exercises – such as whirling – were designed for local use in a particular cultural context.[61] This can be observed in the use of prayer and ritual activity, which has an opposite effect in the West to what it has in the East. In an Eastern context, Sufi adherence to Islamic ritual makes it easier to teach Sufism, whereas in the West, the prevailing secularism – combined with a deep-seated fear of Muslims (the Crusader mentality) – contributes to a situation where stress on adherence to Islamic rituals has a detrimental effect. For this reason, whether or not a Sufi group is genuine one, or not, cannot be assessed in terms of adherence of its members to Islamic rituals. Those groups which stress such a conformity- including dressing in alien dress, the use of customs, which are Persian, Arabic, or Turkish - in a Western country, are what brands it as a cult group. The Sufi shows no such attachment, having passed beyond external forms. A Master may use exercises drawn from a variety of cultures without being a syncretist, at the same time as creating his/her own. But at no time will there be a stress on customs designed to separate the disciple from the surrounding cultural context, or to give the feeling of superiority.

As we have seen, Sufism is an experience, its method being experiential rather than being based upon dogmatic formulation. For this reason a Teacher is essential,[62] for the Teacher breaks through dogmas and so-called infallible truths. The instability of human existence and consequent unbalanced forms of thinking, causes people to become attached to external forms. These are idols that need to be destroyed if the inner reality is to be appreciated. According to the Sufi maxim, "the apparent is the bridge to the Real" and should not be confused with the Real itself. The highly influential great Sufi saint, Muhammad Bahā' ad-Dīn Naqshband (died 1389), said: *"az-zāhir li'l-khalq al-bātin li'l-Haqq"* (the outer is of the world, the inner is **The Real**).[63]

While modern science is discovering the relativity of Nature, dogmatists - of either the materialist or religious kind - continue to assert a belief in so-called unequivocal facts. I would suggest that scientific positivism or religious dogmatism are alternative names for neuroticism. It was against conformity and lethargic thinking that practices such as music and whirling dancing were directed. They were a means of stirring people into awareness and as such have had a limited usefulness in their own time. However, Sufism must continually be presented in new ways, if it is to remain a living way.[64] Cult groups, who imitate *what were once* a spontaneous means for breaking through rigidity of thinking, doing so out of their original, historical, cultural context, cannot be considered Sufi, regardless of what they might call themselves.

Sufism does not seek to provide a religious system in which to live,[65] nor a means for solving all of life's problems. Its aim, if it can be called such, is to provide a means for experiencing **Reality** directly: "receiving", as I have described it. It is a process of deconditioning, creating an awareness of a Greater Reality which lies beyond and behind, our limited perception and concepts. It is the culmination of this that enables one to become a Sufi in the real sense, a gift that cannot be attained by effort alone: The culmination is an experience in which the meaning of life and death, space and time are transcended.

An examination of those calling themselves Sufi leads us to see that they fall into the following three types:

1)**Those who are syncretists**, and who follow a variety of practices, but whose practices and knowledge of the esoteric path is more apparent than real. This group comprises most of the popular Sufi groups (so-called) in the West, who like to dabble in different religious paths without a true commitment to any. Quite often members of this group – like many Westerners – are hostile and/or antagonistic to Islam.

2)Those who are really nothing other than Orthodox Muslims and are differentiated from them simply by their degree of piety, though they may be distinguishable by clothing, meet as a group distinct from other Muslims, or engage in practices additional to following the basic rudimentary requirements of Islam. Members of this group generally pride themselves on being *real Muslims,* and are often compulsive-obsessive personalities. In the West they are looking for a sense of identity, whilst in the East (or Eastern members in Western groups) they are seeking to "belong" and/or are attempting to eradicate guilt. Such groups are often led in the West by non-Westerners, who gather around them an immigrant core who provide the mainstay of the group.

3)It is from this group that the Sufi come. Likely to acknowledge Islam as significant in Sufism's transmission (but not as its origin, nor as equivalent to it) they will be considered to be "innovators", and at variance with Islam. Though they may practise Islam – or any religion – with devotion, they will be equally open to all religions; and

232

their knowledge and practise, being based upon inner experience, will be of great depth.

We may call the first group intellectualists; the second, imitators, while from the third group come the saints. These divisions, though based on experience and analysis of groups existing at the present time, also agrees with that of the so-called *Sufi Saint of the twentieth century* - from the book of the same name [66] - *Shaykh* Al-Alawī:

> The folk (Sufis) may be divided into three groups. The first is the group of those who see that there is no agent but God, thus realizing Oneness in Actions by way of direct intellectual perception, not merely by way of belief, for they see through the multiplicity of actions to the One Agent. The second is the group of those who realize the Oneness in the Qualities, that is, that none hath hearing, sight, life, speech, power, will, knowledge save only God. The third is the group of those who realize the Oneness in the Essence and who are veiled from all else inasmuch as the infinity of the Essence hath been unveiled to them, so that they find no room for the appearance of any created thing. They say: *"In truth there is nothing there but God"*, for they have lost all but Him. These are the essentialists and the Unifying Gnostics; and all others are veiled and unheeding: they have not tasted the flavour of Oneness, nor sensed the perfume of Uniqueness, but they have only heard of this doctrine and imagine because it hath fallen upon their ears, that they adhere to it. Nay, they are remote from the Truth and cut off from it.

So in distinguishing genuine Sufism from Pseudo-Sufism, or from other systems purporting to be mysticism, we need to realise that the goal of all mysticism is to attain the Supreme spiritual state. In Sufism, this means becoming the Perfected, or Complete, Universal wo/man, a state perfectly reflecting the **Creative Reality**, by being in complete harmony with it. That perfection lies in reacting to every situation in life – good or bad – with perfect resignation. This does not mean fatalism, but an actual constant striving *(istislām)*, whilst living according to the inspiration of the moment: neither planning, nor diregarding responsibilities. It is this keen readiness to act at a moment's notice that marks out the true mystic.

Creative action is the hallmark of the Sufi, and behind many activities that have changed our world, has been a Sufi – usually unknown except to the initiated. It is this that marks out the true Sufi, as opposed to the sham Sufi, who is only an imitator, living in the past rather than the present.

Notes and References

1) *Khamriyya* (Wine Ode), in *The Mystical Poems of Ibn al-Farid* translated by A. J. Arberry, Emery Walker, Dublin, 1956.

2) Mysticism is by nature universal, whereas religions are specific. In explaining the mystic experience we necessarily resort to terms that are specific; therefore, *Sufism is realisation, not explanation.*

3) Nor can it be denied; e.g., its catering for the emotional needs of ordinary people as opposed to the dry formalism of legalistic Islam; its ability to harmonise conflicting cultures and cater for minor ethnic groups and the socially disadvantaged – especially women in a male dominated society. Or its fostering and development of folk culture(music, dance, poetry, art)into what became as a result of its influence, the rich tapestry of Islamic civilisation. Plus providing the intellectual basis and motivation for Islamic medicical science, the majority of whose physicians and scientists, were Sufi.

4) From the Persian *tāj* meaning crown, it has connotations of divesting wealth, position, power, and was used as the name for a Sufi hat.

5) Sufism is a living process, continually requiring new Masters who must be sought out, their evidence being the creative spirit which surrounds them.

6) For a history of Sufism, see J. Spencer Trimingham, 1971, pp, 3-30, together with his list of sources.

7) This is reflected in the many Sufi women of the period, for Sufism was the only sphere where they could find a place. See J. Spencer Trimingham, 1971, p,18, for references, and I.M. Lewis, 1971, pp, 72-79, for the present day situation in Islamic countries.

8) Anthropologists have shown that magical power is a universal belief *(mana, nanama, akasa.etc)*. If such a notion had not existed prior to the spread of Islam and Sufism's development, it would have been surprising. That it did is intimated in the *Qur'ān (Sūra;* 113,114).

9) By the idea that it is a direct conveyance of spiritual power, passed on through an *isnād,* rather than a transmission of teaching, etc.

10) Kalābādhī(died 995) discusses the possibilities in *The Doctrine of the Sufis* (see Arberry, Cambridge University Press, 1935,pp,5-11).

11) A.H.= after the *Hegirae* or flight from Mecca by Muhammad, from which time the Islamic calendar is dated.

12) Al-Kindī, *Qudāt Misr,* edited by R.Guest, London, 1912, p,162. The term was used in later times to mean *the elect.*

13) Possibly from *ashāb as-Suffāh,* hence *suffīyya'* 'people of the bench' (adjoining Muhammad's house), where the poor received alms.

14) See note 45 in chapter six.

15) Or a combination of these terms as in the *Brethren of Purity* (for these authors of 40 tracts; see Nasr, 1976, pp,93-95).

16) See Bibliography for details of the following references to terms: Ibn Battūta, 1939, Vol 1, p,234; 'Abd al-Qādir, 1962, p,41; Ikhwān al-Safā; Sulamī, 1945, p,108; Kister, 1954; Riazul, 1955, p,204; Ibn Jubair, 1907,pp,284-287; Suhrawardī, 1939,pp,56-57.

17) This is one of the reasons for researchers misunderstanding the Sufi, e.g., compare the **Glossary** with dictionary interpretations.

18) Many people called Sufi would not be thought of as such by the *Ārifīn;* while some who might not be considered Sufi, actually are!

19) 'Ayn al-Qudāt al-Hamadhānī, **Shakwā' l-Gharīb an al-Awtan ilā *'Ulamā' al-Buldān,*** edited and translated by M.'Abd al-Jalīl, in 'Journal Asiatique', Paris (216), 1930, p,41.

20) **Tarjumān al-Ashwāq,** edited and translated by R.A. Nicholson, London, 1911, p,115 (in brackets mine).

21) Based upon the **Qur'ān** (29:69); where, *"those who struggle for Us, these shall we Guide."*

22) While *states are gifts and stations acquisitions* (in Abū 'l-Qāsim Qushairī **Ar-Risālāt al-Qushairiyya,** Cairo,1319 A.H., p,32) these stations depend on gifts to be attained, so that the station attained is in the end predetermined.

23) The *Rifā'iyya* -named after Ahmad ibn 'Alī ar-Rifā'i(died 578A.H./ 1182C.E.) is the first definitely recorded *silsila* and not 'Abd al-Qādir's, as is generally inaccurately claimed - see e.g., Glassé, 1989, p,398. J. Spencer Trimingham, 1971, has conclusively shown that *tā'ifa* were a later stage of Sufism.

24) J. Spencer Trimingham and others have not realised the emphasis on *silsila* and the consequent establishment of Sufi Orders was to counteract pseudo-Sufis, though the result has been the opposite.

25) Belief in the power of touch, as e.g., in the Christian *laying on of hands,* is universal and often associated with the institution of power (for an account of such during the Puritan period in England see Harvey, 1983,pp,40-46). I also encountered the "power of the breath", amongst the Kwaio of the Solomon Islands, an idea found in Babylonian and Akkadian magical systems of c 4,500-500 years ago. See also Butt, 1956.

26) This paralleled a developing veneration for the *Shī'ah Imāms* as well as a growth in power of the *Sunnī 'Ulamā'* of Islam.

27) Ibn Battūta **Voyages d'Ibn Batouta,** Paris, 1856, Vol.3,pp,52-77. Remembering the dead, a universal practice, is to be distinguished from worship of them- something contrary to Sufism. It is unlikely that any of the Great Masters, would have approved of their disciples building them an elaborate tomb/shrine after their death; nor of the commercialisation that generally goes along with it.

28) J.Spencer Trimingham, 1971, p,98, for references on this.

29) See above, pp,102-104,189,199-200 for references.

30) Acts of homage such as feet-kissing and the like can be witnessed, but this should not be confused with genuine Sufism and *ādāb.*

31) Such as a belief in the power of ritual for obtaining desired ends; the notion that words must be spoken in a specific way, and/or a specific language in order to achieve an effect; the sanctity of certain places for enacting rituals; the use of paraphernalia, such as robes, ritual instruments and sacred texts; plus the authoritative power of the ritual's leader (magician/priest/imām/cult head).

32) Quoted by Lings, as above 1971, p,144.

33) See e.g., Battūta as above, Vol. 3, p,36. Master *Bābā* Dovid Yūsuf chants portions from the scriptures of the religion, and language of the country he is in, as well as translating them.

34) Master *Bābā* Dovid Yūsuf, argues that insisting on using Arabic in in every ritual situation, is contrary to the example of Muhammad, who was instructed by God to recite the *Qur'ān* in *his own tongue* (41:43-44; 16:103; 46:12; 43:3,44).

35) For this reason some Masters, and/or Orders, have forbidden non-initiates from attending *Dhikr*, believing that lack of understanding can lead to misinterpretation (see **Matthew** 7:6).

36) In most of the Islamic world, the smallest child will be able to read, but not understand the *Qur'ān* in Arabic. It is this magical insistence which perhaps, more than anything else, has prevented traditional Muslims from applying their beliefs in a relevant way in the modern world, in contrast to the Sufi, who have provided an intellectual stimulus.

37) The practices of the *kāhin* or *kāhinah*(female) are condemned in the *Qur'ān* (113-114) along with divination and use of talisman(5:4,93).

38) Discussed frequently in the *Talmud,* conclusions are based on the texts: **Leviticus** 19:31, **Deuteronomy** 18:10-11, **Isaiah** 47:11-15.

39) To be distinguished from a belief in Creation's Unity - meaning we can learn by studying it - e.g., Ibn 'Arabī, studied astrology as a rudimentary form of astronomy, not as a means of divination.

40) In Lings work of the same name, 1971, pp, 50-51 & 82ff.

41) See, e.g., Lewis, as above, pp,101-103; and also Crapanzano, *The Hamadasha: A Study in Moroccan Ethnopsychiatry*, University of California Press, Berkeley, 1973, pp,15-21.

42) See note 43 in the previous chapter.

43) Throughout his many writings, and especially his major work: *Le Chamanisme et les techniques archaiques de l'extase*, Paris, 1951.

44) One reason for seeking a Master before attempting Sufi practices.

45) Such phenomena are seen as personified projections of the psyche (either positive or negative), and the failure to explain or deal with them adequately, plus their increasing manifestation in Western society, as another indication of the failure of its psychology.

46) Crapanzano as above, p,208 ff, for a description of such phenomena as observed in a Sufi-derived healing cult. This is not confined to Sufi-derived cults, but was characteristic of initiates into the mystery cults of Classical times (see Lewis, 1971, pp,100-112). It also appears in contemporary Hindu Balinese *kriss* dancers (see Belo 1960, p,223). For Shamanism, see Eliade, 1964 edition as above, p,228 & Shirokogoroff, 1935, p,365.

47) See references in Crapanzano and Lewis as above, and the works on healing in the **Bibliography**. For an association between Sufism and Shamans, see Winsted 1925, Constantinides 1977, Köprülüzadé 1929, Westermarck 1926, & Andrews 1903.

237

48) It is impossible to investigate Sufism without becoming an initiate.

49) See Ansari, 1986, pp, 17,51,192-200.

50) For Ibn 'Arabī, as above note 20, p, 116 ff. For Tirmidhī, see *Kitāb khatm al-wilāya* of Al-Hakīm at-Tīrmidhī, edited by 'Uthmān Ismā'īl Yahyā, Beirut, 1965.

51) There are various accounts of this story but accuracy in this case is not important for the essential elements remain unchanged. The fact that Bilāl was not cured in a conventional sense argues for its essential authenticity, in so far as the point we wish to make here. One version is to be found in Rushbrook Williams, 1973, p,189.

52) in Arberry as above, 1950, p,42.

53) For details of these figures and their influence on medicine, see S.K.Hamarneh, *Health Sciences in Early Islam*, edited by M.A.Anees (2 Vols), Zahra Publications, Blanco, Texas.

54) The definitive source on al-Ghazzī is the biography by grandson Najim ad-Dīn al-Ghazzī(1570-1651); see J.S. Jabbur (Editor), *Al-Kawakīb as-Sa'ira bi-A'yan al-Maya al-Ashīra*, by Najim ad-Dīn al-Ghazzī, Vol. 2, Junyeh, Beirut, 1949.

55) See note 12 in chapter two.

56) Eliade, Mircea, *Shamanism: Archaic Techniques of Ecstasy*, University Press, Princetown, 1964, pp, 71-81.

57) This is not an argument in favour of Freud's notions, for whilst there are animal characteristics responsible for human depravity present within the human psyche, this is not a necessary response. Freud, like Eliade, when drawing upon the vast heritage of our tribal origins in the use of symbols, mythology (and therefore necessarily of dream elements), failed to realise that in preliterate societies, where infant mortality is high - and where for a variety of social and psychological reasons infertility (much more common than in developed societies) is a primary concern - fertility rites are bound to be a major preoccupation. This is because sexuality in such societies (true of our own until relatively recently) is a *social* rather than just an individual concern.

58) For India, see M. Eliade, *Yoga: Immortality and Freedom*, Arkana, Harmondsworth, 1989, pp,104,190; chapter six; and pp,293-306. For the practices of witchcraft as preserved in our time, see J & S. Farrer, *Eight Sabbats For Witches*, Robert Hale, London, 1981.

59) Eliade's inferences (as above, pp, 63, 216-219, 391, 408,) can be dismissed because they disregard Sufism's deterioration in its incorporation of Yogic and allied practices, as has been shown by J. Spencer Trimingham (1971, pp, 98, 197-198, 230, 58). For witchcraft, see I.Shah, *The Sufis*, Octagon Press, London, 1964, pp, 208-216, 382.

60) Husainī, Maulvi S.A.Q., *Ibn Al-'Arabī*, Lahore, 1931, VI: I, p, 38.

61) For explication and confirmation of this, see Shams ad-Dīn Ahmad al-Aflākī, *Manāqib al-'Arifīn: (Acts of the Gnostics)* (1881), translated by J. Redhouse, reprinted as *Legends of the Sufis*, Kingston Publishers, London, 1965, pp,35ff.

238

62) This includes saints and others whose influence can continue after death because of their virtuous acts. In this sense, none of the world's great religious teachers can be said to be dead - the true meaning of *bāraka*. Not because they are ghosts or disembodied spirits that haunt the vicinity of tombs, for the saint being selfless, cannot be so localised.

63) See also **Mathnawī** 5:3257 & 3277.

64) Thus, *Bābā* Dovid Yūsuf, has taught Sufism through alternative medicine, conservation and peace activities, cooking, gardening, hospital lectures, a clinical practice and academic seminars.

65) Sufis may be adherents of any religion (though realising it has its limitations as an external form) or none, depending on culture, context and historical experience, just as Sufism can be taught through any of the world's religions, including the tribal - see note 42 in **chapter six** & note 70 in **chapter seven**.

66) From **Al-Minah al-Quddūsiyah**, translated by Martin Lings, in Lings, 1971, pp, 133-134.

11

TRANSCENDING WESTERN PSYCHOLOGY AND THERAPY

"Psychology springs from the question:What is the difference between oneself and the things outside oneself ?"

E.B. Titchner's *An Outline of Psychology*

The Sufi Master – More than a Psychotherapist

The definition used at the beginning of this chapter from a classical and influential textbook, though outdated, remains as a valid assessment of the foundations of Western psychology and psychotherapy – regardless of its form. Sufism transcends this question by posing another in its place: What is common to all things? The answer given is Their Source and End, in traditional religious language God.[1] The Sufi Master, in addressing this question, is shown to be much more than a psychotherapist. Whilst in answering it, there are likely to be psychological benefits to those who follow the Master's direction, such an answer takes the subject beyond the bounds of psychotherapy, however it may be defined.

The Sufi sees worship as being a recognition of the essential Unity of Life*(Tawhīd)*, and refusal to recognise this Unity as a supreme form of egotism*(shirk)* in which there is a denial*(iblīs)* of **Reality** *(Haqq)*. Such a stance has as its consequence, a disease*(marad)* of the heart*(qalb/dil)*,

240

one of the manifestations of which is mental/emotional/
physical imbalance, disturbance. However, this condition is
common to all humanity in the world of mortality, and not
confined to neurotics, or psychotics:

> Since all will die, from this they run, from freedom
> and existence, to make themselves unconscious of
> this fact. To drug themselves with wine and song,
> that they may rest awhile from consciousness of
> self. To know that they exist is but a trap, for will
> and thought and memory, are naught but hell.[2]

The Sufi Path forces those who follow it to confront death
as a reality; to see that seeking satisfaction in temporal
pursuits or objects is *self*-deception. By acknowledging the
is One permanent unchanging **Reality**(*Haqq),* individuals are
forced to confront themselves and their inadequacies.

> Open your eyes to see!
> Away from whom shall we flee?
> From ourselves can we fly?
> How absurd!
> From what then, God? [3]

When an individual worships self, then death is feared,
for there is a confrontation with limitations. Fear arises
from preoccupation with the limited self and its concerns.
The Sufi experience is more than a therapeutic one - it is a
transcendent experience; the realisation in a complete
sense: intuitively, experientially, holistically, that all life
including one's own, is subject to a **Greater Self.** By
actively acknowledging this - consciously as well as
unconsciously*(wahdat as-shuhūd)* - then peace *(islām)* is
found, for a morbid fear of death no longer exists.

241

This peace is expressed continuously*(istislām)* by ritual prostrations*(Salāh)* that portray in visible form, birth and death – participating in the Cycle of Nature, as all return to their **Source**. Encapsulated within this act is the whole cycle of Creation, from its beginning to its end. Time is annulled, as the Sufi participates in an act of worship, that is at the same time an acknowledgement of all masters, teachers and prophets. In this timeless moment, there is a re-enactment of the death and rebirth of the Shaman [4] and of all the Great teachers/mystics/healers who lie at the basis of the world's religions.[5] In this holistic experience – as lived out in the Sufi's own life – past and future are merged into the EVER PRESENT NOW *(Ya Hayyu al-Qayyūm!).*[6] For the Sufi, there is no religion other than love and no creed greater than compassion. In such an experience, religion and healing (of the whole) cannot be separated – it is the ultimate psychotherapy.

Sufism's Capacity to Overcome Dysfunctional Thinking and Illness

Despite essential differences between the Sufi Path and Western psychotherapy, it does not mean that it has no relevance to psychotherapy. Its value lies in highlighting the deficiencies in Western psychotherapeutic systems, illustrating that all problems arise from dualism, as an expression of an inner division within the self. Western psychology – of whatever school – reinforces this duality, by believing in an inherent and inevitable conflict between two opposing forces: conscious and unconscious, individual and society, stimulus and response, or a number of variants upon this theme. In addition, Western psychology encourages *self*-orientation, which, according to the Sufi, is the root cause of all disharmony, including mental and emotional disturbance. There are other systems utilising practices similar to *Dhikr* and its associated exercises, but only Sufism takes attention away from concern over self without becoming masochistic by promoting asceticism, mortification of the flesh, being a hermit, or activities that are in reality, only forms of *self*-preoccupation.[7]

For the Sufi, the object of devotion/attention/focus is OUTSIDE self, yet not separate from self. God is brought down to earth, so to speak, not as something remote like Jesus or the Buddha, but as something immanent within. The gulf between individual life -- and Life as a whole -[8] is bridged. It is this capacity to transcend the feeling of separateness from Nature and its eternal cycle - yet at the same time to become aware of individual distinctiveness, limitations and mortality - that explains Sufism's amazing ability to *heal the inner divide:* Sufism is much more than either psychotherapy or general mysticism.

Sufism does not ignore the context in which questions and problems confronting individuals and societies arise. To what extent does Western psychology and therapy - including its metaphysical basis - adequately deal with such

243

issues, issues that Sufism does not ignore, obscure, or override? We need to ask why - when it is evident from the multiplication of problems - is Western psychological theory(of any kind, including psychiatry) considered valid? Can a system of psychology and therapy be considered successful, if the members of the society that utilise it, become increasingly unhappy, disillusioned, violent and disturbed? Sufism does not ignore these problems, because it sees that disharmony can only be remedied by harmony, conflict by peace, disunity by Unity. It sees Unity(Tawhīd) as a natural state of affairs, not as an unobtainable Utopia; whilst it recognises that as part of this harmony, there will inevitably be states, places, times of disharmony.

There are numerous documented cases of persons who, having undertaken the Sufi Path, were cured of serious physical, as well as mental illnesses.[9] *Shaykh*, **Mulay** al-'Arabī ad-Darqāwī(died 1823), writing in a letter,[10] refers to the struggle of a person afflicted by the passions of the **commanding psyche**. He indicates that it is the refusal of such persons to acknowledge a superior **Self**(God), so becoming engaged in idle chatter with lower and egotistical(*psychic and satanic*) suggestions, that causes them to be overwhelmed by emotions:

> The soul is an immense thing, it is the whole cosmos since it is the copy of it. Everything that is in the cosmos is to be found in the soul; equally everything in the soul is in the cosmos. Because of this fact, he who masters his soul, most certainly masters the cosmos, just as he who is dominated by his soul is

244

certainly dominated by the whole cosmos.....The sickness afflicting your heart, *faqīr* [11] (i.e.,disciple) comes from the passions which pass through you; if you were to abandon them and concern yourself with what God ordains for you, your heart would not suffer as it suffers now....if you were to abandon your will entirely to Him, you would most certainly be saved from psychic and satanic suggestions and from all trial. But if you begin to reflect in these moments when your soul attacks you, to weigh the factors for and against, and sink into inner chatter, then psychic and satanic suggestions will flow back towards you in waves until you are overwhelmed....

So the Master does not encourage the disciple to dwell on negative thoughts, for preoccupation with them acts to strengthen them; just as for similar reasons, there is no engaging in analytical discussions with the disciple as a means of ascertaining **Reality**, for that only strengthens the ego and consequently the illusion of separateness.[12]

Ashraf 'Alī Thānvī, in his *Bawādir-al-Nawādir*, traced thought through five stages: (1)*Hajīs* – a passing thought (2)*Khātir* – a persistent thought (3)*Hadīth al-nafs* – a thought providing the basis for alternative action (4)*Ham* – preoccupational thought having the power to motivate action; and (5)*'Azm* – the decision to act. He argued that by sticking in stage 3 – subvocal talking – an impetus is given that allows the thought to pass to completion. Simply accepting it and allowing it to pass, rather than dwelling on it, prevents it becoming – in the case of an evil thought – the basis for psychopathy.[13] Or in cases where the thought is obsessive, it can create dissociation, delusions or depression.

It is subvocal chattering*(Hadīth al-nafs)* or self-talk that perpetuates emotion. By such means, natural sorrow over some loss, failure to act, or disappointment with oneself, is turned into a state of depression and despondency. Alternatively, it may become a source of hypocrisy, egotism or dissonance. While some forms of psychotherapy have recognised the role of irrational subvocal monologues in perpetuating mental disease,[14] in no case other than Sufism is there a replacement with a metaphysical system that removes egocentricism.

The Contrast between Sufism and Western Psychological Concepts

Some researchers have mistakenly claimed that Sufism can be equated with Western psychological concepts.[15] The problem with this view is that it does not take into account the differences in people arising from different cultural contexts, societies and belief systems. While it is obviously true that people, despite their differences are basically the same everywhere - i.e., they have the same basic mental apparatus - are able to communicate and learn each other's languages, etc., there are also differences between them in motivations, values, concepts and ideas. This becomes clear when we contrast Sufi concepts with Western psychological categories, using the latter as much as is possible, whilst acknowledging that such categories are in

246

themselves a part of Western psychology and therefore alien to Sufism.[16]

Memory

The aim of Sufi practice is to achieve a state of perpetual awareness of God and of the consequent **Unity of Existence**. One of the very first injunctions revealed to Muhammad was (*Qur'ān* 73:8):

*Invoke in remembrance the Name of your SUSTAINER (Rabb)*Lord/Master *and devote yourself to Him completely.*

وَاذْكُرِاسْمَ رَبِّكَ وَتَبَتَّلْ إِلَيْهِ تَبْتِيلًا

It is upon this and various other passages in the *Qur'ān* and *Ahadīth* that the Sufi places his justification for *Dhikr*, a name referring to the repetitive reciting of Divine Names and similar allied practices, that effect a loss of individual limited conditioned consciousness, thereby inducing a transcendent awareness. This awareness is our natural state – a state transcending limitations of Time and the limited self*(anā')*. Consequently, while through our interdependence with **All that Exists***(Wujūd)* there can be a realisation of other times/places/states,[17] in **Reality***(Haqq)* the only **Truth***(Haqq)* is **God***(Haqq);* all else depends upon this realisation, which can only be attained by negating *(nafī)* the limited self.

Once this stage is achieved*(fanā')*, memory as used in the Western psychological sense has no meaning. For it is a concept based upon limitations of time and experience of the past within the present, whereas the Sufi's orientation is the Eternal Present. It is this that explains the *'Arīf's* frequent precognitive experiences and which replace the non-Sufi's preoccupation with *déjà-vū*.

Consciousness

The Sufi recognises that there are different levels of consciousness. This is not an agreement with Freud's notion of humanity going through different stages in the development of consciousness - which ultimately replaces the necessity for religion in a conventional sense [18] - for the Sufi is speaking of individuals, rather than humanity as a whole. The perfected individual *(Al-Insān al-Kāmīl)* transcends historicalism. It is not that religion becomes outdated in Sufism, as it does in Freud's theory, but rather that through a total absorption of the object of its devotion, it is transcended. The perfected individual embodies this and does not therefore have to rely on an external code. The Teacher, the teaching and the taught have become one.[19]

The Sufi does not believe, as did Freud, that dream symbols are the result of distortions arising from repression;[20] rather, they are considered to be sources of guidance, that proceed from above - **The Transcendent** - and not from our base nature. This is why many Sufi Masters have chosen to be guided by them; Ibn 'Arabī, as one example, wrote in his *The Revelations of Mecca (Al-Futūhāt al-Makkiyya)* on how the decisive stages of his life were all marked out by dreams.

Therefore, in contradistinction to Western psychological theories, the human being is not determined by blind forces - a process in which consciousness emerges as an end product. Rather, it is consciousness itself that determines all activities - not chance - with differences arising from different levels of consciousness/awareness. This fundamentally different approach means any attempt to compare Sufism with Western psychology, is fraught with difficulties.

Cognition

This difference becomes clearer when we consider the Sufi approach to cognition. According to this perspective, it is the inward faculty of perception - **The Intellect**, or process of synthesis itself - that makes cognition possible. Put in another way, we can say that the *Inward Eye* perceives within (is reflected by) the outward organ of perception. This is a cryptic way of explaining what has just begun to be accepted in **Cognitive Psychology**; i.e., that there is an innate faculty of perception (this applies to all senses and language) for unless I know what I am to perceive, then I am unable to perceive it; [21] this in complete contradiction to Behaviourism which posits that perception and language are learnt through a process of experience called 'stimulus and response'.[22]

Conditioning/Habituation

Although Sufis claim that people make idols for themselves

as a result of inner dualism *(shirk)* and outward duplicity; these idols (=conditioned ways of thinking) come about through choice, being the result of ego-traps.

The Sufi confronts the dualist (externalist) with these inner contradictions,[23] not directly in a hostile sense, but by an appeal to transcendent consciousness (the inner Primal Unitary State). Self-contradictory phrases, hidden meanings, together with remarks and behaviour that at first sight seem shocking to the religiously orthodox, are used to *penetrate* dogmatism and the limitations of rational thought.[24] The hearer is challenged to examine the basis of their faith, so that there is no mere token acceptance, for if the meaning of such remarks are to be grasped, *deep and inward* thinking is necessary.

This appeal to transcendent consciousness should not be confused with non-linear thinking, psychoanalysis, rational-emotive therapy, insight therapy, or any Western psychological method. This is because it is not a mental activity (in the usual sense of the word) at all, for it is neither rational nor irrational. Stories or statements, which at first sight appear contradictory or confusing, are used to weaken the control factor*(anā')*, that has been strengthened by the sterility of an arid intellectualism that reinforces the ego or conditioned self. This method is in stark contrast to that of Western psychology, which though it may deal with the emotions, is in the final analysis, intellectually biased and based.

250

In contradiction to Western psychology, the Sufi believes that conditioned ways of thinking/idols/habituation are overcome not by avoidance, or even by decreasing their emotional power - what is called "Flooding" in Clinical psychology [25] - but by an appeal to higher and transcendent values. Sufis believe that the impetus behind such is not subconscious - or at the level of emotion - but rather is freely accessible, being an ego-trap.

One method for dealing with this is called "The law of reverse effect". For example, rather than disregarding the performance of rituals associated with external religion (whether it be Islam, Catholicism, or Orthodox Judaism), which are often equivalent to a compulsive-obsessive trait, the disciple may be encouraged to follow them to the letter - even to go beyond what is required. At the same time, intentions rather than actions are stressed as the ideal. The Sufi is aware that removing the external makes the desire for it even stronger, while carrying it out necessitates an understanding of its inner meaning. An example of this was the insistence by *Bābā* Dovid Yusuf, that a lapsed and suicidal Franciscan monk say his rosary every day and live as a genuine Franciscan. The result was, that, although he came to appreciate the beauty and meaning of the life of St.Francis, in a way he had not previously done, he left the Order and the Church, becoming a more stable and satisfied personality, to realise his gifts as an artist and poet.

251

For similar reasons, different types of practice are used, designed, or have been evolved for different cases, the method depending on the situation, environment and individual - also changing over time. It is because of this that the different Sufi Orders arose. Although not intended to be therapeutic practices, they have had this effect.

Experience

A difference in approach to experience can be seen in the Sufi view of death. Not ignoring the continual presence of death,[26] but continuously re-enacting it through *Dhikr*, as well as proceeding along a path in which there is a deliberate and conscious desire for self-extinction*(fanā')*; the *death instinct* - to use Freud's terminology - is cultivated and encouraged. Thus, there is an implicit, if not stated view, that it's not necessarily experience [22] which moulds a person's response to life, but rather the perception of it. Meaning that often it is more a case of a lack of experience, rather than experience itself, that determines actions. The realised Sufi*('Arīf)* does not fear death, for having experienced it, knows that it is only to be feared, if like life, it is considered in a timebound sense, i.e., in a limiting, non-Unitary way. Death is so often feared, because life is not understood; it has no meaning and is not joyful. Therefore, there is always hope for something more, something better, and it is sustained at all costs in order to achieve this goal. However, for the Sufi life has meaning, purpose and joyfulness*(tūbā)* because

252

there is an awareness of a **Greater Reality***(Wahdat al-Wujūd)* within which all else is subsumed. Sufism is the creation of an awareness of this **Reality**.

The Sufi believe that in pursuit of ego-satisfaction, all teaching is continually being transformed into something unreal, unnatural, institutionalised; causing dissatisfaction, disharmony and lack of orientation. The various forms of experience, of consciousness/developmental stages, have been recognised in different systems, being given different names. The first kind of experience is emotional; the second is intellectual and/or intuitional; and the third transpersonal. While the various religious traditions have acknowledged this latter kind of experience (though using different terms) accepting that there is something which goes beyond usual everyday experience, this is not the case for Western psychology. For even where there has been a token acceptance of the importance of such experience,[27] there has not been a realisation that it is not experience, but the perception of it which is important. Such perception depending upon the fact that it, together with experience, makes each dependent on the other. In other words, we are not determined by our experiences – for WE ARE THE CONSTITUTORS OF OUR EXPERIENCE, as agents of the **Transcendent Reality**.

Causation

Freud based many of his theories upon the notion of repression (continued suppression) of basic drives *(trieb)*,

253

like sex, which he believed arises from the fact that individual desires must be controlled for societies to exist and function.[28] According to this view, anxiety is the result of a conflict between these so-called basic drives and social needs. Though many Western psychologists have rejected Freud, this notion of an inherent conflict between the individual and society, permeates their thinking. Its origin is to be found in the Christian belief in the natural tendency of human beings to sin.

This standpoint is in complete opposition to that of the Sufi who sees Unity *(Tawhīd)* everywhere and conflict more apparent than real. The creation of self is simply a means (illusory and ineffectual) of trying to regain the consciousness of that Unity; a striving to attain an original/primal/pure state. There is no need to *sublimate, create a personal schema,* or partake of a *socially created* one [29] says the Sufi; for by abolishing the ego, or self-created self, Unity can be perceived. It is therefore a question of knowledge, of an expansion of perception – not of emotion – for the only real identity, says the Sufi, is God. Once this is realised (in the fullest sense of the word), the necessity for a personal ego disappears.

Emotion and Motivation

Since there is striving to overcome the ego, *acting-out* or activities with an emotional orientation are discouraged. While cathartic discharge may take place as the result of Sufi practise these outbursts are not encouraged or sought as ends in themselves. Nor are internal conflicts resolved by this method, for emotional discharge only acts as ego-reinforcement.[30] Therefore, even though Sufi physicians have been instrumental in pioneering the use of hypnosis in medicine,[31] Sufis do not employ hypnotherapy as a means for self-knowledge.

While various schools of psychotherapy, in common with Shamanism and healing cults, use techniques of brainwashing, by creating a state of emotional exhaustion and collapse, enabling beliefs and patterns of behaviour to be erased and supplanted with new ideas, while the participant is in a heightened state of suggestibility,[32] this is not the case with Sufism.[33]

Sufism has long recognised the power of emotion, which is why it has limited the use of music in certain contexts.[34] *Mevlana* Rumi, who, following the influence of his *Shams-i-Tabrīz* utilised music in a controlled way,[35] said of emotion:

> ...when you feel desire and a compelling passion –
> then you know there is a controller – this is
> emotion and you are made aware it more than
> anything visible. For example; hunger and thirst,
> anger and delight – all these you cannot see, yet
> you are more aware of them than anything visible.
> For even if you close your eyes you will still be
> aware of hunger as if it were visible and nothing
> you do will be able to make it go away.[36]

Sufism acknowledges the power of the emotions and recognises that in accordance with our basic physiological needs, hunger and yearning – which includes sexual needs – should be dealt with. So nothing is done to over-stimulate the emotions,[37] whilst at the same time these needs are not viewed as animal or sinful in themselves, so that the question of sexual repression does not arise. It could be argued, that rather than sexual repression being central to human culture, it is the creation of hunger (unnecessary) that has been a major factor in systems of social control. Such a need, which is much more basic than the sexual, has been involved in human aberration and anxiety in all cultures and periods of history, yet has not even been considered as a neurotic factor in Western psychology. Sufism not only sees the necessity of feeding the poor – and many Sufi Orders been involved in this *(Zakāt)* – but also employs regular fasting (in a regulated way) so as to be aware of – but not under control of – the power of hunger.

Health, Illness and Cure

Unlike Western psychology and its therapies, including the physical, for the Sufi illness is not seen as something to be afraid of. Rather, it is to be accepted and understood – even welcomed – in that it is a way of drawing us to God by making us aware of our fragility and the impermanence of the material world. It can be THE avenue through which we are forced to acknowledge our dependence on God. So turning to a religious faith is not seen as an escape into fantasy and a symptom of neurosis,[38] but as a positive and not a negative step. [39] Freud is turned on his head, so to speak. Regarding this, Rūmī said:

> There are two veils that hide God from us. From these two all other veils come into being: they are health and wealth. If a man is healthy he will say; *"God where is he - I do not see him!"* But if he becomes sick and in pain, then he cries out; *"Oh God! Oh my God!"* and begins to talk with God. So you can see that health hid God from him. [40]

From the Sufi perspective, the obsession with health to the point of self-indulgence as is manifest in Western culture, including its non-acceptance of death (leading to bizarre practices, like keeping people alive as vegetables), is abnormal. Western psychology not only refrains from dealing with these symptoms of mass neurosis, but more often than not, promotes them.[41]

Potentiality/Growth/Capacity/Ability

Western psychology is obsessed with measurement, so that a multitude of tests have been created to enable people to be placed into categories of management, indicating a preoccupation with monetary control.[42] On the other hand, this is balanced out by therapies offering the possibility of *self-actualisation, individualisation,* or the *fulfilment of human potential.* In addition to this there are religious substitutes in the form of psychology cults, some of which acknowledge that they are, or have become, religions, such as Scientology, and the New Age Church.

If Sufism is compared with these two trends, we discover that it can be placed in neither camp. In the first

257

case (in psychiatric, or general medical practice in Western society)the person remains essentially the same;[43] whereas in the second (the psychological-religious cult) there is a superficial change that takes place through membership of a group conferring a new social status, privileges and responsibilities. Neither case is true of Sufism: the Sufi does not become the *old self* or someone else, but for want of a better word a *true-self*. Abilities are expanded and developed beyond those of a limited conditioned self so as to acquire an *Over-self*, which, while it expresses individual characteristics to full potential, also encompasses a multitude of different possible responses.

It is in this sense, that we can begin to understand Rūmī, writing the *Dīwān-i-Shams-i-Tabrīzī* as if his Teacher had written it himself; as is also the case for a Jewish Doctor writing of his *Bābā*, and a Turkish *Shaykh* who refers to his own words as those of *Grandshaykh*. [44]

It is this transcendent aspect that distinguishes Sufism from Western psychological treatment methods, as well as from becoming a member of a cult group. A genuine Sufi is, at one and the same time, level-headed and rational (without being a cynical, economic-determinist) as well as being a far-sighted visionary. This produces a highly creative individual whose hallmark is originality, and who possesses both determination and ability. Instead of becoming a conformist - which is what membership of a psychological and/or religious cult group induces - there is

258

a striking independence – as can be seen in the writings of Master *Bābā* Dovid Yūsuf, which teach Sufism through all the world's religious traditions, including the tribal.

View of the Body

Western psychology takes a primary view of the body, even when – as in, for example, Symbolic Interactionism – social psychology is the basis of the particular school of thought, for social behaviour is viewed as an extension of the satisfaction of individual needs. The Sufi, whilst acknowledging physical needs – which shows our ultimate dependence on Nature's **Source** – does not believe we are determined by our bodies. Unlike Western psychology, the mental and spiritual worlds are not considered to be developments, additions, or peripheral to the material world. There is no Cartesian dualism in which the body is viewed as more real than other aspects of existence. Instead, the material and physical worlds, including the body, are viewed as manifestations – at different levels – of **One Source of Consciousness**. Consequently, the body is viewed as secondary and not primary. Rūmī explains:

> Why do you regard the body so? What is your connection to the body? You are not the body for you are you without it. When you are asleep you disregard it, whilst when it is daytime you are involved in your activities. Why are you anxious over your body for you are never with it not even for one hour, but are occupied elsewhere? Where is the body and where is the you? [45]

View of the Therapist

Western psychology, including psychoanalysis – as is also the case for folk cults and primitive psychologies of healing – focus responsibility on someone or something else as being the cause of mental aberration. This may be inadequate parents, economic deprivation, poor social learning, a possessing spirit, or witchcraft. In every case, the power, prestige and status of the therapist – whether that be a Clinical Psychologist, Analyst, Pseudo-Sufi or Shaman – is boosted in return for reinforcing the ego of the person concerned. Each one tells the other what they want to hear, whereas, in the case of Sufism, emphasis is on self-responsibility, yet without guilt. Mistakes are viewed as a lack of knowledge, rather than deliberate error; an inevitable self-deception that correct motivation can remedy.

While the Sufi treats the Master/*Shaykh*/*Pīr* with a great deal of respect, this position does not arise from reinforcing the disciple's ego, or from validation by any external agency whatsoever.[46] Quite often, a Master will reject disciples and rather than cultivate support, may actually engender hostility.[47] Furthermore, success is measured not in terms of dependence on the Master, but on dependence on God; a dependence that the Master may induce when the time is right, by terminating the teaching in some way or another.[48]

View of the Self

It is in considering this last aspect that Sufism shows its greatest distinction from Western psychology. Without exception, all psychotherapies in the West are concerned with reinforcement of the self, whether that be through individualisation, ego-psychology, confidence building, assertiveness training, or self actualisation. From the Sufi perspective, this ego reinforcement is – to coin a phrase – *self*-defeating. The Sufi argues that it is this attention to the limited self that is responsible for ALL human ills and miseries, for it creates a dualism within the human mind, making true satisfaction impossible. *This self* has no meaning in Sufism, for the only **Real** personality is God who alone can be said to exist in permanence and stability, and therefore the only **Being***(Wujūd)*, the only **Existence** *(Wujūd);* as summated in the *Qur'ān* (28:88):

Call none god other than God, there is no god but THAT!

Everything perishes except His Face (Self): His is the Authority, to Him will you return.

وَلَا تَدْعُ مَعَ اللَّهِ إِلَٰهًا ءَاخَرَ لَآ إِلَٰهَ

إِلَّا هُوَ كُلُّ شَىْءٍ هَالِكٌ إِلَّا وَجْهَهُ

لَهُ الْحُكْمُ وَإِلَيْهِ تُرْجَعُونَ

Notes and References

1) From God do we come and to God do we return;
   Qur'ān 2:28; 15:23; 19:40; 96:8.

2) *Mathnawī* 6:210.

3) *Mathnawī* 1:956.

4) See notes 28 & 38 in chapter two.

5) One must distinguish between what the figures (mystics) around whom these religions revolve, believed, and what their followers have said about them. Sufis say that none of them - including Muhammad - made the claim that theirs was the only, last, or best (see *Mathnawī* 2:815; 5:200; 3:1259).

6) These words are emphatically invoked by the *Bābā'iyya* during their initiation ceremony. They are said to represent the continuous act of creation - as symbolised by the breath - manifested in a living spiritual tradition (their Master/Order).

7) In other systems showing an outward similarity, the focus is on the practice itself, whereas in Sufism it is on God. Any preoccupation with the method or self-concern, renders the practice invalid.

8) It is this gulf that underlies the theme of all great literature, drama and art, as a little reflection will testify.

9) In addition to the numerous examples of the healing of physical and psychological illnesses, by the spiritual Master *Bābā* Dovid Yūsuf, previously referred to (see **chapter one**), see the cases recorded in the 6 volume *Tarbiyāt al-Sālik*, by the late Sufi Master, Ashraf 'Alī Thānvī, Pakistan Press, Lahore (undated) (Urdu).

10) *Letters of a Sufi Master*, translated by Titus Burckhardt, Perennial Books, Middlesex, 1969, pp, 4 & 9.

11) The name literally means poverty, and it refers to the detachment of the Sufi from the material world and his/her acknowledgement of the lack of spirituality, a precondition for being able to learn. Summated in a saying of Master *Bābā* Dovid Yūsuf: *"He who is to be filled must first be empty."*

12) As Master *Bābā* Dovid Yūsuf put it: *"Truth is to be experienced not talked about."*

13) If this has been understood, it will be seen why, in a culture that indulges itself in preoccupational thought under the labels of "freedom" and of "entertainment", psychopathy is increasing at a phenomenal rate.

14) Rational-EmotiveTherapy. The problem is that rationalism of whatever form, only strenghtens the ego*(anā')*.

15) See e.g., works by Shafii and Deikman, in the **Bibliography**. Many others, like Litvak, and Frager, while acknowledging the difference, indirectly make assumptions that Western psychological concepts are comparable with Sufi concepts.

16) Categories, like psychological theories, are continually changing in Western psychology. Since it is not part of our purpose to choose one above another, the categories as outlined here, are based upon their being fairly representative of the various schools of thought.

Similarly the Western concepts referred to here are simplifications and generalisations, but they suffice to illustrate our point.

17) The Sufi explanation of the Buddhist concept of rebirth and of so-called reincarnation memories or experiences.

18) Freud treated psychoanalysis as if it were a kind of religion, even identifying himself with Moses, in *The Moses of Michelangelo* (1914), Standard Edition Vol. 13, Hogarth Press, London, 1950, believing that psychoanalysis would ultimately replace religion, with himself as its Prophet (see Mannoni, 1971, pp, 163-166).

19) This does not mean that the Sufi shows no allegiance to any kind of religious/ethnic group, but rather that, that specific religion is realised in its fullness, including its esoteric aspects, and not as a rigid dogma. For this reason, Sufis have been found in all of the world's religions, being able to transcend external differences.

20) According to Freud (*The Interpretation of Dreams* -orig pub 1900-Standard Edition, Vol.4, Hogarth Press, London, 1953, pp, 573-574) whilst asleep, repressed desires emerge from the unconscious, which, if not disguised, would shock the individual into wakefulness. It is this, according to him, that explains the *obscure nature of dream contents*, symbols being designed to hide, rather than reveal (1900, pp, 137-193, 277).

21) This point has been argued by the philosopher and psycho-linguist, Naom Chomsky (see **Bibliography**).

22) Sufism does not deny stimulus and response, but would claim that neither stimulus nor response is affective without perception which is *a priori*.

23) One of the reasons why the Sufi have so often been persecuted.

24) As in, e.g., Sufi Master Yesua(Jesus of Christianity), whose speech, the religiously orthodox found shocking(see, **John** 6:51-53; 59-62).

25) A Behaviourist technique for reducing the anxiety threshold (the stimulus/conditioning level) by over-exposure.

26) The very act of living presupposes death - a fact that is stressed continuously, in a variety of ways, in all cultures other than the present day Western one. Regarding the change in the attitude towards death which resulted from the development of Protestantism see Stone, 1965, p, 579 and Garer, 1965.

27) Such as, Abraham Maslow's *"peak experiences"* (see Maslow,A.H. *Towards a Psychology of Being*, Van Nostrand, New York,1962)

28) This notion was continually repeated throughout his writings, its fullest discussion is found in *Civilization and its Discontents* (1930) Hogarth Press, London, 1975.

29) Unlike Rousseau (*The Social Contract*) and his descendants, the Sufi does not believe that human beings came together to create society and culture, in contrast to the natural animal state. In common with Islam(Qur'ān 6:38; 27:16-22; 24:41), they believe that society and culture are together a natural and original state, shared with animals, though theirs is of a different kind, a fact that is no longer disputed in Biology and adequately demonstrated by Animal

Ecology. This is in contrast to the Judeo/Christian belief in man's *dominion* over the animals.

30) Even Western psychological studies, have shown that discharging emotion is not necessarily therapeutic(Gill & Brenman 1966,p,356).

31) See note 43 in chapter four.

32) For further explanation of this point see W. Sargant, *Battle for the Mind*, Pan Books, London, 1964.

33) This technique is not limited to cult groups and fashionable forms of psychotherapy, but is used by films, TV and the pop-music industry in the West. And by military/religious and political forms of government, in the East (particularly Muslim countries).

34) Aware of this fact, *Bābā* Dovid Yūsuf has forbidden his disciples to use musical instruments for *Dhikr*, or when singing the beautiful melodies which accompany his prayers.

35) Members of the *Mevlevi* Order undergo rigorous training for the *samā'*, and its effect is elevating, as anyone who has witnessed it will testify. This is in contrast to pseudo-Sufi cults, whose use of music involves them in head-slashing, animalistic expressions, and other forms of ego-gratification.

36) *Fīhi mā fīhī*, Tehran & Azamargh, 1928, p,128 (Persian).

37) Neither men nor women wear sexually stimulating clothes, watch TV indiscriminately, or engage in activities which encourage greed (ostentatious display of wealth, accumulation of capital, or usury).

38) Since religion is a fundamental and universal characteristic of all human societies - historically as well as geographically - as anthropology testifies, its demise in Western society must be viewed as uncharacteristic and therefore abnormal. That is until one realises that it is not absent, but changed; the religion (value-system) of the West being materialism, a philosophy which viewed historically, has always been associated with civilisation's decline.

39) It is neurotic, when that faith (whatever it might be) is entirely separated from life in general, i.e., is externalist. Sufism realises this and promotes a holistic view leading to an understanding of the inner nature of religious faith.

40) *Fīhi mā fīhī*, as above, 1928, p, 129.

41) A society producing organisations and books that turn the bereaved (an experience common to us all) into victims, but does not offer a natural network of support during such times, is itself sick!

42) This is betrayed in the history of terms used in official bulletins, case conferences, and the like, where *patients* became *clients,* then *customers,* and are now *service users* !

43) A common expression for sickness - *"S/he is not him/her old self"* - expresses the desire to get the patient back to their original state/self.

44) *Shaykh* Nāzim 'Adīl al-Qubrusī, who uses this title for his Teacher (now deceased), *Shaykh* Abdullah ad-Daghistanī.

45) *Fīhi mā fīhī*, as above, 1928, p, 127.

46) One should not confuse *silsila* with becoming a Sufi Teacher, for such validation can only come from God alone, and not through any mediation, for if it did, this would be equivalent to the creation of an instituted priesthood, which Sufism in common with Islam rejects (though the latter practise it). The proof of this is that the Great Sufi Masters, rather than being the member of Orders, were seen as the founders of such. The appeal to a chain of transmission as an *authorisation* is a mark of pseudo-Sufism and can easily be refuted. C. Glassé, writing in **The Concise Encyclopaedia of Islam**, Stacey International, London, 1989, pp,371-372 quotes *Shaykh* Ahmad ibn Mustafā-l-'Alawī (died 1934) the **Sufi Saint of the Twentieth Century**, as having derived his authority from such a line, yet in the book by the same name(1971), Martin Lings shows how 'Alawī founded a new Order independently of his deceased former Teacher and Master.

47) One can witness flattery (the use of titles such as *Shaykh* for new disciples, ego-reinforcement and similar psychological ploys) by the leaders of Islamic cult groups calling themselves Sufi. However, as Master *Bābā* Dovid Yūsuf once said in a discourse to his disciples: *"When you are wanting to run out of the door, when you are feeling uncomfortable, uneasy, or your pride has been assaulted, this one is THE Teacher for you!"*

48) Sometimes, by passing the disciple on to another Master, by death, or as in the case of Rūmī's teacher, by disappearance. This deliberate disappearing is not uncommon on the part of genuine Sufi Teachers, and discussion about who murdered Shams of Tabriz by numerous commentators, is an indication of their lack of knowledge, or involvement, in real Sufism.

265

12

THE TRANSCENDENT SELF

"Your fear of death is really a fear of yourself!
See what it is from which you are fleeing."

Mevlana, Jalāl ad-Dīn ar-Rūmī

Beyond Religion and Psychology on the Path of Transcendence

Sufism is not simply a religious quest in the reductionist meaning of the word - no more than it is an alternative to it. If we examine Sufism in terms of its practical effects, it will be seen that it produces the characteristics of an integrated individual, and therefore fulfils the aims of psychotherapy - even though it is not that:

SUFI PRACTICES & BELIEFS	THEIR EFFECT
Rejection of all forms of idolatory (religious/national/personal)	Overcoming of (ego-traps) & negative, limiting conditioning
No mediatory priesthood, authority internal not by external arbitration	Leads to an inner freedom and acceptance of responsibility
Dhikr, Wird, Tafakkara	Overcoming circular thinking, subvocal entrapment & dualism
Life is eternal, creation continual, Time relative, all but God is impermanent, change inevitable	Destroys fears, hold of desires & excessive ambitions. Effects of success & failure mediated
Prayers, fasting, *Khalwah*, travelling, *Zakāt, Tajrīd*	Creates an inner strength, self-discipline & non-attachment
Devotion without thought reward/punishment	Freedom from self/ego
Belief in the equality of religions	A freedom from bias
No dogma, individual differences permitted, stress on the holistic acquisition of knowledge	Development of spontaneity, creativity and originality
Ittilā', Ta'bīrar-Ru'yā, Inkāral-kasb	Development moral/ethical sense

However, it is also the case, that Sufism cannot be considered to be a psychological/sociological developmental system, that is independent of the spiritual and religious quest. This is clearly shown in the example of Abū Hāmid Muhammad al-Ghazālī – the aforementioned Islamic jurist and theologian – who suffered a nervous breakdown at 38 – what would be defined in Western psychological terms as a *mid-life crisis*. This resulted in him leaving his job, and visiting over a period of ten years, every centre of learning and religious instruction in the Muslim world. That it was religious doubt which caused his mental confusion, is betrayed in his writings[1] where he denounces dogmatic theology *as being opposed to reason,* but the exact sciences – arithmetic, geometry, etc., – he accepted unreservedly, since *they are not open to doubt.* The fact that he regained his belief to become the *Proof of Islam* and *Ornament of the Faith,*[2] in addition to his mental composure, is proof of this fact.

Sufism is holistic and does not separate beliefs from actions, or values from psychological and social well-being. Western psychology can be seen as a development of Aristolian philosophy and the Greek magical formula, becoming over time, the basis of the reductionist, Western medical scientific hypothesis, and verbal psychotherapy.[3] In other medical systems, such as the Chinese, the Indian, and the Persian – and their modern derivatives such as homeopathy– we have an identification between subject and

267

object; each is believed to have an effect upon the other. These systems represent the other extreme, and they are by nature limited in their functional ability to manipulate matter, since detachment from it is discouraged. On the other hand, Sufism is neither reductionist, nor animistic, but truly scientific, in that it takes an overall (holistic) view. In this sense it is truly objective – objectivity, in this case, not being confused with reductionism.

It can be seen from this analysis that the sciences of the psychology of learning, as of psychotherapy in the fullest sense of the word, are interrelated and both inseparable from character development, or what could be called spiritual/moral learning. It is important that we fully grasp this, because it will then become apparent that, despite contemporary assertions to the contrary, we cannot learn or develop without considering the relevance of beliefs. An interest in psychological development methods is NOT an alternative to the spiritual quest, but is in fact the same thing, viewed from a different perspective, using different labels, or terms.

Once this is understood, Sufism can be seen as both a science as well as a philosophy. The difference between it and what is generally termed religion, is that the latter like its materialistic counterpart(pseudo-science) is reductionist failing to consider life as a whole. Sufism aims to break conditioning's hold on the individual, allowing him/her to see beyond the limitations of cultural context, social form, time and space. In this it has much in common with what is called "scientific objectivity", whereas traditional religion is rooted in these limitations, appealing to emotional stimuli, which must first be attenuated for learning and development to take place.

To the scholar of religion, being objective means studying Sufism as an external form, but from the Sufi perspective it can only be understood by practise. The Sufi experience alone that grants this objectivity by it being grounded in a view of the whole. In this sense, Sufism is akin to the empirical method of science, in that it realises that the phenomenal and noumenal worlds are different. This experiential viewpoint makes it more similar to science than to religion, making it possible to argue that Sufism is a scientific approach to religious experience.

In understanding this we can see a difference between general mysticism and the Sufi Path, for unlike most mysticism, it does not require self-mortification or other forms of self-indulgence, designed to produce abnormal psychological experiences. Nor does it centre itself on the individual, but rather on the whole: the community, social unit, historical as well as individual experience - **Total Reality**. By following the Sufi Path to its ultimate, the individual self is dissolved. There is only a concern with, and awareness of, **Total Reality**, i.e., God as the **Source of All**. Salvation does not consist of self-abnegation or self-sacrifice through identification with a saviour of some kind or another, but instead, of a total denial of the self in an individualistic/independent sense. It does not require that there be abnormal experience or demands, but consists of recognising and submitting to what actually IS! It is not abnormal, since it seeks to cut through illusion; it is not even unusual, except to those who seek to run away from, rather than face, reality. The mystic of Hinduism or Christianity will seek to identify with the *other*, the *Thou*, *Christ* or whatever; but the Sufi sees only the Other: *"Lā ilāha ill'a Llāh"*. [4]

Despite these essential differences, there is a common basis to both Western Science and Sufism, for most of the major philosophical ideas upon which the Renaissance was founded, originated with Sufis,[5] especially in the fields of psychology, medicine and science.[6] Jung's theory of archetypes was as we have seen,[7] undoubtedly derived by him from Sufism, via his study of Alchemy. And even though the original concepts were debased, many of Freud's ideas were derived from Jewish mysticism, whose links with Sufism are indisputable.[8]

Therefore, Sufism has a common basis with religion and science (including psychology), the difference is, that in the West the emphasis is on the individual - in religion as well as elsewhere - leading to an emphasis on individualism in therapy. The Christian values, which underlie Western culture, mean that people are not really held responsible for their behaviour, i.e., it is Adam's sin, or in its modern

270

form – circumstances, that are to blame.[9] In addition, the development of Protestantism has as Weber, Tawney, and others showed,[10] contributed to an economic–determinist culture in which the individual reigns supreme.

The result is a psychology that has contributed to the moral decline we now witness in society; its individualism has – to use its own terms – resulted in *narcissism*. The Sufi emphasis on the social, on community, makes religion an entirely different thing for the Sufi than for one following Western philosophy. The social emphasis to be found in Sufism – where there is a loss of self in the group*(tarīqa)*, and in Nature and its Source(God) – makes Sufism something quite different to Western individualism.

The idea of therapy as it exists in Western culture is wrapped up in notions of individualism. The break-up of *Custom*,[11] and the separation between social–explanatory elements(religion) and individual–explanatory ones(science); between socio-healing(ritual) andthose of individual-healing (medicine), has led necessarily to the need for therapy. Previously, religion was psychotherapy (in a social sense), now with religion has been divorced from its roots, therapy becomes religion in an individual sense. Using this socio-cultural-historical-ideological (holistic) framework, gives us a key enabling us to understand Sufism: Sufism is **religion** *and* **therapy** both at one and the same time; it fills the gap between religion, which has become meaningless and outdated, and a medical art divorced from social and

271

emotional reality. It does this by linking birth and death, so transcending the boundaries of the self (its mortality), a factor it holds in common with religion. However, unlike religion, it does not limit this transcendence to belief (i.e., in an after-life) but extends this transcendence into an individual experience in this life. By focusing on this individual experience, rather than on a common belief system, it cuts through the difference between psychology and religion. Yet at the same time, it shows up the differences between the two systems, differences which arise because Western psychology, unlike Sufism, is bodily based. 'Ayn al-Qudāt al-Hamadhānī explains:[12]

> God's concern and love for you, is not directed to the body, but is directed towards your spirit and heart. For... *"God does not consider your form and its activities, for God's attention is focused on your hearts"*.[13] The heart is made by God to direct attention towards the body for a brief moment in this world until death arrives... (but) you are still attached to mortality: How could you ever be Our (God's) friend? [14] The friends of God are not mortal, whereas you (the unrealised) are entirely by your nature within the mortal world.

It was this transcendent approach that enabled Al-Hamadhānī, as we have seen in **chapter one**, to predict, face and endure a gruesome death, his example, indicating Sufism's capacity to both overcome psychological distress, and to transcend the limitations of traditional religion or a reductionist psychology. For this reason, when Al-Ghazālī realised himself as a Sufi, he not only discovered how to

272

transcend religion and refute the narrow philosophies of his time, but he also regained his psychological stability, becoming a prolific, profound and intellectually stimulating writer. Significantly, the last – and to him – the most important book of his 40 volume compendium, *The Revival of the Religious Sciences*, deals with *The Remembrance of Death* ...[15]

Sufism an Holistic Method of Healing

From the foregoing it is clear that Sufism is a holistic system. It is not surprising that it should show an affinity with Shamanism, and other indigenous medical systems, [16] just as it is in sympathy with ultra–modern holistic medicine,[17] for it does not separate the different elements of existence from each other or their **Source**. The Sufi approach to health and healing is not seen as a separate concern from problems of everyday living or social well-being, for all aspects of existence are conceived of as an interdependent WHOLE with consciousness as part and parcel of this continuum.[18] Failure to acknowledge this by the creation of an unreal reductionism – in Sufism equivalent to dualism – is what creates mental/moral/social/physical problems; problems, that according to Sufism, can also be a means for finding solutions, solutions that do not ignore the interdependence of all life, in its dependence on a common **Source**.

This inevitably leads to what could be called 'Divine

Humanism, a recognition that learning about oneself in the world is to see a **Creative Reality** (God's Presence) everywhere. Like the Arabic script, it connects diverse expressions into a harmonious whole[19] in practise as well as concept; while the reductionist approach of the Western methodological framework – in practise – excludes what SUFISM IS!(interconnectedness), including the exclusion of its (and other non-Western systems) validity, by a methodology that refuses to consider what cannot be reduced to its limitations [20] – including an **Infinite Source**. This was aptly expressed by a Western Unitarian poet, when he wrote: *"We have imprisoned our own conceptions, by the lines we have drawn to exclude the conceptions of others."* [21]

The consequence of this is, that, in Western thought, all behaviour and motivation has been reduced to self-satisfaction; the human is seen as no more than an animal, whereas in Sufism, the human is elevated to a level that transcends base animal drives, for the perfected and complete *hu*-man[22] *(Al-Insān al-Kāmīl)* is the measure of all things *(ahsan al-taqvīm).* [23]

For all these reasons, truth is considered holistically in Sufism, that is to say, it can only be apprehended by the whole personality, for it is the result of experience. There is no artificial separation of what is known intellectually, from what is experienced, perceived and acted on. Belief, ritual, and way of life are inseparable aspects. That is why

274

- strictly speaking – one cannot talk about Sufi rituals for they are not something distinct as is the case for religion. Rather, they are practices – exercises – which will change as the practitioner becomes progressively, more and more aware. As explained by Sufi Master, *Bābā* Dovid Yūsuf:

> Truth is beyond any limiting concept for it is Infinite – while we may talk about it, we can only comprehend it by living within it. It is to be experienced not discussed.[24]

We have seen in previous chapters that it is this factor which explains the diverse nature of Sufi phenomena. Contemporary individuals as different from each other as *Shaykh,* Nāzim 'Adīl al-Qubrusī, *Shaykh,* Fadhallala Haeri, Dr. Javad Nurbakhsh, Idries Shah, Martin Lings, Reshad Feild, Laleh Bakhtiar, Irina Tweedie, *Bābā* Dovid Yūsuf and others who have been quoted in this book,[25] express in different ways an underlying Unity, which is in turn a continuation of the Sufi Masters of the past. Yet, *this does not mean that all these individuals,* or their disciples, or members of other groups who attach the label of "Sufi" to themselves, *necessarily are such,* for it is an holistic attitude to life that determines what constitutes a *Sūfī,* an attitude that can be discerned by an holistic approach towards death, for the Sufi in seeing life as a Unity does not fear death. Having experienced death *(fanā')* of the self *(anā'),* there is no fear of bodily death *(idtirārī),* for death is seen as a liberation rather than a tragedy, a natural completion, in which the fruits of action

275

and intention are manifest. Such fear mirrors the duality *(shirk)* present within the mind of the unbeliever,[26] and is the result of an attachment to the limited self. Having transcended such limitations of perspective by realising a **Greater Reality**, the Sufi is aware of abiding *(baqā')* eternally in that **Reality***(Tawhīd)*, which is *experienced personally* as God.[27] Only this **Reality** is certain of **Eternal Existence** – only this is **Truth***(Haqq)*.

It is the fear of death that causes individuals –especially those of an unstable psychological character [28] – to anchor their instability in a symbol of permanence. Religion then becomes a way of avoiding awareness of the fact that change – impermanence – is a characteristic of human life. Such individuals attempt to nullify the effects of time, by assuming that values, rituals, beliefs, concepts and ideas that originated in the past are unchangeable. Conservatism in religion, as much as in politics, is generated by times/places/situations(and in persons) of uncertainty. This can be expressed in many ways, but the fact that each of the world's religions sees itself as the last,[29] indicates to what extent this phenomena is universal. It is against such conditioning, fears and obsolete notions, that Sufism is directed; its exercises aim to break the hold of dogmatism and release the personality from mental rigidity. Looked at from this perspective, not only is it therapeutic – in both an individual as well as a social sense – but it also transcends the notion of religion as it is usually defined.

Death and the Self

Numerous theories have been advanced concerning Sufi origins, but as Burckhardt pointed out:

> Orientalists have attributed the origins of Sufism to Persian, Hindu, Neo-Platonic or Christian sources. But these diverse attributions have ended cancelling one another (out).[30]

From our analysis, it becomes obvious that rather than seeing Sufism as having a specific origin, we are faced with a number of traditions having common elements. The Sufi response is both universal, as well as specific, representing the continuity of an archaic tradition manifesting within certain socio-psychological contexts, that, for historical reasons, have been primarily, but not exclusively, Islamic (see **chapters 2 & 3**). Sufism represents a retainment of the socio-psychotherapeutic elements of religion – yet which at the same time goes beyond them – by focusing on what is common to both religion (in its external form) and psychology (separated from religion in the West). That is, with the self and its boundaries, in psychology its physical and mental boundaries; in religion its mortality. In both cases, there is a concern with the concept of self, and a question of what it comprises. In the case of Sufism, the separation between the two categories is transcended by anchoring the answers to these questions in terms of an individual personal experience of that which lies beyond the individual self. It is able to do this, because it concentrates on religion's basis (the transcendent mystical

277

experience of the Great Teachers) rather than on particular specific, historical cultural forms (laws, dogma, rituals).

The Sufi does not despair, feel hopeless or helpless – resorting to Western psychological illness definitions (i.e., depression or anxiety, etc.) – when experiencing problems or calamities, for there is a recognition that God is the source of all difficulties, as well as of their solution. The Sufi is compelled thereby to recognise transcendent values upon which the Sufi must act (as far as is possible), rather than considering that s/he is obliged to serve base animal instincts, or is at the mercy of blind forces. Therefore – to use a Western phrase – Sufism *empowers people*, rather than as in the case of Western psychological systems, making them either dependent personalities, or selfishly motivated individuals.

This essential difference is illustrated by considering – one of the most open to religious experience systems of Western psychotherapy – Jung's. Despite the similarities between his own system and Sufism, he was unable to pursue his concepts to their logical Sufi conclusion, for he could not reject the individualistic orientation of the Western value-system.[31] Jung's quest for wholeness and integration is resolved in Sufism, not by an emphasis on the individual – *individualisation* – but by the opposite: *selflessness* !

In Farīd ad-Dīn 'Attār's *Mathnawī*, **Conference of the Birds**, an assembly of birds sets out in search of the king

278

of birds – the *Sī-murgh* (a name which is a pun based on the Persian for 30 birds). After passing through seven valleys (symbolic of the Sufi path) only 30 birds remain. When eventually they arrive, they find that the much sought after king is none other than themselves. The 30 remaining birds are transformed into the **One** *Sīmurgh* (the end of the Sufi quest) as they hear the following:

> I am a mirror set before your eyes
> And all who come before my splendour see
> Themselves, their own unique reality;
> .....
> It is yourselves you see and what you are
> Who sees the Lord? It is himself each sees;
> .....
> And since you came as thirty birds, you see
> These thirty birds when You discover Me,
> .....
> Dispersed to nothingness until once more
> You find in Me the selves you were before
> .....
> The substance of their being was undone,
> And they were lost like shade before the sun..[32]

Despite the diversity of individuals who can be thought of as Sufi, as shown by those from whom we have quoted, coming as they do from different cultures, languages, historical periods and geographical locations, there is an essential harmony between them,[33] yet many of these individuals never met, or had any contact whatsoever. This argues we are considering something fundamental and universal, when we speak of *the Sufi experience*. This experienceonly comes about from *Realising Transcendence;*

it is a realisation that ONLY **Ultimate Reality** exists, for all else is impermanent. I would suggest that this is the highest conception of life possible; the concept of the child at birth, and that of humanity in its simplest and purest state, long before religion or psychology were invented. In discovering our origins, we also discover our ends.

Despite all that has been said, it becomes apparent that, while we may study Sufism in terms of what it does, we cannot really study it in terms of what it is. Its essence is only to be discerned through participation. Any conclusion drawn can only be considered interpretational and not actual. We may know that our lover feels the same feelings as ourself, even though we are on the other side of the world and unable to communicate by writing or by telephone. But how can we convey this in words? How can we test this empirically? Similarly; How can we adequately describe in finite terms, the REALISATION OF TRANSCENDENCE?

But who can speak of this? I know if I
Betrayed my knowledge I would surely die;
If it were lawful for me to relate
Such truths to those who have not reached this state,
Those gone before us would have made some sign;
But no sign comes, and silence must be mine.
Here eloquence can find no jewel but one,
That silence when the longed-for goal is won.
The greatest orator would here be made
In love with silence and forget his trade,
And I too cease: I have described the Way –
Now, you must act – there is no more to say.[34]

280

Notes and References

1) See Al-Ghazālī's autobiography(1358/1939) and introductory chapter to his compendium *Ihyā' 'Ulūm ad-Dīn*, and the commentary on the latter by Muhammad ibn al-Husain Murtadā az-Zabīdī, 10 Vols, Cairo, 1311 A.H; Vol. 1, pp, 3-7; also Al-Ghazālī's *Tahāfut al-Falāsifa* edited by M.Bouyges, Beirut, 1927.

2) Safadī, Salāh ad-Dīn Khalīl ibn Aybak(as-); *Al-Wāfī bi' l-wafayāt* edited by H.Ritter *et al*, Wiesbaden, 1962, p,274.

3) The development of this material lies beyond the scope of this book, for an introduction see K. Plantov, *The Word as a Physiological and Therapeutic Factor*, Foreign Languages Publication House, Moscow, 1959 & P. Lain-Entralgo, *The Therapy of the Word in Classical Antiquity*, Yale University Press, New Haven, 1970.

4) This commonly chanted invocation - used in all Sufi Orders - literally means *there is nothing that is God* (Real, Persistent, Stable, Non-Illusory) *other than THAT WHICH IS !*

5) The influence of Humanism - in its essence Sufism, or what can be called Divine Humanism - upon the West, together with the West's debasement of it, is outlined by Sir Muhammad Iqbāl, in his *The Reconstruction of Religious Thought in Islam*, Oxford, 1934. A fuller consideration of this subject, lies outside the bounds of this book; see Ajmal, 1986, pp,11-20 & pp55-63.

6) For an introduction to this subject, see Seyyed Hossein Nasr, *Islamic Science: An Ilustrated Study*, World of Islam Festival Publishing, London, 1976, pp, 153-204.

7) See note 22 in chapter two.

8) Many Sufi have come from places in the world where Jews were in large numbers and able to interact with the local population without too many restrictions or prejudice(unlike Christian Europe), such as e.g., Morocco, Turkey, India and Persia. See also notes 10-12 in chapter three.

9) The Sufi do not fear Divine punishment, sex is not thought of as a sinful act, nor is there a belief in inherited sin. Freud could only have arisen in Western culture, for like Behaviourism and its variants, these ideas are based upon the notion that humans are instinctually driven *like animals.*

10) *The Protestant Ethic and the Spirit of Capitalism* by Max Weber, George Allen & Unwin, London, 1930; R.H. Tawney, *Religion and the Rise of Capitalism*; and Michael Hill, *A Sociology of Religion*, Heinemann, London, 1972, pp, 98-139.

11) A word used in anthropology to apply to the focus of values and mores, as found in traditional societies, i.e., tradition.

12) Al-Hamadhānī as above, 1962, pp,163-164(in brackets mine).

13) A reference to God's promise to *guide the hearts* of the faithful (not their bodies) - *Qur'ān* 64:11.

14) This is a play on a word, applied as a title, to both Abraham and Muhammad, as well as being one of the earliest terms for the Sufi to be found in the *Qur'ān*(10:62-63).It is worth noting as another

281

example of the religious transcendence of Sufism, that the title for the founder of Zoroastrianism, *Zar'dustra* (from which Zarathustra is derived) literally means *Prince of the Friends.*

15) Al-Ghazālī, *The Remembrance of Death and the Afterlife: Kitāb Dhikr al-Mawt wa-Māba'dahu*, translated by T.J. Winter, Islamic Texts Society, Cambridge, 1989.

16) Systems, that in acknowledging their dependence on tradition and custom, for understanding and treating illness, i.e., psychological and social factors, including the transcendent or spiritual, do not separate psychological and physical from social and biological.

17) Many Sufi, apart from myself, have been instrumental in promoting holistic approaches in modern medicine; see e.g., *The Healing Power of Illness – the meaning of symptoms and how to interpret them*, by Thorwald Dethlefsen & Rüdiger Dahlke, as translated by Peter Lemesurier, Element Books, Shaftesbury, 1990.

18) This does not mean that the **Source**, and its manifestation, are the the same thing as in Pantheism. While elements of existence should not be separated and their interdependence recognised, neither are they to be confused, or compounded – this is magic, not Sufism.

19) Differences between flowing Arabic script and European cuneiform writing are not accidental. European characters express the value system of Western culture: individual letters (individualism), separated from each other (reductionism), that are rigid in form (mechanistic) and limited in their expressive capacity (secularism – no sacred or Infinite element). Hebrew writing, like Judaism, is midway between both systems and cultures.

20) As illustrated by expressions such as; *This is not relevant! This cannot be proven!* , or by limitations on time and cost, as anyone who has had experience of research will testify.

21) Samuel Taylor Coleridge, *Biographia Literaria.*

22) The Sufi continually invoke *Hū* in their assemblies and during *Dhikr*, believing that this represents God's breath as was manifest in the creation of humans.

23) *Mathnawī* 4:519; 6:2877.

24) There are those who have called themselves Sufi and who have made a reputation or money from writing about them. However, those whom they wrote about were the ones who have defined it by *living it* – often at great personal expense.

25) Individuals who, while they essentially agree in their approach to life, have different beliefs and practices.

26) *Mathnawī* 3:3438.

27) See note 7 in **chapter four**.

28) The common characteristic of all forms of mental disturbance, is the preoccupation with the morbid, the limited, and with identity. Mental illness, could in fact, be defined as *self-obsession.*

29) The **Qur'ān** (2:115; 4:47; 5:69; 10:47) makes reference to all the religions as being expressions of the **One Truth** or **Source**, which,

as it is **Infinite** (18:109; 31:27), must be forever expressed (see note 5 in **chapter eleven**).

30) In, *An Introduction to Sufism: The Mystical Dimension of Islam*, Wellingborough, 1990, p, 16.

31) Jung's father was a Protestant clergyman; see note 10.

32) *The Conference of the Birds*, translated by Afkham Darbandi and Dick Davis, Penguin Books, London, 1984, pp, 219-220.

33) Which is why it is a misnomer to refer to *Persian Sufism, Islamic Sufism,* the *Sufism of Rūmī,* or whatever. What may be obscure in the teachings of one Master becomes clear in the writings of another. However, as Sufism is not limited to any specific cultural and/or religious context, we can use terms like "an Islmic Sufi," a "Sufi who is Jewish," a "Persian Sufi," a "follower of Rūmī", etc.

34) 'Attar, as above, 1984, p, 229.

GLOSSARY

For the purposes of alphabetical listing, the definite article has been disregarded, or placed after the word, or phrase, in question. Similarly, though minor differences in pronunciation and ending of words (e.g., an H as opposed to a T, etc.) may have been used in the text, the feminine, or plural, or specific, has here – except in certain instances where meaning is crucial – been disregarded. The majority of words are Arabic in origin – unless stated otherwise – but in some instances are compound terms derived from more than one language.

Abad: post-eternity; a condition of the soul infatuated with Divine Love.

'Abd Allāh: 'slave of God' – one who acknowledges an utter dependence on the Sustainer.

Abjad: the science of the relationship between numerical values of Arabic letters and their meanings.

Adab, plural *ādāb:* canon of respect observed by a disciple especially when interacting with a Master.

Ahadīth – see *Hadīth.*

Ahsan al-taqvīm: 'the best of patterns' – a saying of the Prophet Muhammad referring to the human as the measure of all things.

Ahwāl: psycho-gnostic states; plural of *hāl.*

Akhawiyya(al-): 'the Fraternity' –another name for Sufis.

Akhir(Al-): 'The Last' – a title for God.

Alīf: number One; a feminine name; the finger-shaped bead on a Sufi rosary representing the Name *Allāh.*

Amr: the Command of God; the Creative Word that brings into being.

284

Anā': the ego, the 'I' as opposed to the 'ME'.

Anatta: 'No-soul' - a *Pāli* Buddhist term referring to the non-existence of a personal self.

'Aqālā: to tie a camel by the foreleg, to hamstring it.

'Aql: the Divine faculty of *Knowing* ; the Intellect.

'Arīf, plural *'arifīn:* one who has attained the stage of a realised Sufi.

'Arīf bi-Llāh: **'Knower through God'** - a realised Sufi.

Asfal al-sāfilīn: **'the lowest of the low'** - a saying of the Prophet Muhammad referring to the level to which humans can sink.

Aṣhāb(aṣ-): **'the People'** - another name for the Sufi.

Asnāf: Sufi craftsmen's guild.

Awliyā': saints, plural of *Walī.*

Awwal(Al-): **'The First'** - a title for God.

A'yān ath-thābitah: archetypal world; unmanifest potential.

Azal: pre-eternity, a condition of the soul infatuated with Divine Love.

'Azm: a decision to act.

'Azza wa Jall: **'Great and Majestic'** - an Arabic phrase that is used in conjunction with the Divine Name *Allāh,* to indicate the singular Nature of that **One.**

Bābā: **'chief'** - a Central-Asiatic term of endearment used for a Master, derived from the colloquial term for father, older man, or teacher.

Balā': afflictions, worldly trials arising from the pain of separation from God.

Baqā': continuance; persistence in the state of *fanā' fi-llāh,* subsistence in God.

Bāraka: holiness; inherent virtue; spiritual benediction and its dispensation.

Baraqa: 'to shine like lightning' - insightful flashes of recognition.

Baruch: 'Blessed' -Hebrew word usually referring to God.

Basṭ: 'expansion of light' - a spiritual state of joy; the opposite of *qabḍ.*

Bāṭin: deep; interior; hidden from sight.

Bāṭinī: secret and esoteric doctrine.

Bay'ah (noun), *bay'at* (verb): pledge of allegiance made with a Master; or a **Murshid** acting for the Master.

Bid'a: innovation in spiritual practices.

Bila'ḥāl: lunatic.

Bodhisattvas': **'Beings of Enlightenment'** - those destined to become Buddhas who delay doing so in order to assist others to Enlightenment.

Burāq: a representation of the means by which Muhammad and the Sufi attain the Unitary State.

Chasidim: **'the pious ones'**: a Jewish mystical movement showing similarities to Sufism, popularised by Israel Baal-Shem Tov (died 1760).

Darvēsh: Persian form of *dār'wīsh.*

Dār'wīsh, plural *darāwīsh:* 'one without abode' - traveller; a common term for a Sufi.

Dede: Turkish form of *Shaykh,* sometimes also used for a senior *murīd (Murshid).*

Dervis: Turkish form of *dār'wīsh.*

Desacralisation: emphasizing lower aspects of existence; a tendency to disregard or reject the sacred.

Dhamma: Pāli Buddhist term for the Teaching/doctrine as perceived in the nature of existence *in Time.*

Dhanb: unintentional shortcomings.

Dhāt (Adh-): The essence, or essential nature, which lies beyond being.

Dhat-i bashariyyah: human essence; essential nature; the individual personality.

Dhawq: 'the taste of' – direct perception; a state of consciousness transcending mental knowledge.

Dhikr: remembrance; invocation of the Divine Names.

Dil: Persian form of *qalb.*

Dīwān: 'many-leaved book'-collection of poems or verse.

Du'ā': personal prayer.

Dukkha: 'unsatisfactoriness' – a *Pāli* Buddhist term, that is usually rendered as *suffering,* which refers to the nature of existence.

Durbar: Indian form of *majlis.*

Durghah: Turkish form of *majlis.*

Externalists: those who emphasize the performance of rituals and practices, rather than their meaning.

Fanā': annihilation; the process of dying to self.

Fanā' al-fanā: self-negation; the stage of merging with God in *consciousness* (not substance).

Fanā' fī-Llāh: 'living in God'.

Fānin: 'perishing' – root of the Sufi term *fanā'*.

Faqīr (feminine form *faqirāt*): one who is aware of their poverty before God.

Fiṭrah: inner primordial nature.

Fiṭrat: the primal State of Unity.

Fuqarā': plural of *faqīr*.

Ghaybah: absence from all but God.

Ghazal: a poem in which God is symbolised by a lover.

Gnosis: esoteric knowledge, the inner meaning of which is not known to the uninitiated. Not to be confused with the dualistic philosophy of *Gnosticism*.

Ḥabība: 'Beloved' – the Sufi expression for God.

Ḥabību'llah: 'Beloved of God' – a title usually applied to the Prophet Muhammad.

Ḥadīth, plural *Aḥadīth:* a saying of Prophet Muhammad.

Ḥadīth al-e-Qudsī: a saying of Prophet Muhammad that reproduces what he said, God said to him.

Ḥadīth al-nafs: discursive thought; subvocal talking; or self-talk.

Ḥadrah: 'Presence' – a name for sacred dance and other practices associated with it.

Hāhūt: world of the Absolute.

Hajīs: a passing thought.

Hajj: the journey to God in Sufism, to be distinguished from the trip to Mecca as in Islam (though some Sufi, *may also* undertake the latter).

Hakīm: 'the Wise' - a practitioner of traditional medicine in Islam; in Sufi parlance, a *spiritual therapist* (see *Tibb-i-rūhānī).*

Hāl: a transitory state of illumination.

Halakhah: 'the way to go' - Jewish religious law as applied to the whole of life.

Halqah: Sufi circle of devotees; a course of Sufi study.

Ham: preoccupational thought.

Haqīqah: essential truth, esoteric knowledge.

Haqq: Truth; Reality; Absolute.

Hāqq'anī(al-): 'the people of Reality' - Sufis who claim descent from the teachings of Mansur al-Hallāj.

Hasad: envy; begrudging.

Hijāb: veil which covers the heart - not the garment worn by Muslim women.

Hikmah al-ilāhiyya: Divine Wisdom - Sufism.

Himmah: courage; concentration; resolve to persevere on the Sufi Path.

Hiss: noise; sensation; cause of distraction from God.

Hiya: 'She' - in Sufi parlance, a Name for God.

Hū: 'that' - the sacred breath as manifest in the perfect human (see *Huwa*).

Hudūr: a state of awareness of God's Presence.

Hulūl: spiritual transformation by an infusion of the Divine essence; to dwell in God.

Hunafā': a group of monotheists existing in Arabia prior to the Prophet Muhammad; Sufi forebearers.

Huwa: 'He' – the Source beyond being manifest as the active principle.

Iblīs: 'Slanderer' – the Denier of God's essential Unity.

Idtirārī: physical death; death of the body.

Ikhlāṣ: sincerity; purity of intention – the necessary requisite for following the Sufi Path.

Ikhtiyār: to choose that which is chosen by God.

Ikhwān: 'Brethren' – another name for the Sufi.

Ilhām: inspiration.

'Ilm: 'knowledge' obtained through the five senses.

'Ilm al-kasbī: acquired knowledge.

'Ilm al-laddunī: direct knowledge from God.

'Ilm al-wahab: knowledge resulting from Sufi practices.

Imāms: Leaders of prayer (see *'Ulamā '*). In *Shī'ah* Islam, those who claimed the right to political/religious leadership of all Muslims, as descendants of 'Alī.

Īmān: the holistic profession of faith as demonstrated by one's actions.

'Imārah: North African term for sacred dance.

Inkār al-kasb: to cut the ties of acquisition (personal, or material reward, acculumative action, fame, etc).

Insān al-Kāmīl(Al-): The perfected, or complete wo/man; the Universal Teacher.

Interiorisation: an awareness of one's inner motivations and their spiritual source.

'Irfān: 'Gnostics' – another name for the Sufi (not to be confused with Christian, Manichean, or Mandaean groups, who go by this name).

Islām: accepting God's Direction in all affairs. Finding peace through submission.

'Ismah: without sin, or *wilful* transgression.

Isnād: chain of transmission.

Isrā'(Al-): 'The night journey' – Prophet Muhammad's ascent to the heavens.

Istighrāq: absorption in God; acceptance by Him.

Istinbāt: 'a drawing out', i.e., of the inner, complete, and holistic meaning of a *Qur'ānic* text or *hadīth.*

Istislām: going forward to meet the Divine Will; desire to submit to it with utter compliance.

Ithm: wilful transgression.

Ittihād: the timeless unified state when the stage of realisation is reached.

Ittihād-i-nur: union with God's Light.

Ittilā': the admission of personal problems by a disciple to a Master.

Jabarūt: the world of emanations.

Jadhb: a state of Divine attraction preceded by a discharge of nervous tension; ecstatic fixation.

Jālāl: Majesty of God; severity – the masculine aspect.

Jalwah: 'being filled by God' – the spiritual experience that marks the culmination of *khalwah;* a realisation of the **Transcendent Self**.

Jamāl: Kindness of God; beauty; clemency.

Jinn: personified mental projections; psychic phenomena; the powers inherent in Nature; elementals (can be positive or negative).

Ka'aba: the place of spiritual orientation; the heart.

Kabbalah: 'received tradition'– Jewish mystical and esoteric teachings based upon the *Zohar*, other medieval writings, oral tradition and visions of the prophets.

Kāfir (Al–) 'one who covers over' – or hides the truth from themselves; disbeliever (see *Kufr*).

Kāhin (feminine form *Kāhinah*): the *Qur'ānic* term for the folk healers of pre-Islamic Arabia, who used divination, clairvoyance and associated practices.

Kalimat: 'Word or command of God' – in Sufi parlance it is Destiny. Not to be confused with the Turkish word *Kismet* (Fate), a belief which Sufism rejects.

Karāmah: Grace of God to saints.

Karāmat: charitable acts.

Karāmāt: charismatic influences exerted by saints as a result of their spiritual radiance.

Karma: *Sanskrit* term for the Hindu belief that the results of one's actions are reciprocated and carried forward from one lifetime to the next.

Kashf: revelation; true intuition.

292

Kathra: multiplicity.

Khalq (al-): the Creation.

Khalwah: 'abode of solitude' – spiritual retreat, or a place used for that purpose.

Khāriq al-'ādah: 'that which breaks the habit' (of the mind) or miracles; Sufi expression for overcoming conditioning.

Kharj al-aḥwāl: 'out of conditions'; ecstasy.

Khaṭi'ah: sin.

Khāṭir: a persistent thought.

Khawājagān (Al-): 'The Masters', a name usually applied to the *Naqshbandī* Sufi.

Khawātāt: female dervishes.

Khiḍr (Al-): 'the green one' – Wisdom personified; the archetypal Teacher who eternally *renews* the ancient esoteric tradition.

Khushū': humility – the first virtue to be internalised by a Sufi initiate.

Kibr-i-Azīm: subliminal pride; literally **'Grand Vanity'**.

Kōan: Riddle given in Zen Buddhism to assist transcending the logical mind.

Kufr: a state of unbelief; denial of **Reality**; ingratitude; blasphemy; a rejection of God's Infinite Mercy.

Lāhūt: world of the Manifest.

Laṭā'if: subtle centres in the body; organs of higher perception – also a Name of God.

Logos: Greek term, first used by the Jewish *'Universalist'* Philo, to refer to the *Creative Power* of the **Divine Word**.

Maftirim: mystical Hebrew hymns and poems, usually sung in addition to, or before, formal Jewish Sabbath worship.

Maghrib(al-): '(where) the sun sets' – a term surviving from the heyday of the Islamic Empire. Nowadays it roughly corresponds to Morocco, Mauratania, Algeria, Tunisia and Libya; also used as a reference to the Islamic evening prayer which is said a few minutes after sunset.

Maggid: 'preacher' Hebrew term for a wandering Jewish teacher; also a spiritual mentor who communicates through visions, dreams or the speech of mystics.

Maḥabba: devotional love for God; sacrifice of self.

Maḥbūb: 'Beloved' – a Sufi name for God.

Majdhūb: one who is affected by *jadhb;* a fool of God.

Majlis: Sufi assembly, based upon the word for a meeting of Arab Bedouin in a tent; also used as a name for the personal audience of a disciple with a Master.

Mākhāfa: a reverence for God, that leads to purification.

Malakūt: the mental world.

Malāmati: Sufis who distinguish themselves by word or deed from other Sufi, in order to further the Sufi Cause.

Maqāmāt: 'standpoints'; stations of spiritual development, manifestation and orientation.

Maraḍ: disease; sickness; imbalance.

Ma'rifa: the *experienced* knowledge of God's essential Unity; transcendent knowledge

Masjid: place of prostration or prayer.

Mathnawī: a classical form of Persian poetry.

Mawāfaqa: 'Master of own law', internalisation of balance; equanimity; a stage of attainment on the Path in which there is neither hope for, or fear of, anything.

Mawlawiyya: 'followers of the Master'; the Whirling Dervishes or disciples of Rūmī.

Māyā: Sanskrit word for the illusory nature of existence.

Mevlana: 'our Master'; Turkish term for Jalāl ad-Dīn ar-Rūmī, derived from the Arabic *Mawlā -'my Master'.*

Mi'rāj: the Ascent of Muhammad, or the Sufi, in spiritual development.

Misbaḥah: prayer beads.

Mishkāt: tabernacle; receptacle; niche.

Mokṣa: Sanskrit word denoting *liberation* or *release* from mortal existence.

Moshelim: a Hebrew poet/bard and singer of ballads.

Muezzin: traditional name for the one who calls to prayer from the minaret(mosque tower) – in Arabic *Mu'adhdhin.*

Muftī: practitioner of, and authority on, Islamic law.

Mujāhada, plural *mujāhida:* effort; struggle on the Sufi path; purification by striving.

Mu'jizāt: 'marvels' – miracles of the prophets.

Mulay: North African term derived from the Arabic *Mawlā -'my Master'* and used for descendants of Muhammad.

Munāfiq: 'a concealer', or hypocrite.

Muqaddam (feminine form *muqaddama*): the deputy of a *muqtadā* (Master).

Muqtadā: 'Exemplary' a leader or Guide along the path.

295

Muqtaṣedon: 'those who follow a middle path' (between establishment Islam & Sufism) as opposed to those who exemplify - *muqtada'īm* (*realised* Sufis).

Murāqaba: a state of vigilant awareness.

Murāqiba: examination of conscience.

Murīd, plural *murīdīn:* disciple; follower; initiate on the Sufi Path.

Murshid: Teacher.

Mystic: one who lives eternally in the Presence of God as an *Everliving present Reality.*

Muwaḥḥid: one who is unified with God's Will and Purpose.

Nafas: breath; freedom; liberty.

Nafas ar-Raḥmān(Al-): The breath of God.

Nafī: negation of the limited, individually-orientated, self.

Nafs: soul; psyche; self.

Nafs-ammārah: commanding psyche.

Nafs-ḥaywāniyah: instinctual animal nature.

Nafs-lawwāmah: accusing psyche.

Nafs-muṭma'innah: integrated psyche.

Nafs-i-nāṭiqah: - the faculty of choice; the mind including its non-logical operations.

Nafs al-Wāḥida: The Undivided Self; First Manifestation - the Knower.

Nāsumā: material Soul - the vehicle through which the differing stages of the self are manifest.

Nāsūt: the world of differentiation and form.

296

Nibbāna: *Pāli* Buddhist term for 'extinction' of desire and the attainment of a state of Absolute Truth.

Nifāq: 'to dissociate and dissemble' - hypocrisy.

Nifās: childbirth.

Pīr: a Sufi Master in Persian or Indian, Sufi Orders.

Qabḍ: 'contraction' -a condition of spiritual dejection often *accompanied* by psychological states of depression; the opposite of *basṭ.*

Qadar: the capacity to choose in Time, a destiny chosen outside of it.

Qalandarī: Sufis who disregard social conventions.

Qalb: heart; the organ of supra-rational intuition and orientation.

Qawm: 'Folk or mystic people' - another name for Sufis.

Qawwālī: sung Ghazal accompanied by music.

Qinā'at: contentment in all situations; a state of beatitude.

Quṭub: 'spiritual centre' as present within a particular Master, at a specific time/place/state.

Rabb: Lord; Sustainer; Master (God).

Ramaḍān: the Islamic calendar's 9th month, when there is abstinence from food, drink, sexual activities, pleasure pursuits or anger, during daylight hours, for 30 days. In some Sufi Orders, it is extended to 40 days, including sexual abstinence for the whole of the period.

Rūḥ: spirit; vital energy; the principle of Reality; Source of consciousness and life.

Rūḥ al-ilāhī (Ar-): The Divine Spirit or Creative energy.

297

Rūḥ al-kullī (ar): The Universal spirit or soul; the created manifestation of the uncreated Divine Energy.

Rūḥ al-Qudūs: Holy Spirit; the divine force as manifest in the created world.

Ṣafwa: uncontaminated/original; without deviation; *spiritual* purity.

Ṣaḥw: one who is not drunk – the opposite to *sukr.*

Saj': the rhythmic prose chanted by the *Kāhin/Kāhinah* of pre-Islamic Arabia.

Ṣalāh: 'Glory' – an holistic form of ritual prayer, during which the *Cycle of Existence* (in all its forms) is enacted/participated in.

Ṣalawāt: communal prayers.

Sālik, plural *sālikūn:* a seeker of God on the path of Sufism.

Ṣalla: to hallow, sanctify or bless.

Samā': the use of music for contemplation or spiritual inspiration.

Samsāra: Buddhist, *Pāli* term, for the cycle of existence.

Sayoshants: Avestanic term for the *saviours* who appear at the beginning of every Zoroastrian cycle.

Shafaqat: affection or kindness shown to kinfolk (Sufis).

Shahādah: the statement expressing a belief in God's essential Unity.

Shakk: doubt; uncertainty; misgiving.

Shaman: Healer (male or female) in tribal societies, who calls on spirits for assistance.

298

Shamon: Japanese female Shaman.

Sharī'ah: Islamic religious law.

Shaṭhuyyāt: ecstatic expressions; utterances made when in a state of ecstasy.

Shaykh: Spiritual Elder.

Shayṭān: The Ultimate Ego.

Shī'ah: 'faction or party'(of 'Alī), whose adherence is based upon the claim that the cousin and son in law of Prophet Muhammad was his only rightful heir (about 17 per cent of all Muslims).

Shirk: associating partners with God – Dualism.

Ṣiddīqūn: 'truthful ones' – a hierarchy of 40 saints (symbolic of completeness) in the invisible worlds, who maintain cosmological equilibrium.

Ṣidq: truthfulness, one of the essential virtues the Sufi initiate is required to internalise.

Sidrat al-muntahā: a representation of the end of the Sufi's and Muhammad's quest – the revelation of Cosmic Unity, through Self-realisation.

Silsila: Sufi initiatic chains.

Sīmurgh: mythical bird of Persia derived from the *Phoenix* of Ancient Egypt.

Sirr: 'secret mystery' – innermost consciousness, the place at which *ittiḥād* occurs.

Subḥah: prayer beads.

Ṣūfism: the path of Oneness; a Way to God through devotion and selflessness (the Way of transcendence).

Ṣūfiyya (as-): the Elect or Chosen.

Ṣuḥba: 'Fellowship, Companions' - a name for Sufis.

Sukr: 'drunkeness' - a temporary state of ecstatic rapture in which the Sufi may unwittingly cry out or babble.

Sunna: example of a living Master and not as in Islam, the customs of Prophet Muhammad.

Sunnī: those who claim to follow Prophet Muhammad's example and consequently derive much of their beliefs from his sayings. The major divisional group.

Sūra: 'steps' classical division of the *Qur'ān* into portions = chapters.

Tabar: double-headed axe, a symbol pertaining to Sufism's active nature.

Ta'bīr ar-Ru'yā: 'Dream interpretation' - as a spiritual message of guidance to an individual on the Path by a realised Master in private.

*Tafakkara(noun Tafakkur):*to contemplate/ponder/meditate.

Tahajjud: night vigils.

Ṭāhir: 'Pure one' (in conduct) a saintly person, sometimes used as a title of respect.

Taḥlīl: 'lawful'; saying the statement of Unity-*"there is no god but The God!"*

Taḥliya: strengthening virtues to assist self-purification.

Ṭā'ifa: an organised, established and formally constituted, association of Sufis (or those who purport to be such).

Tāj: 'crown'- Persian word for a Sufi hat.

Tajallī: Illumination of the heart by the Divine Presence.

300

Tajrīd: divestment of worldy attachments.

Takhannus: annual retreat and withdrawal by the Ḥunafā.'

Takhliya: self-examination to eliminate moral weaknesses.

Talmud: Jewish laws and ethical teachings, collected over centuries and finally compiled about 500 C.E.

Talwīn: flux; transition; state of impermanence.

Tamkīn: rest; repose; stability.

Tanakh: 'Bible'- Hebrew term composed of the first letters of 3 words referring to *Torah, Prophets* and *Writings.*

Taqwā: fearful-awareness; piety.

Ṭarīqa: the Way or mystic path - also a specific Order.

Tark-i-sabab: cause-abandonment.

Taṣawwuf: mysticism; esotericism; pertaining to purity.

Tasbīh: Turkish name for prayer beads derived from the Arabic invocation - *Subhāna 'Llāh* (Glory be to God).

Tashbīh: assimilating; likening; making of comparisons.

Tasir al-anzar: hypnotism.

Ṭawā'if: organisational associations; Sufi Orders - plural of *Ṭā'ifa.*

Tawajjuh: 'to turn one's face' - the Master's attention, concentration, confrontation, contemplation of a disciple.

Tawakkul: relying on God to increase awareness of Her.

Tawatur: an *hadīth* whose authenticity is vouched for by an unbroken line of Sufi oral transmission, and consequently repeated in writings of their Masters.

Tawbah: to turn away from duality to the One - in Islamic parlance, repentance.

Tawḥīd: Divine Unity.

Ṭibb–i–rūḥānī: **'spiritual therapy'** – holistic healing; that which Sufi Masters practise.

Transcendent Self: The only Being; seat of Consciousness and Source of experience, going beyond the limitations of personal existence.

True Self: a state in which the limited self of everyday experience is in harmony with the **Transcendent Self**.

Tūbā: **'Blessed Joy'** – an inward state of tranquillity and equanimity that is unaffected by external conditions.

Ṭuruq: Sufi Orders; plural of *Ṭarīqa*.

Tzaddik: **'Righteous man'** – Hebrew term for a holy man, one of the spiritual hierarchy by whose merit the world is sustained (see *Ṣiddīqūn*). In each Age one of this number, possesses the capabilities of ushering in the Messiah if that generation is worthy. In *Chasidism*, the name for a pre-eminent Master.

'Ulamā': the clerics of Islam; see *Imāms*.

Unfoldment: the attainment of human capacity achieved by effort and experience according to inner potentiality (see *True Self*)

Waḥad: **'One'** – i.e., God.

Waḥdat: the Unity of Being.

Waḥdat ash–shuhūd: the Unity of consciousness.

Waḥdat al–Wujūd: the Oneness of Being.

Wahhābī: a Sa'ūdi version of Islam based on Muhammad ibn 'Abd al-Wahhāb's (1703-1787) teachings, that by its

302

socio-economic power, dominates Islam's interpretation in most of the Muslim world, and by its donations, that of Islamic Studies Departments in Western universities.

Wajd: ecstasy.

Walī: 'a friend of God' – a saint; or a Sufi Master.

Wasāwis: obsessional thoughts.

Wilādat 'l-ma'nawiyya : spiritual begetting; the parent and child relationship between a Master and a disciple.

Wilāyah: God's friendship towards a saint.

Wird: invocatory prayer; formula or litany, to orient the mind towards God. Derived from *wārid* (inspiration), as symbolised by a rose *(ward)* signifying the heart.

Wujūd: Existence; Being; a term only applicable to God.

Yahweh: a derived name for Israel's God, composed from 4 consonants (YHWH) indicating the inexpressible and unlimited nature, of the Divinity.

Yanuka: wonder child of Jewish medieval literature, possessing suprarational cognitive powers.

Yaqilun: understanding; wisdom; the verbal form of *'aql.*

Yaqīn: assurance or certainty; a stage of attainment along the Sufi Path.

Yogi: Hindu ascetic who desires to attain union with the Universal Soul.

Ẓāhir: the outer; external.

Zahrā'(az-): 'the Resplendent one' – title given to Fātimah, daughter of Prophet Muhammad

Zakāt: to be free from material encumberances by the charitable disposal of excess.

Zeker: 'that which fixes the mind upon' – Hebrew form of the Arabic *Dhikr*.

Zikr: Persian form of *Dhikr*.

Zohar: 'Illumination' – the most influential book of Jewish mysticism; a pseudographic work that purports to be by 2nd century Judean Rabbi, Simeon ben Yohai, but which has been shown to have been compiled by Moses de Leon (died 1305) in Islamic Spain.

Zuhhād: 'Renouncers' – another name for Sufis.

APPENDIX 1: 99 NAMES OF GOD

Al-Ḥayyu al-Qayyūm

The Ever-Living, the Everlasting, the Self-Subsisting (The Greatest Name of God);
Qurān 20:111 & 3:2

Ar-Raḥmān
The Giver of Mercy, the Most Kind (the Name Muhammad used most frequently for God); *Qur'ān* 55:1

Ar-Raḥīm
The Most Merciful
Qur'ān 2:143

Al-Aḥad
The One and Only
112:1

Al-Awwal
The First
57:3

Al-Wāḥid
The Unique
74:11

Al-Badī'
The Originator
2:117

Al-Bāri'
The Evolver
59:24

Al-Mubdī'
The Producer
85:13

Al-Khāliq
The Creator
13:16

Al-Wāsi'
The All-Encompassing
2:268

Al-Bāqī
The Ever Abiding
20:73

As-Samad
The Eternal
112:2

Al-Muḥyī
The Life Giver
30:50

Al-Muqīṭ
The Determiner
4:85

305

Al-'Alī The Exalted 2:255		Al-Malik The King 59:23	
Al-Muta'ālī The Most High 13:9		Mālik al-Mulk The Possessor of Sovereignty 3:26	

Dhū-l-Jalāli wa-l-Ikrām
All-Majestic and
Generous Lord
55:27

Al-Wahhāb The Bestower 3:8		Ar-Razzāq The Provider 51:57-58	
Al-Karīm The All-Sufficing and Bountiful 27:40		Al-Ghanī The Self-Sufficient 2:267	
Al-Mughnī The Enricher 9:74		Al-Bāṣit The Enlarger 13:26	
Ar-Rāfi' The Exalter 6:83		Al-Fattāḥ The Decider 34:26	
Al-Ḥakam The Judge 40:48		Al-'Adl The Just 6:114-115	
Ash-Shahīd The Witness 5:120		Ar-Raqīb The Watcher 5:120	

Al-Khabīr
The All-Aware
6:18

Al-Baṣīr
The All-Seeing
57:3

As-Samī'
The All-Hearing
17:1

Al-'Alīm
The All-Knowing
2:29

Al-Ḥasīb
The Accounter
(of all)
4:6

Al-Muḥsī
The Numberer
19:94

Al-Muqsiṭ
The Just
Reckoner
21:47

Al-Ḥafīẓ
The Preserver
11:57

Al-Wakīl
The Protector & Disposer
6:102

Al-Muhaymin
The Guardian
59:23

Al-Wārith
The Inheritor
(of all things)
19:40

Al-Wāli
The Governor
13:11

Al-Jāmi'
The Gatherer (of all)
3:9

Al-Jabbār
The Compeller
59:23

Al-Bā'ith
The Raiser
(from death)
16:89

Al-Ḥayy
The Living
20:111

Al-Mumīt
The Bringer of Death
15:23

307

Al-Muntaqim The Avenger 30:47	**Al-'Afuw** The Pardoner 4:99
Ar-Ra'ūf The Compassionate 2:143	**Al-Ghaffār** The Forgiver 2:235
As-Salām The Peace 59:23	**Al-Ḥalīm** The Lenient 2:235
Aṣ-Ṣabūr * The Patient 16:127	**At-Tawwāb** The Relenting 2:37
Al-Ghafūr The Forgiving 2:235	**Al-Mujīb** The Responsive (to prayer) 11:61
Ash-Shakūr The Appreciative 64:17	**An-Nāfi'** * The Profiter 48:11
Al-Mu'īd The Restorer 85:13	**Al-Muṣawwir** The Modeller 59:24
Al-Qābiḍ * The Restrainer 48:20-24	**Al-Muta'akhkhir** The Deferrer 14:42-44
Al-Muqaddim The Promoter 50:28-31	**Al-Mu'izz** * The Honourer 3:26

Al-Mudhill *
The Dishonourer
3:26

Al-Khāfiḍ *
The Abaser
3:26

Al-Māni' *
The Controller
25:2-3

Ar-Rashīd *
The Director
15:24-25

Aḍ-Ḍār *
The Distresser
48:11

Al-Qahhār
The Almighty Subduer
13:16

Al-Qādir
The Capable
17:99.

Al-Muqtadir
The All-Powerful
54:42

Al-Qawī
The Strong
22:40

Al-'Azīz
The Mighty
59:23

Al-Jalīl
The Majestic
55:27

Al-Kabīr
The Great
22:62

Al-Majīd
The Glorious
11:73

Al-'Aẓīm
The Magnificent
2:255

Al-Mutakabbir
The Supreme
59:23

Al-Wājid *
The Noble
31:26

Al-Laṭīf
The Gracious
42:19

Aẓ-Ẓāhir
The Manifest
57:3

309

Al-Bâtin The Hidden 57:3	الوالي	**Al-Ḥaqq** The Truth 20:114	الحق
Al-Ḥakīm The Wise Physician 6:18	الحكيم	**Al-Mu'min** The Preserver of Faith 59:23	المؤمن
Al-Walī The Friend 4:45	الولي	**Al-Wadūd** The All-Loving 11:90	الودود
Al-Hādī The Guide 22:54	الهادي	**An-Nûr** The Light 24:35	النور
Al-Barr The Beneficient 52:28	البر	**Al-Ḥamīd** The Praiseworthy 2:267	الحميد
Al-Quddûs The Holy 62:1	القدوس	**Al-Matīn** The Invicible 51:58	المتين
Al-Qayyûm The Self-Subsistent 3:2	القيوم	**Al-Âkhir** The Last 57:3	الآخر

• These are traditional Names, which whilst not actually used in the *Qur'ānic* passage given, are implied therein.

310

APPENDIX 2: The *'Ilm-i-Abjad* system

Arabic Letter	Number assigned	Arabic Letter	Number assigned
ا	1	س	60
ب	2	ع	70
ج	3	ف	80
د	4	ص	90
ه	5	ق	100
و	6	ر	200
ز	7	ش	300
ح	8	ض	400
ط	9	ت	500
ي	10	ث	600
ك	20	خ	700
ل	30	ذ	800
م	40	ظ	900
ن	50	غ	1,000

APPENDIX 3: Examples of *Ādāb* to be observed by Sufi disciples when interacting with a Master*

Requirements for Initiates of the *Chishtiyya Order*

1. Reliance on the *Pīr* must be total, to turn to another would be to be deprived of this *Pīr's* blessing.

2. There must be total obedience and service to the *Pīr*, with the whole of one's life and property, for this is the mark of love.

3. The *murīd* should observe only the *wird* that is given, abandoning all other exercises and devotions.

4. Stepping on the *Murshid's* prayer mat is not permitted.

5. There shall be no using of the *Murshid's* utensils.

6. The *Murshid's* place of ablutions and purifications shall not be used.

7. Feet should not be turned towards the *Murshid*, or in his absence towards his seat.

8. When standing, there shall be no overshadowing of the *Murshid*, his clothes, or even his shadow.

9. Eating, drinking, or the performance of ablutions while the *Murshid* is present, shall only be done with his express permission, and to attend to anybody, or anything else other than him, is not allowed.

10. While the *Murshid* is present, there shall be no leaving of the room without permission or necessity.

11. Anything the *Murshid* says, or does, shall not be objected to.

12. The *murīd's* voice shall not be raised above that of the *Murshid*, and speech should be brief, waiting attentively for the answer.

13. The *murīd* should know that the *Murshid* only answers questions that deserve a reply. If the reply is not satifactory, the *murīd* should regard this as a deficiency in understanding on his part, rather than by the *Murshid*.

14. Actions, or statements by the *Murshid*, shall not be contradicted, even if the *murīd* is right. The *murīd* must believe that the *Pīr's* mistakes are better than the virtues of the *murīdīn*.

15. All the *murīd's* doubts should be expressed to the *Murshid*, as well as dreams, and what their interpretation is believed to be.

16. The *Pīr* shall be considered as a physician of the heart, and all the *murīd's* states and conditions should be described to him, that he might suggest their remedies.

312

17. Whatever the *Murshid* relates to the *murīd*, shall not be disclosed without his express permission, and then only that which can be understood by others without difficulty or interpretation.

18. The *murīd* should not expect the *Pīr* to perform a miracle for him.

19. Whatever blessings the *murīd* receives shall be thought to have come from the *Pīr* and not someone else; even if in a dream the *Pīr* should visit the *murīd*, as some other *Murshid* or saint.

Requirements for Initiates of the *Ni'matu'llāhī Order*

1. The disciple must be sincere in faith and pure in intention.

2. The disciple must take only the Master as a guide.

3. The disciple must keep the Master's secrets, not divulging his power, or disclosing any miraculous occurrence he might witness.

4. The disciple should not draw attention to himself, but be silent in the presence of the Master.

5. The disciple should not seek precedence over the Master, even by quoting his words to others whilst in his presence.

6. There should be no criticism, by either word or action, of the Master's direction. And there must be patience in waiting for a reply to a question, accepting the answer given unconditionally.

7. The disciple should not show ignorance by testing the Master in any way, for to do so shows the Master is not accepted as such, making teaching impossible.

8. In the Master's presence, the disciple must abandon all pride and self-esteem, realising by comparison, his own spiritual poverty.

9. The Master's peace and tranquility must be put before a disciple's.

10. Surrender of possessions and soul to the Master, must be total.

11. The disciple must not display his abilities or knowledge in the Master's presence, including what has been gained through Sufi practice, for this is self-affirmation not self-negation.

12. The disciple must address the Master in a correct way and at the correct time, avoiding mention of worldly affairs, or useless chatter and asking God to assist him in correct behaviour when doing so.

13. The disciple must never feel the Master is in any sense indebted to him for his devotion, but should see that he owes the Master for the Divine blessings and spiritual nourishment he receives.

14. The disciple should not expect the Master to take him beyond whatever state he is capable of, or that God has ordained.

15. The disciple must be employed and free from financial dependence on either the Master, or on others.

16. Should the Master expel the disciple, he should not go away, but persist in accepting the Master's approval and rejection equally, thus showing his true nature to both himself and the Master.

17. A disciple must obtain permission before undertaking any course of action of consequence, realising that to to rely on his own ideas, even if correct, is to reject the Master as his guide.

18. The disciple should not take advantage of the Master's tolerance or forgiveness, but must obey all instructions given explicitly, never taking them lightly, for progress will be affected by disobedience.

19. A disciple must never rely on his own interpretations of signs, events, dreams or visions, but must relate them to the Master in order that their validity and meaning can be assessed.

20. The disciple must listen intently to the Master's direction accepting that his words are God inspired; attempting at all times to discern the relationship between them and his own spiritual state.

21. The disciple must at all times act respectfully towards the Master, avoiding familiarity; never praying in front of him, or laughing loudly whilst in his presence.

22. Questions should not be asked about what the disciple is unable to understand.

23. The disciple must disclose all his secrets, spiritual experiences and whatever God ordains for him, to the Master. Should he not do so his progress will be prevented.

24. The disciple must not undermine the Master's position as a Guide, by speaking to others about things, or in a way that is beyond their capacity to understand. Nor should he assume that directions given to him will necessarily be applicable to others.

Requirements for Initiates of the *Bābā'iyya Order*

1. Only the Master must be taken as a guide – all dreams, personal experiences, spiritual knowledge, or signs in life, are only to be understood in the light of the teachings and not by other means.

2. There shall be no attempt to instruct the Master in any way, either by word, intonation, or by ignoring his advice or counsel.

3. There shall be no teaching of others without permission, and if given, teaching shall be seen as coming from the Master, not self.

4. It is forbidden to disagree with the Master even if he is wrong, or to dispute with him in any way, including discussing his instructions with others.

314

5. When the Master is present there shall be no engaging in talking to others, or any other activity whatsoever.

6. Speech to the Master should be direct, truthful and with an attitude of respect, not burdening him with gossip, useless chatter or irrelevant questions.

7. All advice, counsel and instructions received, shall be considered to be personal and must not be disclosed to others, including dreams and their interpretation.

8. It is forbidden to sit in the Master's seat, or use any of his books, or personal belongings, even if he is not present.

9. It is necessary to be employed, or have a regular source of income and not to depend on the Master's, or his disciples, resources.

10. All one's resources including time, health - and if necessary life - should be given to the Master, just as he does for his disciples.

11. There must be no feeling of indebtedness for devotion given to the Master, for he is only a guide to direct attraction to God; without his assistance, spiritual blessings and progress are not possible.

12. Whatever the Master says or does, should be accepted without any conditions, for he is the Master, and what may be unclear will in time be understood.

13. No course of action, commitment, or change in circumstances, should occur without consulting the Master.

14. Personal well-being, peace of mind, material, or any form of self-benefit must take second-place to furthering the Cause. For this reason the Master's interests must be put before one's own. To do otherwise is to reject the path of selflessness and to hinder the Master's endevours, since he will always put the Cause and the interests of the disciples, before his own.

15. Fraternity activities, exercises learnt, the Master's personal life, and prophecies, are not to be divulged without permission. To violate this secrecy is to automatically terminate membership.

16. The Master's approval, rejection, praise or displeasure arising from the disciples actions, shall all be accepted equally as being part of the Divine Plan and the means by which progress is possible.

---

* In the original written statutes on which these individualised and simplified versions are based (a Master makes his own rule according to circumstances and the needs of his group) there will be **Qur'ānic** or other scriptural references, and elaborate explanations and justifications for the rules given. For an example of complete codes, see Meier, 1957, Suhrawardī, **Bounties of Divine Knowledge** (chapters 30-53), Ajmal, 1986, pp, 30-31, and Nurbakhsh, 1978, pp, 128-135.

E	J	I	S	T	Actions Taken During the Period	Symbolic Items
Candidate	Giyoret ♀	Muslim	Candidate	12 mths.	**CANDIDATE** learns to accept, understand and implement three guiding principles in life (see p, 318).	A red, yellow and white armband is worn on the left wrist at all times, until the stage of **DISCIPLE** is attained.
Approacher	Ger ♂	Sālik	Seeker	2 years	The **SEEKER** becomes a community servant at meetings. Personal and community *Zeker* and *Wird* are learnt.	Men grow their beards and women have long hair. A hat and prayer beads are used by both sexes.
Associate	Chaver	Murid	Disciple	3 years	10% of all income is pledged to the Cause. There are periods of full-time service and on-going study.	Clothes of three colours are worn at Fraternity meetings, and during all periods of full-time service.
Navi	Nis'ta'rim	Dervish	Initiate	3 years	Periods of travelling without means; living simply and developing a trust in Divine Providence.	A golden cord with three knots and clothes of the three colours, are worn during the periods of full-time service.
Essene	Chasid	Sūfi	Companion	3 years	Circumcision, or blood-letting for circumcised males; women shave their whole body and head.	Pure white garments are used by both sexes, for all activities that are connected with the Fraternity.
Theraputae	Nazār'ite	'Arif	Realised One	Time period known only to God	19-99 weeks of withdrawl, fasting during daylight hours, and abstaining from animal foods, sex, alcohol and contact with the dead.	The hair and beard are not cut for the whole period. A minimum of clothes are worn, no money is carried, and the begging-bowl used for food and donations.
Homilites	Hakham/Rav	Shaykh/Murshid	Elder	Time period known only to God	**MASTER** (alive), and/or **SAINT** (dead or alive) **S** A *Muqtadā* can become a *Walī* **I** *Tzaddik* " *Maggid* **J** Master *(Maskil)* / Guardian *(Mebakker)* **E**	

* Individual differences are taken into account and the completion
The first two stages are probationary, and the last two stages are
being the result of election, or choice by God, and so determined

THE *Bābā'iyya* (The Fraternity of the Universal Way)

The Ritual Indicating Completion of a Stage and the Commencement of the Next One	Z
After reciting **Qur'ān** 2:285 and making a public pledge of loyalty to the **Fraternity** (at least three **INITIATES** must be present), the **CANDIDATE** becomes known as a **SEEKER** and is given a specific, appropriate personal Name of God, to be used in individual *Zeker* (see **Appendix 1**).	Repentance
The **SEEKER** reads out **Psalm** 51:10-17, then is given a new name after being baptised (in living water), so becoming known as a **DISCIPLE**. Men receive a yellow shirt that is worn with a white scarf and green trousers. Women receive a red waistcoat that is worn with a white blouse and a green skirt.	Reform
Men shave their head and beard, and women cut their hair very short. An Initiation vow is said publicly (see the next page for details) and the community recites a special prayer. The new **INITIATE** then reads out from the *Avatamsaka Sūtra* (see p, 318) and is given a golden knotted cord.	Sacrifice
There is a Retreat at the end of the period *(Khalwah)*, after which the golden cord is handed back and its symbolism explained by the new **COMPANION**, who reads out *Svetasvatara Upanishad* 4-6 (see the next page), and is then given white garments. The community shows its acceptance by a ritual chant - see pp, 242 & 262, note 6.	Trust
Having successfully completed all the requirements, the **COMPANION** now becomes a full member of the Fraternity. **John** 13: 13-17 is read out, and its instructions followed by the new member. A blue/black cloak for men and a dark red/brown for women is given together with a begging-bowl.	Obedience
At the end of the period, the **REALISED ONE** having *received* such as a gift (see pp, 76 & 232) reads out **Acts** 2:42-47, renouncing publicly personal ownership of time or goods. The cloak is retained to signify the desire to exemplify the Path in *everyday life,* whatever the occupation, and a stick is given to indicate authority as an **ELDER** (see note 67, p, 161).	Submission

The Key to Table

				Praise	Piety – Hope
E = Essene	**J** = Jewish	**I** = Islamic	**S** = Stages		
T = Minimum Time Period		**Z** = Stations (see pp, 120-121)			

of all stages is not obligatory, but considered to be *Kalimat* (Destiny). additional - as they are unlikely to be attained by most candidates, before birth (for further details of these stages see p,318).

APPENDIX 4: THE INITIATION STAGES EXPLAINED

The names in capitals designate the terms used by the *Bābā'iyya*, who are called the **Fraternity of the Universal Way** in recognition of the fact that they show a continuity with other esoteric systems. Those familiar with *Freemasonry*, *Kabbalah* or *Rosicrusianism* will notice parallels. This is also indicated by the Arabic terms, used alongside Hebrew and other associated systems, that *roughly* correspond to them. Scriptural quotations are deliberately drawn from various religions in order to emphasize to the initiate that it is not these religions as such, that the Path is concerned with, but the meaning that underlies them. The seven basic stages are symbolic, equating with the week completed by the Sabbath (peace & fulfilment); the seven heavens; cycles of revelation; major religions and stages of consciousness.

THE THREE PRINCIPLES LEARNT AT THE CANDIDATE STAGE

The Unity and Sanctity of Life
The Oneness of the Human Family
The Common Basis of Religion

THE INITIATION VOW

The Divine Messengers of all Revealed Religions do I respect and honour, seeking to love all humanity as they have taught. All forms of conflict and division do I resist, and violent action will I not initiate. With all nations and all peoples I wish to be at peace; that all beings in all worlds of existence may come to know the Joy of Unity in the service of All. Let Love, Peace and Joy be within myself, and may it be so for all I meet.

The Avatamsaka (Garland) Sūtra: 23 (last part)

"I vow to protect all beings and never to abandon any. What I say, I say sincerely, truly and without being false. Why? Because my mind is set on realisation that I might free others; I do not seek the All-surpassing Way for my own sake. Therefore I shall be like the sun, shining Universally on all, without seeking thanks or reward. Taking care of all sentient beings, even if they are bad, never giving up my vows on this account, not abandoning All, because one being is evil. This I vow before All".

INITIATION INTO THE COMPANION STAGE

Svetasvatara Upanishad (4-6)

" May the mysterious visionary power that transforms pure light into the rainbow coloured creation; and from whom all things come and to whom all return, grant us the grace of pure vision...for in this vision of Love there is everlasting peace...When creation was ended He rested, making a bond of Love between His Self and all self's; giving to each its place in nature...now this work is done a greater work can now begin...May we know You Lord of lords, Ruler of rulers, God of gods; the Supreme Sovereign of Love...Pure Consciousness of conscious beings, the ONE who fulfils the prayers of many - when You are known, we are free of all fetters....If one has supreme Love for You, and also loves their master, then the radiance of The Self illuminates the teaching; illuminating the world - for that one is a Great soul."

318

BIBLIOGRAPHY

For the purposes of alphabetical listing, the definite article has been placed after - rather than before - the Arabic name in question. Occasionally, Arabic or Persian names have been abbreviated, but sufficient information has been given to make location possible.

'Abd al-Qādir, A.H. (1962), Editor, *Rasā'il al-Junaid,* London.

Abu-Nasr, J.M. (1965), *The Tijaniyya: A Sufi Order in the Modern World,* Oxford University Press, London.

Abū Nu'aym al-Isfahānī, *Hilyat al-Awliyā' wa Tabaqāt al-Asfiyā'* (10 vols.), Cairo, 1351-1357/1932-1938.

'Adīl, Haji Amina(1988), *Forty Questions: asked of Prophet Muhammad by the Jews of Medina and his answers,* Arafat, Sri Lanka.

Aflākī (al-), Shams ad-Dīn Ahmad (1959-1961), *Manāqib al-'Ārifīn,* edited by T.Yaziji (2 vols.), Ankara, translated by C.Huart as, *Les Saints des derviches tourneurs* (2 vols.), Paris, 1918-1922.

Aini, M.A. (1926), *La Quintessence de la Philosophie de Ibn-i-Arabi,* translated by A.Rechid, Paris.

Ajmal, Muhammad (1986), *Muslim Contributions to Psychotherapy and Other Essays,* Psychology Research Monograph (5), National Institute, Islamabad.

'Alī,'Abd Allāh Yūsuf (1938), *The Glorious Kur'an* (translation and commentary), 3rd Edition, Lahore.

Altizer, T.J. (1959), "Science and Gnosis in Jung's Psychology", in *The Centennial Review,* Summer Edition, pp, 304-320, London.

Amuli, Sayyid Haydar, *Inner Secrets of the Path,* translated by A.D.Yate, Element Books, Shaftesbury.

Anderson, P.E.(1974),"SufiStudies", in *Library Journal of the American Institute for Continuous Education,* in Shah, 1966, 2nd edition.

Andrews, J.B. (1903), *Le cult des fontaines de Sebba Aioun à Alger,* Jordan.

Annett, S. (1976), *The Many Ways of Being: A Guide to Spiritual Groups and Growth Centres in Britain,* Abacus, London.

Ansari, M. Abdul Haq (1986), *Sufism and Shari'ah: A Study of Shaykh Ahmad Sirhindi's Effort to Reform Sufism,* Islamic Foundation, Leicester.

Ansārī (an-), Abū Ismā'īl 'Abd Allāh al-Harawī *Manāzil as-Sā'irin,* edited and translated as *'Les Etapes des itinérants vers Dieu'* , by S.de Laugier de Beaurecueil, Institute Orientale, Paris, 1962.

Apuleius, *Metamorphoses and other writings,* trans. by W.Adlington (1566) and revised by S.Gaselee, Loeb Classical Library, William Heinemann, London.

Arberry, A.J. (1969), *A Sufi Maryr: the Apologia of Ain al-Qudāt al-Hamadhānī,* George Allen & Unwin, London.

-------(1966), *Muslim Saints and Mystics: Episodes from the Tadhkirat al-Auliya' of Farid al-Din Attar* (trans.), Routledge & Kegan Paul, London.

319

-------(1961), *Discourses of Rumi*, John Murray, London.

-------(1956), *The Mystical Poems of Ibn al-Farid* (trans.), Emery Walker, Dublin.

-------(1950),*Sufism:An Account of the Mystics of Islam*, Allen & Unwin, London.

-------(1950b), *The Spiritual Physick of Rhazes* (trans.), University Press, Cambridge.

-------(1937), *The Book of Truthfulness* (a translation of the *'Kitāb as-Sidq'* of Abū Sā'īd al-Kharrāz), Oxford University Press, London.

-------(1935), *The Doctrine of the Sūfīs* (translation of Al-Kalābādhī's, *Kitāb*), University Press, Cambridge.

Archer, N.P.(1980), Editor, *The Sufi Mystery*, Octagon Press, London.

Astour, M.C. (1967), *Hellenosemitica*, E.J.Brill, Leiden.

'Attār, Farīd ad-Dīn, *The Conference of the Birds*, translated by Afkham Darbandi and Dick Davis, Penguin Books, London, 1984.

-------*Ilāhi-Nāma*, edited by Helmut Ritter, Tehran, 1980.

-------*Tadhkirāt al-Awliyā'* (2 vols.),trans by R.A.Nicholson, London, 1905-1907.

Badri,Malik B.(1979),*The Dilemma of Muslim Psychologists*, MWH Publishers, London.

Bakan, D. (1958), *Sigmund Freud and the Jewish Mystical Tradition*, Schocken Books, New York.

Bākhrazī, Abū'l-Mufākher, *Aurād al-ahbāb wa Fusūs al-ādāb*, edited by Iraj Afshār, Tehran 1975.

Bakhtiar,Laleh (1976), *Sufi:Expressions of the Mystic Quest*, Thames & Hudson,London.

Balikci, A.(1963), "Shamanistic Behaviour Among the Netsilik Eskimos", in *South Western Journal of Anthropology*, 19 (4), pp, 380-396.

Barks, Coleman & Moyne John (1988), *This Longing: Poetry, Teaching Stories and Letters of Rumi*, Threshold Books, Putney, Vermont.

Basilov, V.N. (1981), "Some Results of the Study of the Vestiges of Shamanism in Central Asia", *International Congress of Anthropological & Ethnological Sciences Intercongress papers*, Holland.

Bassetti, S. (1981), *St.Francis in Islam*, published in New York and subsequently suppressed. Original Italian version in Bodelian Library (censored works), Oxford.

Beidler, W. (1975), *The Vision of Self in Early Vedānta*, Motilal Books Delhi, Oxford.

Belo, J.(1960), *Trance in Bali*, Columbia University Press, New York.

Bennett, J.G.(1969), *Sufi Spiritual Techniques*, Coombe Springs Press, Ripon, Yorks.

Benson, H.(1975), *The Relaxation Response*, Morrow, New York.

Berger, L.,Hunter, I. & Lane,R.(1971),"The effects of stress on dreams", *Psychological Issues Monograph* (27), International University Press, New York.

Bernal, Martin(1991), *Black Athena: The Afroasiatic Roots of Classical Civilization*, Vintage Books, London.

Bible, *The New English Bible*, University Press, Oxford & Cambridge.

Birge, J.K(1937),*The Bektashi Order of Dervishes*, Luzac & Co, London.

Blacker, C. (1975), *The Catalpa Bow*, London.

Bourguignon, E. (1976), *Possession*, San Fransisco.

------(1968),"Divination, transe et possession en Afrique trans-saharienne", in *La Divination*, Vol.2, edited by A.Caquot & M.Leilovici, pp, 331-358, University Presss, Paris.

Bowra, C.M. (1952), *Heroic Poetry*, Macmillan, London.

Brockelmann, C.(1979), *History of the Islamic Peoples*, translated by J. Carmichal & M. Perlmann, Routledge & Kegan Paul, London (orig. pub. 1948).

Brody, H.(1977),*Persons and Placebos: Philosophical Implications of the Placebo Effect*, Ph.D Dissertation, Dept. of Philosophy, Michigan State University.

Brown, Norman O.(1957),*Life Against Death*, Random House, New York

Browne, E.G.(1927),*A Persian Anthology*, translations from the Persian, edited by E.D. Ross, Methuen, London.

----(1902-24),*A Literary History of Persia*(4vols.),London &Cambridge.

-----(1921),*History of Arabian Medicine*, University Press, Cambridge.

Budge, E.A. Wallis(1904),*The Gods of the Egyptians: Or Studies in Ancient Egyptian Mythology* (2 vols.), Methuen, London.

-----(1911),*Osiris and the Egyptian Resurrection* (2 vols.), Lee & Warner, New York.

Bukhārī (al-),*Sahīh al-Bukhārī*(12 vols.), compiled & edited by Muhsin Khān, Hilāl Yayinlari, Ankara, revised edition, completed 1976.

Burckhardt, Titus (1990), *An Introduction to Sufism*, Crucible, Wellingborough (orig. pub. 1976)

-----(1986), *Alchemy*, Element Books, Shaftesbury.

-----(1969),*Letters of a Sufi Master*(trans.), Perennial Books, Middlx.

Burriss, E.E(1931),*Taboo, Magic, Spirit: A Study of Primitive Elements in Roman Religion*, Macmillan, New York.

Butt, A.(1956),"Ritual Blowing: Taling - a causation and cure of Illness among the Akawaio", in *MAN* (61), pp, 49-55.

Chadwick, N.K.(1942), *Poetry and Prophecy*, Univ. Press, Cambridge.

Chadwick, H.M.(1912), *The Heroic Age*, University Press, Cambridge.

Chessick, R.(1969), *How Psychotherapy Heals: the process of intensive psychotheraspy*, Science House, New York.

Chomsky, A.N.(1957), *Syntactic Structures*, Mouton, The Hague.

------(1972), *Language and Mind*, Harcourt Brace Jovanovich, New York (enlarged edition orig. pub. 1968).

------(1976), *Reflections on Language*, Pantheon, New York.

Church, J.(1961),*Language and the Discovery of Reality*, Random House, New York.

Cicero, *Tusculan Disputations,* translated by J.E. King, Loeb Classical Library, William Heinemann, London.

Clare, Anthony(1976), *Psychiatry in Dissent,* Tavistock Publications, London.

Cleary, Thomas F.(1984-1987), *The Flower Ornament Scripture: A Translation of the Avatamsaka Sūtra* (3 vols.), Shambhala, Boston.

Cole, M & Scribner, S.(1974), *Culture and Thought: A Psychological Introduction,* John Wiley, New York.

Coleman, Vernon(1986), *How to Use your Mind to Heal your Body,* Century Press, London.

Constantinides, P.(1977),*"Ill at ease and sick at heart": Symbolic Behavior in a Sudanese Healing Cult,* in Lewis (1977).

Conze, Edward(1959),*Buddhist Scriptures* (selection & trans.) Penguin Books, Harmondsworth.

Cowan, James(1991),*Letters from a Wild State: An Aboriginal Perspective,* Element Books, Shaftesbury.

------(1989), *Mysteries of the Dreaming,* Prism Books, New York.

Crapanzano, V. & Garrison, V.(1977), Editors, *Case Studies in Spirit Possession,* New York.

Crapanzano, Victor(1973),*The Hamadasha: A Study in Moroccan Ethnopsychiatry,* University Of California Press, Berkeley.

Czaplicka, M.A.(1918), *The Turks of Central Asia in History and the Present Day,* University Press, Oxford.

------(1914), *Aboriginal Siberia,* University Press, Oxford.

Dabbāgh, Abd-al-Azīz.(undated), *Al-Ibrīz: Khazā'in-i-Ma'rifa,* Mehtab Publishers, Lahore.

D'Andrade, R.(1961),"Anthropological Studies of Dreams", *Psychological Anthropology,* edited by F. L. Hsu, Dorsey Press, Homewood.

Darqāwī(ad-), Mulay al-'Arabī, *Letters of a Sufi Master,* translated by Titus Burckhardt, Perennial Books, Middlesex.

Davidson, R.W.(1966-1967), *Documents on Contemporary Dervish Communities,* London.

Deikman, A. (1966), "Deautomatization and the Mystic Experience", in *Psychiatry* (29), pp, 324-338.

------(1966b), "Implications of Experimentally Induced Contemplative Meditation", *Journal of Nervous & Mental Diseases*(142), pp,101-116.

------(1977),"Sufism and Psychiatry", *Journal of Nervous & Mental Diseases* (165), pp, 318-329.

Dethlefsen, Thorwald & Dahlke, Rüdiger(1990), *The Healing Power of Illness: the meaning of symptoms and how to interpret them,* translated by Peter Lemesurier, Element Books, Shaftesbury.

Dietrici, A.(1879),"Der Darwinismus", *Jahrhundert* (10,19), Leipzig; in Shah 1966, p,13.

Dioszegi, S.(1968), *Tracing Shamans in Siberia,* Holland.

Eckley, T.R.(1981), *An exploration of the possible analogies between religious experiences and sense experiences, with a view to determining the relative cognitive value of the former,* unpublished M.A. Thesis, University of Wales, Bangor.

Edelstein, L.(1949),"The Function of the Myth in Plato's Philosophy", *Journal of the History of Ideas* (10), pp, 463 ff.

Eggan, D.(1955), "The Personal use of Myth in Dreams", *Journal American Folklore* (68), pp, 445-453

Eliade, Mircea(1951), *Le Chamanisme et les techniques archäiques de l'extase*, Paris.

-----(1964),*Shamanism: Archaic Techniques of Ecstasy*, University Press, Princetown (orig. pub. in French as above).

-----(1989), *Yoga: Immortality and Freedom*, translated by W.R.Trask, Arkana, London (orig. pub. 1958).

Emre, Yunus *The Drop That Became The Sea*, trans.by Kabir Helminski and Refik Algan, Threshold Books, Putney, Vermont, 1989.

-----*The City of The Heart: Yunus Emre's Verses of Wisdom & Love*, translated by Süha Faiz, Element Books, Shaftesbury, 1992.

Encyclopaedia of Islam (5 vols.), Luzac & Co, London, 1913-1938.

Encyclopaedia Judaica (16 vols.), Macmillan, New York, 1971-1972.

Epstein, Isaac(1961), Editor, *The Babylonian Talmud* (18vols.), Soncino, London.

Erikson, M.(1964),"The Confusion Technique in Hypnosis", in *American Journal of Clinical Hypnosis* (6), pp, 183-207.

Erman, A.(1966), Editor, *The Ancient Egyptians: A Source Book of their Writings*, Harper Torchbooks, New York.

Evans, R.J.(1979),*Jung on Elementary Psychology*, Routledge & Kegan Paul, London.

Evans-Wentz, W.Y.(1960),Editor, *The Tibetan Book of the Dead*, Galaxy Edition, Oxford University Press, New York (orig. pub. 1927).

Fabrega, H.(1974),*Disease and Social Behaviour: An Interdisciplinary Perspective*, MIT Press, Cambridge, Mass.

Fairchild, W.P. (1962), "Shamanism in Japan", *Folklore Studies* (21), pp,1-22, Tokyo.

Fairley, John & Simon Welfare(1984), *Arther Clarke's World of Strange Powers*, Guild Publishing, London.

Fārābī(al-), Abū Nasr *Risālah fi'l-'Aql*, edited by Maurice Bouyges, Beirut (undated).

Farrer,J. & S.(1981),*Eight Sabbats For Witches*, Robert Hale, London.

Faulkner, R.O.(1969),*The Ancient Egyptian Pyramid Texts*, Clarendon Press, Oxford.

Feild, Reshad(1988), *Breathing Alive: A Guide to Conscious Living*, Element Books, Shaftesbury.

-------(1983), *Steps to Freedom: Discourses on the Alchemy of the Heert*, Threshold Books, Putney, Vermont.

Festinger, L. Riecken, H.W. & Schachter, S.(1956), *When Prophecy Fails*, Harper & Row, New York.

323

Festus, *Pilae Effigies; Macrobius Saturnalia,* in Burriss 1931, p, 107.

Finley, M.I.(1977),*The World of Odysseus,* Chatto & Windus, London.

Flinders Petrie, W.M.(1899-1905), *History of Egypt* (3 vols), Methuen, London.

Frager, Robert & James Fadiman(1976), *Personality and Personal Growth,* Harper & Row, New York.

Frager, Ragip(1987), Editor, *'Love is the Wine': Talks of a Sufi Master in America,* Threshold Books, Putney, Vermont.

Frank, J.(1961), *Persuasion and Healing,* Schocken, New York.

------(1974), "Therapeutic Compoɪents of Psychotherapy", *Journal of Nervous & Mental Diseases* (159), pp, 325-342.

------(1975), "Psychotherapyof Bodily Disease", *Psychotherapy & Psychosomatics* (26), pp, 192-202.

Frankl, V.E.(1964), *Man's Search for Meaning: An Introduction to Logotherapy,* Hodder & Stoughton, London.

Freud, Sigmund (1953-1973), *The Standard Edition of the Complete Psychological Works of Sigmund Freud* (24 vols.), edited by James Strachey, Hogarth Press & Institute of Psycho-Analysis, London.

------(1975), *Civilization and its Discontents,* Standard Edition, Vol. 17, Hogarth Press, London (orig. pub. 1930).

------(1974), *Moses and Monotheism: three essays,* Standard Edition, Vol. 33, Hogarth Press, London (orig. pub. 1939).

------(1927), *The Future of an Illusion,* Standard Edition, Vol. 21, Hogarth Press, London, 1962.

------(1924), *An Autobiographical Study,* Standard Edition, Vol.20, Hogarth Press, London.

------(1914), *The Moses of Michelangelo,* Standard Edition, Vol. 13, Hogarth Press, London, 1950.

------(1925), *Letter to the Editor of the Jewish Press Centre in Zürich,* Standard Edition, Vol. 19, Hogarth Press, London.

------(1900), *The Interpretation of Dreams,* Standard Edition, Vol. 4, Hogarth Press, London, 1953.

Fromm, Erich, D.T. Suzuki & Richard De Martino(1960), *Zen Buddhism and Psychoanalysis,* Harper & Row, New York.

Furūzanfarr, Badī' al-Zamān (1982), *Ahadith-i-Mathnawī,* 3rd Edition, Amir Kabir, Tehran.

------(1932), *Sharh-i hāl-i Maulānā,* Amir Kabir, Tehran.

Gallus, Thomas *Theologia Mystica Dionysii Areopagitae* (Latine interpretata), Folio, Oxford, 1634.

Gardner, Edmund *The Cell Of Self-Knowledge: Seven Old English Mystical Works,* New Medieval Library, London, 1910.

Garer, G.(1965), *Death, Grief and Mourning in Contemporary Britain,* London.

Gellner, E.(1969),*Saints of the Atlas,* Weidenfeld & Nicolson, London.

------(1981), *Muslim Society*, Weidenfeld & Nicolson, London.

Ghazālī (al-), Abū Hāmid Muhammad *The Remembrance of Death and the Afterlife*, translation of *Kitāb Dhikr al-Mawt wa-māba 'dahu* by T.J.Winter (1989), Islamic Texts Society, Cambridge.

------*Al-Munqidh min ad-Dalāl*, Damascus Edition, 1358/1939.

------*Ihyā' 'Ulūm ad-Dīn* (40 books in 5 vols.), Mustafā al-Halabī, Cairo, 1347 A.H.

------*Mishkāt al-Anwār*, Cairo, 1322 A.H.

------*Tahāfut al-Falāsifa*, edited by M.Bouyges, Beirut, 1927.

Gibb, H.A. & Bowen, H.(1957), *Islamic Society and the West: A Study of the impact of Western civilization on Moslem culture in the Near East* (Vol. 1), Oxford University Press, London.

Gill, M.M. & Brenman, M.(1966), *Hypnosis and Related States: psychoanalytic studies in regression*, Science Editions, New York.

Gilsenan, M.(1973), *Saint and Sufi in Modern Egypt*, London.

Ginsburg, C.D.(1955), *The Essenes: their history and doctrines & The Kabbalah: its doctrines, development and literature - 2 Essays*, Routledge & Kegan Paul, London (orig. pub. 1863-1864).

Glassé, C. (1989), *The Concise Encyclopaedia of Islam*, Stacey International, London.

Godwin, J.(1981),*Mystery Religions in the Ancient World*, Thames & Hudson, London.

Good, B.(1977),"The Heart of What's the Matter: the Semantics of Illness in Iran", *Culture, Medicine & Psychiatry* (1), pp, 25-58.

Gorgias the Sophist, *Eulogy of Helen*, in Lain Entralgo 1977, p,93 ff.

Grof, Stanislav(1976), *Realms of the Human Unconscious*, Dutton, New York.

------(1980), *LSD Psychotherapy*, Hunter House, Pomona, California.

------*Journeys Beyond the Brain*, unpublished manuscript available from the author.

Haas, W.S. (1943), "The Zikr of the Rahmaniya Order: A psychophysiological analysis", *The Moslem World* (33), pp, 16-28.

Haeri, Shaykh Fadhallala(1991), *Decree and Destiny: the freedom of no choice*, Element Books, Shaftesbury.

----(1990), *The Elements of Sufism*, Element Books, Shaftesbury.

----(1989), *The Journey of the Self*, Element Books, Shaftesbury.

----(1989b),*Living Islam, East and West*, Element Books, Shaftesbury.

----(1988),Editor, *Leaves From a Sufi Journal*, Element, Shaftesbury.

----(1987), *Beginning's End*, Routledge & Kegan Paul, London.

----(1983), *Songs of Iman: On the roads of Pakistan*, Zahra, Texas.

----(1983b), Editor, *Nuradeen: An Islamic Sufi Journal, Selections*, Zahra Publications, London.

----(1980), *Self Knowledge*, IQRA, Houston, Texas.

325

Hāfiz, Shams ad-Dīn *Tongue of the Hidden,* translated by Paul Smith, New Humanity Books, Melbourne, 1986.

-----*Rubā'iyyāt,* translated as *Love's Perfect Gift* by Paul Smith, New Humanity Books, Melbourne, 1986.

-----*Mathnawī,* translated as *Book of the Winebringer* by Paul Smith, New Humanity Books, Melbourne, 1986b.

Hall, C. (1951), "What people dream about", *Scientific American* (5), pp,1-5.

Hallaj, J. (1962), "Hypnotherapeutic Techniques in a Central Asian Community", *International Journal of Clinical & Experimental Hypnosis* Vol. 10 (4), Oct., pp, 271-274.

Hamadhānī (al-), 'Ayn al-Qudāt (1962), *Zubdat al-Haqā'iq; Tamhīdāt; Shakwā 'l-Gharib,* edited by Afif Usayran, Tehran.

-----(1930),*Shakwā 'l-Gharīb 'an al-Awtan ilā 'Ullamā' al-Buldān,* edited & trans. by M.'Abd al-Jalil, *Journal Asiatique,* Paris, (216), pp, 1-76 & 193-297.

Hamarneh, S.K.(1983), *Health Sciences in Early Islam* (2 vols.), edited by M.A. Anees, Zahra Publications, Blanco, Texas,

Hammūdah, 'Abd al-Atī (1977), *The Family Structure in Islam,* American Trust Publications, New York.

Haqqani (al-), Shaykh Nāzim 'Adīl (see also al-Qubrusī) (1987), *The Secrets Behind the Secrets Behind the Secrets,* Duru, Berlin.

-----(1989),*Mercy Oceans:Sapphires from Serendib,* Arafat, Sri Lanka.

Hardy, Sir Alister(1979),*The Spiritual Nature of Man,* Clarendon Press, Oxford.

-----(1966), *The Divine Flame: An Essay Towards a Natural History of Religion,* William Collins, London.

Hartmann, E.(1973), *The Functions of Sleep,* Yale University Press, New Haven.

Harvey, David(1983), *The Power to Heal: An Investigation of Healing and the Healing Experience,* Aquarian Press, Wellingborough.

Hebrew Bible, *The Soncino Books of the Bible,* Soncino Press, London.

Heinemann, D.J.(1995), Editor, *Leaves from the Tree of Life: Sayings, Meditations & Prayers For a New Age,* Rainbow Trust Publications, Northampton.

Herodotus (4 vols.), translated by A.D.Godley, Loeb Classical Library, William Heinemann, London.

Hertz, Joseph H.(1960), translator, *The Pentateuch and Haftorahs,* including commentary, Soncino Press, London.

Hesiod and the Homeric Hymns, translated by H.G.Evelyn White, Loeb Classical Library, William Heinemann, London.

Heusch de, L.(1962),"Cultes de possesssion et religions iniatiques de salut en Afrique", *Annales du Centre d'Etude des Religious,* Brussels

Hill, Michael (1973), *A Sociology of Religion,* Heinemann, London.

Hinnells, John R. (1984), Editor, *Dictionary of Religions,* Penguin, Harmondsworth.

326

Hodgson, Phyllis(1944), Editor, *The Cloud of Unknowing and the Book of Privy Counselling*, Early English Texts Society, Oxford University Press, London.

Homer, *Iliad*, trans. by A.T.Murray(2 vols.), Loeb Classical Library, William Heinemann, London.

-----*Odyssey*, trans. by A.T. Murray (2 vols.), Loeb Classical Library, William Heinemann, London.

Honko, L.(1969), "Role-taking of the Shaman", in *Temenos* (4), Turku.

Hoppal, M.(1981), "Traces of Shamanism in Hungarian Folk Beliefs", in *The Comparative Study of the Early Forms of Religion*, Sarospatak, Hungary.

Howell, D.(1970), "Health Rituals at a Lebanese Shrine", *Middle East Studies* (6), pp, 179-188.

Howells, J.G.(1971), Editor, *Modern Perspectives in World Psychiatry*, Brunner-Mazel, New York.

Hsu, J. & Tseng, H.S.(1972), "Intercultural Psychotherapy", *Archives of General Psychiatry* (27), pp, 700-705.

Hujwīrī (al-), Abū-l-Hasan 'Alī *Kashf al-Mahjūb*, translated by R.A. Nicholson, Gibbs Memorial Series & Luzac & Co, London, 1959 (orig. pub. 1911).

-----*Kashf al-Mahjūb li-Arbāb al-Qulūb*, Edition by V.A. Zhukovsky, Leningrad, 1926 (Persian).

Hultkrantz, A.(1973),"A Definition of Shamanism", *Temenos*(9), Turku.

-----(1957), *The North American Indian Orpheus Tradition: A Contribution to Comparative Religion*, Stockholm.

Husainī, Maulvi S.A.Q. (1931), *Ibn Al-'Arabī* (6 vols.), Lahore.

Ibn al-Fārid *Dīwān*, edited with commentary by Hasan al-Būrīnī & 'Abd al-Ghanī an-Nābulusī, Būlāq, Beirut, 1289 A.H.

Ibn 'Arabī, Muhyī-d-Dīn *"Whoso Knoweth Himself..."* a translation from *Risale-t-ul-wujudiyyah* by T.H.Weir, Beshara Publications, London, 1976.

-----*The Wisdom of the Prophets (Fusūs al-Hikam)*, translated by Titus Burckhardt & A. Culme-Seymour, Beshara Public., Gloucester, 1975.

-----*Fusūs al-Hikam*, edited by Abū 'l-'Alā' 'Afīfī. Al-Halabī, Cairo, 1365/1946.

-----*Al-Futūhāt al-Makkiyya* (4 vols.), Cairo, 1329 A.H.

-----*Tarjumān al-Ashwāq*, edited and translated by R.A.Nicholson, London 1911, Beirut edition by Dār Sādar, 1386/1966.

-----*Kitāb al-Alīf*, translated by J.Weir, *Journal of the Royal Asiatic Society* 1901.

-----*Kitāb al-Isrā' ilā 'l-Maqām al-Asrā*, Beirut (undated).

Ibn 'Atā'illāh, Ahmad ibn Muhammad *Kitāb al-Hikam*, translated by Victor Danner, E.J.Brill, Leiden, 1973.

Ibn Battūta (1939), *Rihla Ibn Batūta*, edited by A. al-Awāmirī & M.A. Jād al-Mawlā (2 vols.), Cairo.

-----*Voyages d'Ibn Batouta,* trans. by C.Defrémery & B.R.Sanguinetti (4 vols), Paris, 1853-1858.

Ibn Ismā'īl, M. Sā'īd *Al-Fuyūdāt ar-Rabbāniyya,* Cairo, 1353 A.H.

Ibn Jubair, Abu'l-Husain Muhammad(1907), *Rihla,* edited by W.Wright & M.J. de Goeje, Gibbs Memorial Series, Leiden-London.

Ibn Khaldūn, *Kitāb al-'Ibar* (7 vols.), Būlāq, Beirut, 1956-1959 (orig.pub.1284/1868).

Ibn Paquda, R.Bachya ben Joseph(1996), *Duties of the Heart,* translated by Daniel Haberman (2 vols.), Feldheim Publishers, Jerusalem.

Ibn Rushd, Abū-l-Walīd Muhammad *Bidayah al-Mujtahid* (2 vols.), National Publications, Cairo, 5th Edition, 1981.

Ibn Sīnā, Abū 'Alī Husayn ibn Abd Allāh *Isharāt* (Persian), Seminary Publications, Karachi, 1498 A.H.

Ibn Taymiyyah, *Kitāb al-Radd 'alā al-Mantīqīyyin,* edited by Sharf ad-Dīn al-Kutubī, Dār al-Ma'rifa, 1368 A.H.

Ikhwān al-Safā', *Dispute Between Man and the Animals,* translated by J.Platts, London, 1869.

Inayat Khan, Pīr Vilayat(1982),*Introducing Spirituality into Counselling and Therapy,* Omega Publishing, Santa Fe.

Iqbal, Sir M.(1962), *The Reconstruction of Religious Thought in Islam,* Ashraf Press, Lahore (orig. pub. 1934).

-----(1908), *The Development of Metaphysics in Persia,* Luzac & Co, London.

Izutsu, I.(1984), *Sufism and Taoism: A Comparative Study of Key Philosophical Concepts,* University Cambridge Press, London.

Jabbur, J.S. Editor, *Al-Kawakīb as-Sa'ira bi-A'yan al-Maya al-Ashīra,* Najim ad-Dīn al-Ghazzī, Vol.2, 2nd edition, Junyeh, Beirut, 1949.

Jacobs, Louis(1995), *The Jewish Religion: A Companion,* University Press, Oxford.

James, William(1902), *The Varieties of Religious Experience,* Fontana, London, 1960.

Jāmī, 'Abd ar-Rahmān Nūr ad-Dīn *Salaman and Absal,* translated by Edward Fitzgerald, in *Four Sufi Classics,* Octagon, London, 1980.

-----*Kitāb Nafahāt al-Uns,* edited by M.Tawhīdīpūr, Tehran, 1337/1919.

-----*Bahāristān,* translated as *The Abode of Spring* by D.Pendlebury, in *Four Sufi Classics,* Octagon Press, London, 1980.

Jochelson, V.(1924),*The Yukaghir and the Yukaghirized Tungus,* Vol. 1, American Museum of Natural History, New York, *Memoirs* 13, (2).

Jones, Joseph, "From Abraham to Andrenio: Observations of the Evolution of the Abraham Legend, its Diffusion in Spain and Relation to the Theme of the Self-Taught Philosopher", *Comparative Literature Studies* 6 (1969), pp, 69-101.

Jung, C.G.(1977), *Memories, Dreams, Reflections,* William Collins, Fount Paperbacks, Glasgow (orig. pub. 1963).

-----(1977b), *Psychology and the Occult*, University Press, Princeton.

-----(1964), Editor, *Man and His Symbols*, Aldus Books, London.

-----(1961), *Modern man in Search of a Soul*, Routledge & Kegan Paul, London, (orig. pub. 1933).

-----(1958), *The Undiscovered Self*, Routledge & Kegan Paul, London.

Kalābādhī(al-), Abū Bakr *Kitāb at-Ta'arruf li-madhab ahl at-Tasawwuf*, Cairo, 1934.

Karrar, A.(1985), *The Sufi Brotherhoods in the Sudan, until 1900, with reference to the Shrāyqiyya region*, Ph.D. Thesis, University of Bergen, Norway.

Keddie, N.(1972), Editor, *Saints, Scholars and Sufis*, University of California Press, Berkeley.

Kelly, G.A.(1963), *A Theory of Personality: The Psychology of Personal Constructs*, Norton, New York.

Kharrāz(al-), Abū Sā'īd *Kitāb as-Sidq*, translated by A.J.Arberry, Oxford University Press, London, 1937.

Khosla, K.(1987), *The Sufism of Rumi*, Element Books, Shaftesbury.

Kindī(al-), Abū Yūsuf Ya'qūb ibn Ishāq *Qudāt Misr*, edited by R.Guest, London, 1912.

Kister, M.J.(1954), Editor, *Kitāb ādāb as-Suhba As-Sulami*, Jerusalem.

Kleinmann, A.(1980), *Patients and Healers in the Context of Culture: An Exploration of the Borderland Between Anthropology, Medicine and Psychiatry*, University of California Press, Berkeley.

Kluchkhohn, C.(1942),"Myths and Rituals: A General Theory", *Harvard Theological Review* (35), pp, 45-79.

Köprülüzadé, M.F.(1929) *Influence du Chamanisme Turco-Mongol sur les Ordres Mystiques Musulmans*, Turkish Institute, University of Istanbul.

Lain-Entralgo, P.(1970), *The Therapy of the Word in Classical Antiquity*, Yale University Press, New Haven.

Laing, R.D.(1965),"Transcendental Experience in Relation to Religion and Psychosis", *Psychedelic Review* (6), pp, 7-15.

-----(1959), *The Divided Self*, Tavistock Publications, London.

Landau, R.(1959), *The Philosophy of Ibn Arabi*, New York.

Lapidus, I.(1988), *A History of Islamic Societies*, University Press, Cambridge.

Lefort, Rafael(1969), *The Teachers of Gurdjieff*, Gollanz, London.

Lévi-Strauss, C. (1963), *Structural Anthropology*, Basic Books, New York.

Lewis, I.M.(1982),"What is a Shaman?" a revised version of a paper originally published in *FOLK* (Vol. 23) 1981, available from personal contact with the author.

-----(1981), "What is a Shaman?" in *FOLK* (Vol. 23), pp, 25-35, Copenhagen.

-----(1977), Editor, *Symbols and Sentiments*, London.

329

-----(1971), *Ecstatic Religion: An Anthropological Study of Spirit Possession and Shamanism*, Penguin, Harmondsworth

Lings, Martin(1984), *The Secret of Shakespeare*, Aquarian Press, Wellingborough (orig. pub. 1966).

-----(1975), *What is Sufism*, George Allen & Unwin, London.

-----(1971), *A Sufi Saint of the Twentieth Century: Shaikh Ahmad al-Alawī his spiritual heritage and legacy*, George Allen & Unwin, London.

Litvak, Stuart(1984), *Seeking Wisdom: the Sufi path*, Samuel Weiser, Maine.

Lord, A.B.(1960), *The Singer of Tales*, University Press, Harvard.

Luborsky, L.*et al*(1975),"Comparative Studies of Psychotherapy: Is it true everyone has won and all must have prizes", *Archives of General Psychiatry* (32), pp 995-1008.

Mach, Rudolf (1957), *Der Zaddik in Talmud und Midrasch*, E.J. Brill, Leiden.

Maimonides, Moses *The Guide of the Perplexed*, translated by S. Pines, University Press, Chicago, 1963.

Maimonides, 'Obadyāh(1981), *The Treatise of the Pool: Al-Maqāla al-Hawdiyya*, translated by P.Fenton, Octagon Press, London.

Manerī, Sharafuddin *The Hundred Letters*, translated by Paul Jackson, SPCK, London, 1980.

Mannoni, O.(1971), *Freud:the Theory of the Unconscious*, Pantheon Books, London.

Maslow, Abraham(1962), *Towards a Psychology of Being*, Van Nostrand, New York

Maspero,G.(1904-1906), *History of Egypt, Chaldea, Syria, Babylonia and Assyria* (13 vols.), edited by A.H. Sayce & translated by M.L. McClure, Grolier Society, London.

Massignon, Louis(1921),*Al-Hallaj Martyr Mystique de L'Islam*, Librarie Orientaliste Paul Geuthner, Paris.

-----(1922), *La Passion d'Al-Hallaj* (2 vols.), First edition, Paris.

-----(1957), *Akbar 'Al-Hallaj*, the edited Arabic text, Paris.

-----(1982), *The Passion of al-Hallāj: Mystic and Martyr of Islam*, translated by H.Mason (4 vols.), University Press, Princeton.

Meier, F.(1957), "Ein Knigge für Sūfi's", *Rivista degli studi orientali* XXXII pp, 485-524.

Merton, Thomas *Contemplative Prayer*, Darton, Longman & Todd, London, 1973.

Mironov, N.D. & Shirokogorov, S.M.(1924) "Sramana-Shaman: Etymology of the Word 'Shaman'", *Journal of the Royal Anthropological Society* (North China Branch) (55), pp, 105-130, Shanghai.

Mischel, W. & F.(1958), "Psychological aspects of spirit possession", *American Anthropologist* (60), pp, 248-260.

Moody, R.A.(1975), *Life after Life: the investigation of a phenomenon - survival of bodily death*, Bantam Books, New York.

Morphy, H.(1984), *Journey to the Crocodile's Nest*, Australian Institute of Anthropological Studies, Canberra.

Muhāsibī (al-), Abū 'Abd Allāh Harith ibn Asad *Kitāb Mahīyat 'l-'aql wa ma 'anāhū was ikhtīlaf al-nas fīhī*, MS. Carullah 1101, Istanbul.

Müller, Max (1962-1976), Editor, *The Sacred Books of the East* (various translators, 50 vols.), Moltilal Banarsidass, Delhi (orig. pub. 1882 ff, by Oxford University Press).

Munawwar (al-), Muhammad ibn *Asrār at-Tawhīd fi Maqāmāt ash-Shaykh Abū Sā'īd*, edited by Dhabihu'llāh Safā', Tehran, 1928.

Murphy,E.(1979),*Life events, psychiatric disorder and physical illness*, unpublished Thesis for M.D., Manchester University.

Mutahhari, Morteza Allama(1980),*Master and Mastership*, translated by M.A. Ansari, Ahl-ul-Bait Publications, Dubai.

Nadel, S.F.(1946), "A Study of Shamanism in the Nuba Mountains", *Journal of the Royal Anthropological Institute* (76), (1), pp, 25-37.

Nasr, S.H.(1976), *Islamic Science: An Illustrated Study*, 'World of Islam' Festival Publishing, London.

-----(1976b), *An Introduction to Islamic Cosmological Doctrines*, Cambridge University Press, London (orig. pub. 1964).

-----(1972), *Sufi Essays*, George Allen & Unwin, London.

-----(1972b), *Living Sufism*, George Allen & Unwin, London.

Nawawi (an-), Imam *Forty Hadīth*, Holy Koran Publishing House, Damascus.

Needleman, Joseph (1982), *The Sword of Gnosis*, Baltimore Press.

Neher, A. (1962),"A physiological explanation of unusual behaviour in ceremonies involving drums", *Human Biology* (34), pp, 151-160.

Neidjie, B. (1986), *Kakadu Man*, Resources Managers, Darwin.

Nicholson, R.A.(1989),*The Mystics of Islam*, Arkana, London (orig. pub. 1914).

-----(1950), *Rūmī, Poet and Mystic*, George Allen & Unwin, London.

-----(1925-1940), *The Mathnawi of Jalalu'd-Din Rumi* (trans. 8 vols.), Gibb Memorial Trust and Luzac & Co, London.

-----(1923), *The Idea of Personality in Sufism*, Reprinted by Mehtab Publishers, Lahore, 1987.

-----(1911), *Interpreter of Longings*, translation, including Ibn Arabī's own commentary of *Tarjumān al-Ashwāq*, London.

-----(1905-1907), *Memoirs of the Saints*, a translation of 'Attār's *Tadhkirāt al- Awliyā'*, London.

-----(1906),"An Historical Inquiry Concerning The Origin & Development of Sufism", *Journal of Royal Asiatic Society*, pp, 303-348.

-----(1898), *Selected Odes from the Dīwān-i-Shams-i-Tabrīz.*, University Press, Cambridge.

Nurbakhsh, Javad *Sufi Symbolism: the Nurbakhsh Encyclopaedia of Sufi Terminology* (6 vols.), Khaniqahi-Nimatullahi Publications, London, 1988 (orig. pub. in Persian 1927).

331

-----(1983),*Sufi Women*, Khaniqahi-Nimatullahi Publicts., New York.

-----(1983b), *Jesus in the eyes of the Sufis*, Khaniqahi-Nimatullahi Publications, London.

-----(1978), *'In the Tavern of Ruin'* : *Seven Essays on Sufism*, Khaniqahi-Nimatullahi Publications, New York.

-----(1978b), "Sufism and Psychoanalysis, Part One: What is Sufism?" *International Journal of Social Psychiatry* (24), pp, 204-212.

-----(1978c), "Sufism and Psychoanalysis, Part Two: A Comparison Between Sufism and Psychoanalysis", *International Journal of Social Psychiatry* (24), pp, 213-219.

Oden, T.C.(1972), *The Intensive Group Experience: the New Pietism*, Westminster, Philadelphia.

Ogden, C.K. & Richards, I.A.(1923), *The Meaning of Meaning*, Kegan Paul, London.

O'Leary, D.L.(1949), *How Greek Science Passed to the Arabs*, Routledge & Kegan Paul, London.

Omar (al-), Prof Abdul Rahman Ben Hammad, *Islam the Religion of Truth*, Supreme Head-Office for Religious Guidance, Saudi Arabia (current edition).

Önder, Mehemet, *Mevlana Jelaleddin Rumi*, Amfora Publications, Ankara, undated (abridged version).

Ornstein, R.E.(1973), Editor, *The Nature of Human Consciousness*, London.

Ovid, *Fasti*, translated by Sir James G.Frazer, Loeb Classical Library, William Heinemann, London.

Park, W.Z.(1938), *Shamanism in Western North America: A Study in Cultural Relationships*, Chicago.

Parry, A.(1970), Editor, *The Making of Homeric Verse*, University Press, Oxford.

Peel, J.(1969),"Understanding Alien Belief-Systems",*British Journal of Sociology* (20).

Philo, "The Contemplative Life", in *The Complete Works* (10 vols.), Loeb Classical Library, William Heinemann, London.

Philostratus and Eunapius *Lives of the Sophists*, translated by Wilmer Cave Wright, Loeb Classical Library, William Heinemann, London.

Plato (I), *Euthyphro, Apology, Crito, Phaedo, Phaedrus*, translated by H.N. Fowler, Loeb Classical Library, William Heinemann, London.

----(VI), *Cratylus, Parmenides, Greater Hippias, Lesser Hippias*, translated by N.H. Fowler, Loeb Classical Library, William Heinemann, London.

----(VIII), *Charmides, Alicibiades, Hipparchus, The Lovers, Theages, Minos and Epinomis*, translated by W.R.M Lamb, Loeb Classical Library, William Heinemann, London.

Platonov, K.(1959), *The Word as a Physiological and Therapeutic Factor*, Foreign Languages Publication House, Moscow.

Pliny *Natural History*, translated by H. Rackham (Vols. I-V), Loeb Classical Library, William Heinemann, London.

Polanyi, Michael & Prosch, H.(1975), *Meaning*, University of Chicago Press, Chicago.

Potapov, L.P.(1978), "Altaic Shamanism: Essay in Historical Dating", in *General Problems of Ethnography*, Editor S.A.Arutyunov, Moscow.

Prince, R.(1968), Editor, *Trance and Possession States*, R.M.Bucke Memorial Society, Montreal.

Qubrusī (al-), Shaykh Nāzim 'Adīl (see also al-Haqqani) (1981), *Mercy Oceans Hidden Treasures: Teachings of Sheikh Ad-Dhagistani*, Sebat, Konya.

-----(1980), *Mercy Oceans (Book Two)*, Sebat, Konya.

-----(1982), *Mercy Oceans Endless Horizons*, Sebat, Konya.

-----(1982b), *The Naqshbandi Way: A Guidebook for Spiritual Progress*, Sebat, Konya.

-----(1983), *Mercy Oceans Pink Pearls*, Sebat, Konya.

-----(1984), *Mercy Oceans Divine Sources*, Sebat, Konya.

-----(1985), *Mercy Oceans of the Heart*, Sebat, Konya.

-----(1986), *Mercy Oceans Rising Sun*, Sebat, Konya.

-----(1987), *Mercy Oceans Lovestream*, Medina Trust, London.

-----(1987b), *Oceans of Unity*, Medina Trust, London.

-----(1987c), *Mercy Oceans (Serendib edition)*, Arafat, Sri Lanka.

Qunawī(al-), Sadr ad-Dīn *Mirat 'l Ārīfin* (Reflection of the Awakened), edited by Sayyid Hasan Askari, Zahra Trust, London, 1983.

Qushairī(al-), Abū 'l-Qāsim,*Ar-Risālāt al-Qushairiyya*, Cairo, 1319A.H.

Rahman, F.(1968). *Islam*, Anchor Books, New York.

Redhouse, J.(1965),*Legends of the Sufis*, a translation of Al-Aflākī's, *Manāqib al-Ārifīn*, Kingston Publishers, London.

Renouf, P. Le Page(1896), Translator, *The Egyptian Book of the Dead*, Society of Biblical Archeology, London.

Reynolds, D.(1976), *Morita Psychotherapy*, University of California Press, Berkeley.

Reza Arasteh, A.(1980),*Growth to Selfhood: the Sufi Contribution*, Routledge & Kegan Paul, London.

Riazul, Islam(1955), "A Survey in Outline of the Mystic Literature of the Sultanate Period", *Journal Pakistan Historical Society* (3), pp, 201-208.

Richard of St.Victor, *Opera Omnia* (Migne, Patrologia Latina, T 196), Paris.

Roazen, P.(1971), *Freud and His Followers*, Knoff, New York.

Rodinson, M.(1971), *Muhammad*, translated by A.Carter, Pantheon, New York.

Róheim, G.(1951), "Hungarian Shamanism", *Psychoanalysis and the Social Sciences*, Vol. 3 (4), pp, 131-169.

Rohl, David(1999), *Legend: The Genesis of Civilisation*, Arrow Books, London.

Rosen, R.D.(1979), *Fast Talk and Quick Cure in the Era of Feeling*, Aion, New York.

Roszak, T.(1977), *Unfinished Animal: the Aquarian Frontier and the Evolution of Consciousness*, Harper & Row, London.

Rousseau, Jean-Jaques(1750), *The Social Contract and Discourses*, translated by G.D.H.Cole, J.M.Dent, London, 1973.

Royster, J.E.(1979),"Sufī as psychotherapist", *Psychologia* (22), pp, ,225-235.

Rūmī (ar-), Jalāl ad-Dīn *Dīwān-i-Shams-i-Tabrizī*, Amir Kabir Press, Tehran, 1972 (Persian).

-----(1928), *Fīhi mā fīhī*, Tehran & Azamgarh (Persian).

-----*Mathnawī* (8 vols.), translated by R.A. Nicholson, Gibb Memorial Series, Luzac & Co, London, 1925-1940.

-----Abridged version of the above in Persian, Tehran, 1977.

Rushbrook Williams, L.F.(1973), Editor, *Sufi Studies: East and West*, Octagon Press, London.

Rushd (ibn-), Abū-l-Walīd *Bidayah al-Mujtahid* (2 vols.), National Publications, Cairo, 5th Edition, 1981.

Sa'adi, Muslah ad-Dīn *Gūlistān*, Khalil Khatīb Rahbar, Tehran, 1969, (Persian).

-----*Gūlistān*, translated as *Le Jardin de Roses*, by Omar Ali-Shah, Paris, 1966.

Sabom, M.B.(1982), *Recollections of Death: A medical investigation*, Corgi Books, London.

Sādiq, Imām Ja'far *The Lantern of the Path*, translated by Muna Bilgrami, Element Books, Shaftesbury.

Safadī (as-), Salāh ad-Dīn Khalīl ibn Aybak *Al-Wāfī bi' l-wafayāt*, edited by H. Ritter *et al*, Wiesbaden, 1962.

Sanā'ī, Hakim Abū 'l-Majd Majdud,"The Way of the Seeker"*(Sair al-Ibad ila'l Maad)* by *Ibad ila'l Maad)* translated by D.Pendlebury, in *Four Sufi Classics*, Octagon Press, London, 1980.

Santillana, G. de & H.von Dechend(1969), *Hamlet's Mill: an Essay in Myth and the Frame of Time*, Gambit, Boston.

Sargant, William(1964), *Battle for the Mind*, Pan Books, London.

Saunders, N.(1975), *Exploration: A Guide to Groups Involved*, Wildwood House, London.

Scholem Gersham(1978),*The Messianic Idea in Judaism & other esays on Jewish spirituality*, Schocken Books, New York.

Schroeder, Eric (1955), *Muhammad's People*, Bond Wheelwright, Portland Maine.

Schuon, Frithjof(1969), *Dimensions of Islam*, George Allen & Unwin, London.

-----(1963), *Understanding Islam*, George Allen & Unwin, London.

Sell, E.(1920), *The Faith of Islam*, London & Madras, 4th edition (orig. pub. 1880).

334

Sell, G.E., *Essays on Islam*, SPCK, Madras, 1901.

Sezgin, F.(1971),*Geschichte des Arabischen Schrifttums*, Brill, Leiden.

Shabistarī, Sa'd ad-Dīn Mahmūd (717 A.H.), *Gulshan-i rāz*, translated as *The Secret Garden* by A.D.Yate, Zahra, Blanco, Texas, 1982.

Shafii, Muhammad(1985), *Freedom from the Self: Sufism, Meditation and Psychotherapy*, Human Sciences Press, New York.

-----(1968),"The Pīr(Sufi Guide) and the Western Psychotherapist", *Newsletter Review of the R.M. Bucke Memorial Society*, Montreal (3), pp, 9-19.

Shah, Idries(1964), *The Sufis*, Octagon Press, London.

-----(1968), *Oriental Magic*, Octagon Press, London.

-----(1968b), *The Way of the Sufi*, Jonathan Cape, London.

-----(1966), *Special Problems in the Study of Sufi Ideas*, Octagon Press, London.

-----(1977), *Neglected Aspects of Sufi Study : On the Nature of Sufi Knowledge*, Octagon Press, London.

-----(1980), Editor, *Four Sufi Classics*, Octagon Press, London.

-----(1982), *Seeker after Truth*, Octagon Press, London.

-----(1978), *Learning How to Learn: Psychology and Spirituality in the Sufi Way*, Penguin, Harmondsworth.

Shah, S.I.A. (1933), *Islamic Sufism*, London.

Shakoor, Muhyiddin(1987), *The Writing on the Water: Chronicles of a Seeker on the Islamic Sufi Path*, Element Books, Shaftesbury.

Sha'rānī (ash-), 'Abd al-Wahhāb ibn Ahmad *Latā'if al-Minan* (2 vols.), Cairo, 1357 A.H.

Shirokogoroff, S.M.(1935), *The Psychomental Complex of the Tungus*, London (there are only 4 copies of this book in existence, obtainable through the *Royal Anthropological Institute*, Library).

Shor, R.E. & Orne, M.T.(1965), Editors, *The Nature of Hypnosis: Selected Readings* (Vol. 6, pp,453 ff), Science Editions, New York.

Shushud, Hasan Lufti(1983), *Masters of Wisdom of Central Asia*, trans. by Muhtar Holland, Coombe Springs Press, Ripon, Yorks.

Siegel, B.S.(1985), *Love, Medicine & Miracles*, Rider, New York.

Simac, R.(1967),"In a Naqshbandi Circle", *Hibbert Journal* Vol.65, 258.

Sirāj ad-Dīn, Abū Bakr (1952), *The Book of Certainty*, London.

Skoruptski, J. (1976), *Symbol and Theory*, London.

Smart, Ninian(1977), *The Religious Experience of Mankind*, William Collins, Glasgow.

Smith, Paul(1988), *Hafiz: Tongue of the Hidden* (translation), New Humanity Books, Melbourne.

-----(1986), *Book of the Winebringer*, a translation of Hāfiz, New Humanity Books, Melbourne.

-----(1986b), *Love's Perfect Gift*, a translation of Hāfiz, New Humanity Books, Melbourne.

Spencer Trimingham, J.(1971), *The Sufi Orders in Islam*, Clarendon Press, Oxford.

Sperber, D.(1975),*Rethinking Symbolism*, University Press, Cambridge.

Steingass, F.A.(1963), *A Comprehensive Persian-English Dictionary*, Routledge & Kegan Paul, London.

Stone, L.(1965),*The Crisis of the Aristocracy*, Univer. Press, Oxford.

Suhrawardī, Shihāb ad-Dīn Abū Hafs 'Umar *'Awārif al-Ma'ārif*, 'Alāmiyya Press, Cairo, 1358/1939.

Sükala, A.L.(1978), *The Rite Technique of the Siberian Shaman*, Helsinki.

Sulami (as-), Abū 'Abd ar-Rahmān *Risālat al-Malamatiyya*, edited by Abū 'l-'Alā' 'Afīfī, Cairo, 1364/1945.

-----*Kitāb ādāb as-Suhba*, edited by M.J.Kister, Jerusalem.

Tambiah, S.J.(1969),"The Magical Power of Words", *MAN* 3(2), pp.175-208, London.

Tanakh, *Tanakh, a new translation of the Holy Scriptures according to the traditional Hebrew text*, Jewish Publict. Society, Philadelphia.

Tart, C.T.(1969), Editor, *Altered States of Consciousness: a book of readings* John Wiley & Son, New York.

Tawney, R.H.(1926), *Religion and the Rise of Capitalism*, John Murray, London.

Thānvī, Ashraf 'Alī *Tarbiyat-al-Sālik* (6 vols.,Urdu), Pakistan Press, Lahore(undated).

-----*Bawādir-al-Nawādir* (Urdu), Lahore (undated).

-----(1965), *Al-Sihat- al- Wasāwis*, Deoband.

Tholuck, F.A.G.(1921),*Sufismus sive Theosophia Persarum pantheistica* (Latin), Berlin, in Shah, 1966, 2nd edition.

Thomas, K.(1978), *Religion and the Decline of Magic*, Peregrine, Harmondsworth.

Thomson, Ahmad(1989),*Blood on the Cross*, Ta-Ha Publishers, London.

Tibullus, translated by J.B. Postgate, Loeb Classical Library, William Heinemann, London.

Tirmidhī (at-), Al-Hakīm *Kitāb khatm al-wilāya*, edited by 'Uthmān Ismā'īl Yahyā, Beirut, 1965.

Titchener, E.B.(1896), *An Outline of Psychology*, Macmillan, New York.

Todorov, I.(1972),"Introduction à la symbolique", *Poétique* (11), Paris.

Tompkins, P.(1978), *The Secrets of the Great Pyramid*, Penguin, Harmondsworth.

Ubicini, M.A.(1856), *Letters on Turkey*, translated by Lady Easthope, London.

Underhill, Evelyn(1911), *Mysticism: the Nature and Development of Spiritual Consciousness*, Oneworld Publications, Oxford, 1993.

Upanishads, *The Upanishads*, translated by Juan Mascaro, Penguin Classics, Harmondsworth, 1965.

Valiuddin, Mir(1980), *Contemplative Disciplines in Sufism,* East-West Publications, London.

Van Grunebaum, G.E.(1954), Editor, "Islamic studies and cultural research", *Studies in Islamic Cultural History,* Memoirs of the American Anthropological Association (76), pp, 1-22.

-----(1970), *Classical Islam, a History 600-1258,* translated by K. Watson, George Allen & Unwin, London.

Vitray-Meyerovitch, E. de(1973), *Odes Mystiques of Djalāl od-Dîn Rûmî* translated with collaboration of M. Mokri, Klincksieck, Paris.

-----(1987), *Rûmî and Sufism,* translated from the French by Simone Fattal, Post-Apollo Press, Sausalito, California.

Voight, V.(1977),"Shamanism in Siberia", *Acta Ethnographica Academiae Scientiarum Hungaricae* (26), pp, 385-395.

Walad, Sultan *Walad-Nāma,* Homāi Edition, Tehran (undated), Persian.

Waliullah, Shah(1980), *Sufism and the Islamic Tradition: the Lamahat and Sata'at of Shah Waliullah,* translated by G.N. Jalbandi & edited by D.B. Fry, Octagon Press, London

Wallace, A.F. (1956), "Mazeway Resynthesis: A bio-cultural theory of religious inspiration", *Transactions of the New York Academy of Sciences* (18), pp, 626-638.

-----(1958),"Dreams & the Wishes of the Soul: a type of psychoanalytic theory among the seventeenth century Iroquois", *American Anthropologist* 60 (2), pp, 234-248.

-----(1959), "Cultural Determinants of Response to Hallucinatory Experience", *American Medical Association Archives of General Medicine* (1), pp, 74-85.

Weber, Max(1930), *The Protestant Ethic and the Spirit of Capitalism,* George Allan & Unwin, London.

Wehr, Hans(1960), *Arabic English Dictionary,* edited by J.M. Cowan, Cornell University Press, New York.

Westermarck, E.(1926), *Ritual and Belief in Morocco* (2 vols.), Macmillan, London.

White, K.(1973), "Life and Death and Medicine", *Scientific American* 229 (3), pp, 23-33.

Widengren, G.(1950), *The Ascension of the Apostle of God and the Heavenly Book,* Leipzig.

Wineman, Aryeh(1998), *Mystic Tales from the Zohar,* translated with notes & commentary, Mythos, Princeton University Press.

Winstedt, Sir R.O.(1925), *Shaman, Saiva and Sufi: a study of the evolution of Malay magic,* London.

Wuthnow, R.(1976), *The Consciousness Reformation,* University of California Press, Berkeley.

Yagan, Murat(1988), *The Caucasian Book of Longevity and Well-Being,* Threshold Books, Putney, Vermont.

Yerkes, R.K.(1953), *Sacrifice in Greek and Roman Religions and Early Judaism,* A. & C. Black, London.

337

Zabīdī (az-), Muhammad ibn al-Husain Murtadā *Ithāf as-Sāda* (a commentary on Al-Ghazālī's *Ihyā' 'Ulūm ad-Dīn*, in 10 vols.), Cairo, 1311 A.H.

Zunz, S., *Die gottesdienstlichen Vorträge der Juden*, Berlin, 1832.

GENERAL INDEX

345

Ignorance 154,182,227
Ikhlās (see Sincerity)
Ikhtiyār 164,219
Ikhwān as-Safā' 214
Ilhām (see Inspiration)
Illiterate Sufi 133,167
Illness: 2,17,23,57,62,141,185,197;
  Western view of 10,257,278; Sufi
  concept of 17-19,66,68,197,218-
  219,227-228,257,278
'Ilm (see Knowledge)
Illusion: 101,128,176,193,219,245,270;
  as a limitation of perspective 57,68,83,
  91,164,191,227,254; reason for anxiety
  64; overcoming of in Sufism 111,165
Image 67,128,133,151,176-177,200-201
Imagination 11,78,84,90,155,165,201,
  234
Imān 83
'Imārah 173
Imitators - Sufi 231,233,234
Immanent 55,57,101-102,205,243
Immanent Transcendent - The 87-88,
  91-92,106,110,151,205
Impermanence 68,257,276
Implicit 53,90,139,150
Inaccurate 91
Incarnation (see *Hulūl*)
Incomplete 191
Independence 81,85,132,137,155,193,
  227,259
India 3-4,28,53,87,105,195,217,229,267
Indigenous 221
Indirect 149,168
Individual: - The 19,54,57,87-88,98,119,
  129-130,134,137,142,178,185,195,212,
  241,244,252,259,266-272,275-279;the
  perfected 194,248-249,258-259,269-270;
  Individualisation 254,261,278; Individu-
  alism 1,241,254,269-271,278; Individu-
  ality, nature of 20,51,54,57,59,119,134,
  166,193-194,243,247-248,277,279
Industrial Revolution 19
Infinite nature of Self 18,43,62-63,101,
  193-194,202,274
Infinity 41,53,55,66,77,79,84,100,102,
  138,202,205-206,275
Influence 51,69,103,165,175-176,201,
  228,231
Inherent 80,243,254
Inhibitory restraints, positive nature of
  174
Initiation 30,100,136,139-145,217,225
Initiative 55
Inkār al-kasb 180
Innate 172,250

Innovator, Sufi as 233
Insān al-Kāmīl (Al-) 26,39,90,116,134-
  135,146,152,178,248,274
Insight 110,115,186,226,251
Inspiration 28,77-78,219,220,225
Instinct 55,88-89,102,184
Institutions 21-22,212-216,218,253
Integrated psyche 54,60,101-102,223,
  266
Intellect - The 46,50,54,57,118,202,249,
Intellectual: 133,140,146,150,167-168,
  216,241,250,253,273-274; Sufism tran-
  scends 52,58,76,166-169,172-174,241;
  Intellectualism not Sufism 77,167,201,
  251
Intelligence 60,90
Intentions 109,252,275
Interaction 57
Interdependence 227,248,273-274
Interiorisation 128,135,139,143,213,217
Interpretation 113,165,217,243,280
Interviews with Master 129-130,143-
  144,183
Intuition 57,70,78,137,169,186,241,253
Invocation 36,53,109-112,117,129,141-
  143,164,177-179,247
Iranian revolution 222
'Irfān 214
Irrational 246,250-251
Isāwīyya 222
Isis (Egyptian goddess) 115
Islam 1,5,10,44,85,129,147,150,175,
  191,197,242,251,267; differences to
  Sufism 58,191,197,202-206,251;
  origins of 36-46; as a transmitter of
  Sufism 36-39,42,66-67,277
Isnād 279
Isolation 36-37,179
Israel 38,192,199
Istighrāq 179,218
Istislām 83,234,242
Ittihād 56,60,107-108,118,152,164,199
Ittilā' (see Confession)
Jadhb 174,218,224
Jainism 196
Jalwah 180
Jappa beads (see Rosary)
Jealousy 182,218,228
Jerusalem 38,113,119
Jester 170
Jetzira - Book 41
Jewish 15,38,41,44,47,51,107,115,
  180,192,198,216,259,270
Jinn (see Elementals)
Journeying 180,179-180
Joy 66,68,165,253

346

Mental health 88,97-98,104,128,141,143, 242,267
Mercy 107,149,185,227
Messenger 45,116,128,220
Metaphysics 55,70-75,81,87,91,244,246
Methods: ancient 25,213; holistic 273; Muhammad's 216-217; psychotherapeutic 144,242,255,259; - Sufi 90,97, 112,145,149,172,177-178,186,251; - Transcendent 52,168-169,186,217; variable 155,181,252
Mevlana 256
Mid-life crisis 267
Mind: 11,76,88,132,137-138,142-143, 167; cannot perceive God 201; charming of 27; cluttering of 105; discipline of 165,244-246; duality of 261,276; - opening exercises 132,144,171; - Peace of 64,177; - States of 22-23
Miracles 4,24,75-76,79,221
Mi'rāj 113,194
Misbahah (see Rosary)
Miseries -Human, the origins of 260-261
Mishkāt 81,90
Moksa 191
Monastic 218
Money 11,22,85,156,170,258
Monk, Christian 200-202
Monotheism 37
Moon 44,78,110,137,166
Morals 22,62,67,104,129,137,174,185, 198,266,271,273
Mosques 176
Mother, God as a 129,145-150
Motivation: 69,76,99,245-246,260; based on values 22,274; becoming aware of 128,130; changing of 128,130,149,181- 182; determiner of experience 121; of the heart 79
Mujāhida 129,164,212
Mu'jizāt (see Miracles)
Multiple-perspective 67,97,113,166
Muqtasedon 204,221-222
Murāqaba 129
Murīd 129
Murshid (see Teacher)
Music, view of 175,178,231,256
Musicians 28,178
Muslim 2,38,51,66,67,83,86,105,107, 112,113,116,134,150,192,194,198,202- 204,211,217-221,226,230,232-233,267
Muwahhid 59,60,108,122
Mystery cults 222
Mystical experience: independent of religion 192,214,277; inducing of 178- 179,194,199-200; termination of 194;

universal nature of 199; and Sufi initiation 141,212-213; and Revelation 115-119,138; and the sonambulistic state 174; of death 6,193-194,204-205; of God 59,201; of Transcendent Self 10-20,29,202
Mysticism: 243; Arabic 61,113; Christian 41-42,148,200-201,270; Egyptian 37; Hindu 270; Jewish 41-42, 47,69,148,199,270; Sufi 137-138,166, 212,217-218,225,269-270; Pseudo 224; different than mystical experience 174; and ancient esoteric tradition 45,141; and humour 148; and practicalities 234
Myths 4,27,28,37,225
Nafas (see Breath)
Nafī 180-181,218,248
Nafs 29,50-56,60-61,69,100-102,107- 108,111,118,122,129,155,176,183,200, 245
Names of God 36,45,89-90,109,129,166, 171,177-179,219-220,247
Name, change of 143,213-214
Narcissism 271
Nāsūt 56
Nationalism 23,51-52,85-86,113,266
Natural: 22,29,76,142,155,178,224,253; basis of creativity 55; capacity to be human 61,87; completion - Death as 275; harmony 70,244; impulses 19,102; laws 84; powers of children 146; primal state 223,247,254; sorrow 246
Nature: 57,98,192; alienation from 103, 243; Animal 51,104,118,129,155,249; Creative 29,53,147; Cycle of 242-243; dominating of 138; Essential 29,53-54, 57,102,118,146-147; Human 102,147, 150,195; individual 57,118; Love of 57; Physical 195-197,272; Primal State of 129,147,199,260; relativity of 231; Supreme World of 89; Transcendent 56, 62,80,104,118,130, 184,249; Unitary 54,97,103,146,199; and God 271; is eternal 193,243
Near Death Experience 223
Needs: economic 83; emotional/psychological 153,156,212,254-255; individual /personal 147,179,185-186; natural 19, 147,196,256; overcoming of 121,156, 256; reason for 196-197; social 254, 259-260; spiritual 254,259-260; spiritual 153,185; therapeutic 271; of the time 27,156;
Negative 64,69,100,103,183-186,245, 257,266
Nervous:breakdown 267;tension 174,224

242-245,278; reductionist 19-20,22,81, 267,277; therapeutic limitations of 17, 140,144-145; unable to explain mystic experience 11-12
Psychotherapist 278
Psychotherapy: Insight 186; Personal Construct theory 52-53; radical forms of 168,255; replacement for religion 17, 271; substitute for parent 145; & Sufism 240-246,255,261-268,271-272,278; metaphysical ignored in 55,246
Psychotics 241,246
Public 186,220
Punishment 20,98,110,153,266
Purification: of intentions 107,129,151-152; of self 76,101,130,143,151,172, 178,180; of thinking 55,111,131,164-165; Way of 212
Puritans 202
Purity: ethnic 51; of Master 92,133,149; path of 113,122; Primal 206,254,280
Purpose: 153; of life 55,138; of Master 154, of repentance 107; of spiritual states 120; of Sufi practices 52,155, 166,180,225
Purposer - God as 196,200;
Pythagoreans 26,115,206
Qabd 101
Qalandarī 214
Qalb (see Heart)
Qawm 214
Qinā'at 84
Quack 17
Qualifications of a Master 131-133,139
Quest 50,57,266-268,279
Questioning 70,105,156,173,196-197, 251
Qu'rān 36,38-39,45,53,86,132,138,199-200,204,216,219-220,247
Rabb 247
Rapture (see Ecstasy)
Rational 39,59,69,88,166,177,183,250-251,259-260
Rational-Emotive therapy 250
Ray of light 137
Reaction 136,222,234
Reality: consciousness of 59-60,79,103, 232,248,253; denial of 206,240-241; discovering of 47,58; experiencing of 82,84,102,231-232,276; God as 66-68, 80,82,86,91,98,132-133,191,199,202-206,248,261,269; knowledge of 58,61, 68,77,100,245; nature of 29,84,89,196, 227; principle of 57,68,88-89; transmission of 135; unification with 59,199
Realisation 10,29,191,194,196,197,204-

208,224-225,241,248,253,255,279-280
Reason 30,53,77,82,90,135,139,144,153, 156,201-202,267
Reassertion 222-223
Rebirthing Therapy 168,242
Recall 22,112
Receiving Sufism 76,133,169,205,232
Recite 90,171,177,220
Recollect 22,36,54,90,164,223
Reductionist 10,22,24,70,76,97,106,171, 229,266-268,272-274
Reflection 36,65,92,111,115,131,133,135-137,148,151,152,155,164,182,185,245
Reformulation 172
Regression 106,222-223
Reincarnation 248
Reinforcing 143-144,186-187,242,255, 260-261
Reintegration 222-223
Relationship to Master 128-129,139-141, 144-153,260
Relativity 231,266
Religion, Sufism transcends 191-210, 212-215,242,248,266-271,276-277,280
Religious authorities 4,22,198,215,266
Remembrance (see *Dhikr*)
Remorse 111
Renaissance 270
Renunciation (see Ascetism)
Repentance 106-109,120,137,178
Repetition 36,111,143,166,170,178-180, 247
Repository, Egypt as a 25-27,41
Representation 117-118,121,149,176-179
Repression 30,69,88,104,229,249,254, 256
Reputation 203
Research 3,17,50,52,104,174,191,212, 222-239,244,246,258,274-275
Resentful 183
Residence of the Sufi 180
Resignation 234
Resistance 103,111,133,172
Respect 144-145,149-150,260
Responsibility 62,181,226-227,239,258, 260,266,270
Resurrection/Restoration 4,6,32,81,108, 110,116,141,204-205
Retreats 37,179
Revelation 36-37,58,68,89,97,118-121, 185,247,249
Reverence 107
Reverse effects, law of 251-252
Revolution 22,85,198
Reward 147,153,169,180,192-193,200, 220,266

353

355

INDEX OF PERSONS

In the case of Arabic names, to assist in location, where a person was generally known by their first name, this name has been used to determine alphabetical listing. Where a person was usually referred to by additional names, or titles, these have been added first as indicated by a comma, as is also the case for non-Arabic names.

Apart from honorary titles which could be added in later life, in Arabic (as is also the case in Hebrew) a person could be referred to as the son of someone - ibn - (in Hebrew ben), or as the father of someone - Abū. In addition, there could be a reference to the place from which they came; the school of Islamic law they followed - and in the case of Sufis their membership of an Order - or even a personal characteristic e.g; n-Nūn (meaning black) or ibn-'Arabī (of Arab descent). These added names were given the prefix al (of) which in Arabic is modified according to the consonant which follows it, as e.g; ash-Shāfi'ī, ar-Rahmān, ad-Dīn, etc. The latter term meant that the person referred to was seen as an exemplary follower of God's laws, just as 'Abd meant 'servant of' (God usually). In some cases the standard Arabic has been altered in accordance with the regional dialect of the area from which the individual came and therefore how he was known. So that in the Maghrīb, al- became l- (=el). Persons who were not Muslim in origin could also have Jewish, Christian, or Hindu names; or be the child of such an individual, e.g; ibn Ishaq (son of Isaac = a Jew), ibn Sahl Rabban (son of Saul, a pre-eminent Rabbi).

The practice of adding additional names over time, so as to distinguish a person from others with a similar name, or as honorific titles, was customary in the Islamic world and accounts for the inordinate length of such names as compared to European ones. In the following, sufficient has been given to indicate who is being referred to, so that additional names have not always been included; e.g., Titus Burckhardt and Frithjof Schuon both had Arabic names and Bābā whose name Dovid is Yiddish, and Yūsuf Arabic, also has honorary Islamic, Jewish, Hindu and Tribal names, which have been omitted here. The title Shaykh has been generally excluded, except where this is a distinguishing feature of that name. Prophet Muhammad has also been omitted, as there are numerous references to him throughout the text.

356

357

358

359

References to Classical, Ancient, & Religious Texts

The extensive use of Sufi writings throughout this book - some of which are very old- has precluded their use in the following and you are advised to consult the Index of Persons. However, although it is unlikely to be admitted publicly, texts such as Rūmī's *Mathnawī*, are considered to have as much sanctity as the Bible. or *Qur'ān*.

Qur'ān (continued)

KEY TO PRONUNCIATION

It is not possible to explain in writing, how to pronounce non-European words exactly. The following is only an approximation and guide to the transliteration I have used here. Non-Arabic academics, are themselves often wrong in their pronunciation, for the reason that there are considerable regional differences, and since the time of Muhammad and the spread of the Islamic Empire, Arabic has been influenced by Persian and other languages; e.g., in Turkey, Muhammad is written as "Mehmet", and in India he is called "Mohamet". The so-called *"correct pronunciation"* used in mosques and *Wahhābī* endowed Universities, would have sounded strange to the Prophet, who having been raised by Bedouin, likely spoke with an accent. It should also be realised that Bilāl – the *first muezzin* – and therefore influential, was an Abyssinian.

ā = aa as in f<u>a</u>ther; the unaccented a is short as in r<u>an</u>.

ī = ee as in f<u>ee</u>t; the unaccented i is short as in n<u>et</u>.

ū =oo as in r<u>oo</u>t; *Arabic* unaccented u is as o in p<u>o</u>rt.

â = eh as in r<u>a</u>y.

In *Arabic* ḥ is a hard h as in ḥat and not a soft h as in hair; but it should not be confused with the guttural h – here rendered as kh, and pronounced as ch in lo<u>ch</u>. In *Hebrew* there is a soft h and a guttural form, pronounced similarly to the Arabic, but neither should be confused with the k, or kh sounds, also found in Hebrew.

Arabic ṣ = ts as in boo<u>ts</u>; in Sanskrit ṣ =sh as in <u>sh</u>ould.

ḍ = td; with the t as in <u>pt</u>yalin and the d as in ḍarn – made at the back of the throat. Not as the d in <u>d</u>eal in English, made with the tongue and pronounced through the teeth.

ṭ = dt, with the t pronounced as in ṭar, not as in <u>t</u>eam.

ẓ = tz as in <u>Ts</u>ar.

363

ABOUT THE AUTHOR

Dr.David Heinemann D.Psy.(Hon)., Dip.A.P., B.A.Soc.Sc., M.Sc., M.Phil., M.Phil., M.Phil., F.Inst.S.M., F.R.A.I., F.I.A.T., F.C.A.M.S., is the Jewish Rabbi for the Kibris community of Turkey. Also an holistic medical practitioner and psychotherapist, he spent most of his life as a psychologist, distinguishing himself as a pioneer in a new medical field – Psychoneuroimmunology – (the interactions between the neurological and immunological systems).

Described as the *"Nostradamus of our time"*, he has possessed since childhood, a natural gift for healing. After experience in the orthodox establishment – which he describes as *"an institutionalized form of drug-pushing"* – he turned to alternative medicine, setting-up centres and instigating new approaches. A founder member of the group that promoted the world-famous, U.K., Bristol Cancer Help Centre and an initial member of the Institute of Complimentary Medicine – and the first person to be listed as an authority on alternative approaches to cancer by the B.M.A. – his experience with cancer patients gave him an understanding of the neccesity for an holistic approach, including spiritual factors, in the treatment of chronic illness. Ultimately, resulting in an examination of Asian, Persian, Arabic, tribal and non-Western systems of medicine. Investigating treatment procedures, he soon came to realise that the psychological and social, are not separated from the physical in these systems, and that they are often *"much more effective in the treatment of psychological ailments."* Struck by a link between psychic phenomena, unusual behaviour, social conditions, beliefs and illness in such societies, he came to the conclusion *"there is something radically wrong with the way the self is defined in Western psychology–no consideration is given to the collective psyche and its influence on events."*

It is – the transcending of the individual self – that is the subject of this book. Taking 12 years to compile, it draws on over 30 years of investigation; from the Egyptian desert, to the islands of the Pacific and the jungles of South East Asia. Drawing on ancient and diverse sources, as well as on a lifetime of psychological, clinical, personal and *Transcendent* experience.

364

1. *'It all began in Malaysia'*
The Al-Arqamī Sufi of Sarawak.

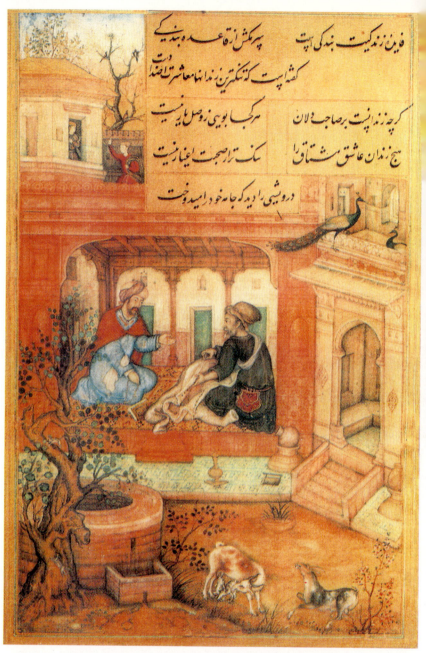

2. An Islamic cleric *(Mulla)* rebukes a Dervish
A well-to-do hypocrite, condemns a poor practitioner:
an early edition of the Sufi poet Jāmī's, *Bahāristān*.

The Egyptian god Thoth

Notice symbols that appear in later religions; the Christian cross and water of life, and the Buddhist lotus (temple of Amon at Karnak).

3. The Egyptian god Osiris

A painting from the tomb of Sennutem.

4. Sufi craftsmen leave cryptic messages in their designs
Madrasah (*Qur'ānic* school) of Shah Sultan Husayn, in Isfahan, Iran.

5. Sufi craftsman's Guilds are of ancient origin
A metalworker in Iran, uses Zoroastrian,
Babylonian, and Islamic motifs in his work.

**6. Transcending all
divisions, including Life
and Death**
Tomb of the Sufi Master,
Bābā Sayyīd Shah Waris
at Diva, India (who
counted Queen Victoria
amongst his disciples)
is visited by Hindus and
Muslims alike.

7. The temple of Abraham
The *Ka'aba* at Mecca.

8. A Perfect Master radiates the Divine Light
The original Sai Baba (a Sufi Master) 1858-1918.

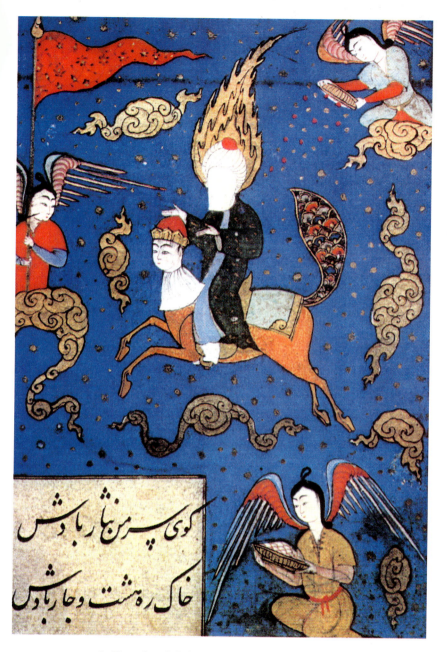

9. Prophet Muhammad's Night Journey

A 16th century manuscript of *'Arifi's Gūy-u-Hawgan*.

10. The Sphinx of Giza, Egypt
The world's oldest and largest sculpture, basis for the Greek legend and
of which the *Burāq* of the 'Night Journey' of Muhammad, is reminiscent.

11. *'Love is the Wine'*
Persian miniature on ivory, inspired by the poetry of the
Sufi Master Sa'adī.

12. Inside a Sufi Centre
A 16th century manuscript depicting Mevlevi
dervishes reciting poetry and dancing.

13. God as the Beloved as a Universal symbol
Krishna the god-man and Radha his lover
(detail from a painting in Rajasthan, India).

14. Wool(*sūf*) symbolising the mystics (*sūfī*) self sacrifice
Sheep dipping and shearing - Niriz, Iran.

15. The Brethren of Purity *(Ikhwān as-Safā')*
An esoteric society founded in Iraq, over 1,000 years ago,
teaching a *Universal Way* that influenced Dante.

**16. Though the rose
dies its perfume remains**
Graves of Sufi poets
Sa'adi and Hāfiz, in
Shiraz, Iran.
Roses - a symbol of the
Sufi Path - are used by
them in their poetry.